MARKED

MARKED

Legacy Builders

A 12-Month Workbook for Fathers

"Legacy is not what you leave for others —
it's what you leave in them."

Jay S. Miller

Senior Pastor · Host, Legacy Builders Podcast

ISBN 979-8-9963430-0-3

MARKED: Men Who Leave an Imprint

Published by Legacy Builders

Lafayette, Louisiana

ISBN (Softcover): 979-8-9963430-1-0

ISBN (Hardcover): 979-8-9963430-2-7

ISBN (Ebook / EPUB): 979-8-9963430-0-3

Legacy Builders Podcast · jaysmiller.com

First Edition

Printed in the United States of America

A note on Scripture: Unless otherwise noted, all Scripture quotations are from the English Standard Version (ESV). The author has chosen this translation for its faithfulness to the original languages and its clarity in English. Occasional paraphrases are the author's own and are noted as such.

For Tessy.

Thirty-three years and still counting. Five sons. Three
daughters-in-law.
Three grandchildren and counting.
You are the reason any of this is true.

ACKNOWLEDGMENTS

This book exists because of people who believed in it before there was a book.

To Tessy — thirty-three years and still counting. You have been the most patient, the most faithful, and the most honest voice in my life. You did not just support this project — you are this project. Everything I know about covenant, about staying, about building something that lasts, I learned by watching you. This book is yours as much as it is mine.

To my sons — the Miller Boyz. You were my first congregation. You are my most important legacy. Watching each of you become men of God, husbands, fathers, and leaders has been the greatest privilege of my life. You did not give me material for a book. You gave me reasons to believe every word of it.

To my daughters-in-law — you married into a loud, passionate, opinionated family and you have loved us well. Thank you for making my sons better men.

To my grandchildren — you do not know it yet, but you are the reason Poppa Jay is still building.

To The Family Church — twenty-four years of Sunday mornings, Wednesday nights, hospital rooms, weddings, and funerals. You have been my people. You have tested these principles in real life and proven them true. This book belongs to you as much as to anyone.

To the men who have spoken into my life — coaches, mentors, pastors, and fathers who modeled what this book describes. You marked me. I am still carrying what you gave me.

To every father who picks up this book and decides to stop drifting — this was written for you.

— Jay S. Miller

Lafayette, Louisiana

Table of Contents

Twelve principles. Twelve months. One legacy.

"Two and a Half Acres of Faith"

ISBN 979-8-3850-6087-0

"A River, A Radio, and A Rocking Chair"

ISBN 978-1-964794-47-1

Available at jaysmiller.com and wherever books are sold.

MARKED is designed to be worked through one month at a time —
twelve months, twelve principles, one chapter per month. Do not rush
it. Do not read ahead. Give each principle the full thirty days it
deserves.

Each month includes:

The Core Principle — The biblical teaching behind the month's principle
— the foundation everything else is built on.

Scripture Deep Dive — A focused look at the passage that drives the
principle, with teaching points to study and apply.

The Illustration — A personal story from the author's own marriage and
fatherhood that brings the principle to life.

Implementation Steps — Five specific, practical actions to take during the
month — not theory, not suggestions. Assignments.

Family Experiences — Four activities to do with your family that make
the principle tangible and memorable.

Daily Bible Reading Plan — A 20-day Scripture reading plan built around
the month's theme.

Reflection Questions — Five questions that will not let you off easy.
Write your answers. Be honest.

Monthly Challenge — A single focused challenge to complete before the
next chapter. Sign it. Mean it.

*A note on the reflection questions and commitment boxes: they only work if
you use them. Write in this book. Mark it up. Dog-ear the pages. The men
who get the most from MARKED are the men who treat it as a working
document, not a reading experience.*

A Word Before We Begin

I need to say something to you before you read a single chapter of this book.

Most men who pick up a book like this do it because someone gave it to them. Their wife. Their pastor. A friend who thought they needed it. They flip through the first few pages, set it on the nightstand, and never open it again. It becomes a monument to good intentions — which is another way of saying it becomes a monument to nothing.

I am asking you not to do that.

Not because I need you to read my book. Because your family needs you to become the man this book is going to ask you to be. And those are two very different things.

Let me be honest with you about something.

I have been in ministry for over thirty years. I have preached thousands of sermons. I have counseled hundreds of marriages. I have sat across from men who had everything — the career, the house, the reputation, the church attendance — and watched them lose the thing that mattered most. Not in a dramatic moment. Not in a crisis anyone could have pointed to. Just slowly. Quietly. The way a fire goes out when no one is adding wood.

And I have been that man.

Not the man who walked away. Not the man with the obvious failure. The man who was present and checked out at the same time. The man whose wife could feel the distance even when he was sitting right next to her. The man whose sons were watching him — and getting a picture of manhood that was less than what they deserved.

I know what that feels like. I know the particular shame of a man who loves his family and has still, somehow, allowed himself to drift from them. And I know what it costs to stop drifting — because I paid that price. Tessy and I paid it together. It was not cheap. It was worth every hard conversation, every moment of honest confession, every uncomfortable look in the mirror.

That is why I wrote this book. Not from a place of arrival. From a place of survival — and the deep conviction that what God built in our family is available to yours.

Now let me tell you what this book is going to ask of you.

It is going to ask you to be honest. Not the performance of honesty — the real thing. The kind that costs you something. The kind that requires you to look at your life, your marriage, your children, and your own soul without flinching away from what you see.

It is going to ask you to show up. Every month. Every week. Every day. Legacy is not built in a retreat or a conference or a single defining moment. It is built in Tuesday evenings when you are tired and your son wants to talk and every part of you wants to sit down and be left alone. It is built in the decision — made again and again — to be present on purpose.

It is going to ask you to fight. For your marriage when it is hard. For your children's faith when the world is louder than you are. For your own soul when the drift feels easier than the discipline.

The men who finish this workbook will look back on this year as one of the most significant decisions they ever made. The men who put it on the nightstand will not remember it at all.

———————————————

I want to speak directly to a few of you.

To the man who has already failed — whose children are older, whose marriage has scars, who is reading this and wondering if it is too late: it is not too late. The best time to start was twenty years ago. The second best time is today. Legacy is written until your last breath. Start writing.

To the man who thinks he is doing fine — whose family looks good from the outside, who has not had any major crises, who is reading this out of mild curiosity: you are the man I am most concerned about. The slow leak does not announce itself. It just empties everything quietly until one day you look up and realize the people in your house feel like strangers. Do not wait for a crisis to take this seriously.

To the young father holding this book with small children in the house: you are holding something that can change the trajectory of your entire family line. The decisions you make in the next twelve months will still be producing fruit — or consequences — forty years from now. Do not waste this season.

____

Here is what I know after thirty-plus years of marriage, five sons, three daughters-in-law, three grandchildren, and more than two decades of pastoring families:

The men who leave the deepest marks are almost never the most talented. They are the most faithful. They are the men who decided — quietly, stubbornly, without applause — that their family was worth showing up for. Every day. Even when no one was watching. Especially when no one was watching.

That man is not born. He is built. Chapter by chapter. Month by month. One hard decision at a time.

This book is the blueprint.

But blueprints do not build anything. Men do.

So let's get to work.

— Jay S. Miller

Lafayette, Louisiana

Jay S. Miller

Senior Pastor · The Family Church, Lafayette, LA

Host, Legacy Builders Podcast · Husband · Father · Grandfather

To the Father Holding This Book,

I want to tell you something before you read a single chapter: the fact that you are holding this book already says something about the kind of man you are. Most men drift. They wake up one day and realize their children are grown, their marriage has gone quiet, and the legacy they meant to build somehow never got started. You are not that man. Or if you were — you are deciding right now not to be anymore.

I know this territory because I have lived it. I married my high school sweetheart, Tessy, on July 15, 1994. For over 32 years she has been my partner, my anchor, and the co-architect of everything we have built together. We have five sons. All five are still walking in faith. All five are musicians, singers, and public speakers. My top three are married to three remarkable women. And I now hold three grandchildren in my arms who are watching what legacy looks like up close.

I do not tell you this to impress you. I tell you this because legacy is not just what I speak about — it is what I have lived, fought for, prayed over, and in some seasons, wept over. Every principle in this workbook has been tested in a real home, with real sons, in real seasons of pressure and joy.

This workbook is not a theory book. It is a field manual. Each month gives you one principle, the honest story behind it, five practical steps, four family experiences, a daily reading plan, and reflection questions that will not let you off easy. Do the work. All twelve months. The man you will be on the other side of this year is worth every sacrifice it requires.

Now let's build something that lasts.

For the fathers who refuse to be forgotten,

Jay S. Miller

Legacy Builder · Husband · Father · Grandfather · Pastor

Legacy Builders Podcast · jaysmiller.com

ABOUT THE AUTHOR

Jay S. Miller

SENIOR PASTOR · THE FAMILY CHURCH, LAFAYETTE, LA
HOST, LEGACY BUILDERS PODCAST

Jay S. Miller has served as Senior Pastor of The Family Church in Lafayette, Louisiana since 2002. He is the President of Lafayette Christian Academy and the host of the Legacy Builders Podcast. He has been married to Tessy since 1994. They have five sons, three daughters-in-law, and three grandchildren.

He is the author of Two and a Half Acres of Faith, A River, A Radio, and A Rocking Chair, and MARKED.

01

The Legacy Code

---

*""Legacy is not what you leave for others —
it is what you leave in others.""*

— J.S.M.

There is a difference between inheritance and impartation.

Some men leave assets. Others leave impact.

Some leave property. Others leave convictions.

Some leave bank accounts. Others leave faith that survives storms.

The question is not what you are accumulating. The question is what you are becoming — and what that will mean for the people who come after you.

Every man has a code — a set of values, habits, and beliefs that quietly govern his life. Most men never examine it. They inherited it from their fathers, absorbed it from culture, or assembled it from wounds they never healed. They are passing something on — they just do not know what it is.A Legacy Builder is a man who writes his code on purpose.

""The most powerful thing a man can give his children is not money in the bank — it is a life worth imitating. My parents understood that before they had a word for it.""

The Legacy Code is not a list of rules posted on the refrigerator. It is the invisible architecture of your family — the answer to the question your children will one day ask:"What did my father believe was worth building?"It is written not in words but in the thousand daily decisions a man makes when no one is watching. How he treats his wife on an ordinary Tuesday. What he does with his money when he could do anything with it. Whether he shows up when showing up costs him something.

Most men drift through fatherhood reacting — to schedules, to crises, to whatever is loudest. They are not building deliberately. They are surviving daily. And the tragedy is not that they failed spectacularly. It is that they drifted quietly — and never noticed what was being built by default in the absence of intention.

The Legacy Builder does something rare and costly:he decides.He decides what kind of man he will be. He decides what his home will feel like. He decides what will pass through him to the next generation — not by accident, not by default, but by deliberate, sustained, daily intention. He does not wait for the perfect season to start building. He starts with what he has, where he is, right now.

There are two kinds of fathers in this workbook. The first kind talks about legacy. The second kind builds it. The difference between them is not talent or income or opportunity. The difference is a decision — made once, and then made again every single morning.Legacy is written daily. In the ordinary moments most men overlook.

SCRIPTURE DEEP DIVE

Deuteronomy 6:4–7 · ESV

> *""Hear, O Israel: The Lord our God, the Lord is one. You shall love the Lord your God with all your heart and with all your soul and with all your might. And these words that I command you today shall be on your heart. You shall teach them diligently to your children, and shall talk of them when you sit in your house, and when you walk by the way, and when you lie down, and when you rise.""*

God's Blueprint for Impartation Has Always Been the Same

01 It Starts in Your Own Heart

Notice the sequence. God does not say "teach your children first." He says "these words shall be on your heart" — then teach. You cannot impart what you do not possess. The Legacy Code begins not with your children's behavior but with your own transformation.

02 Legacy is Transferred in Ordinary Moments

God describes the classroom: when you sit, when you walk, when you lie down, when you rise. Not just Sunday mornings. The most powerful discipleship happens in the car, at the dinner table, during the bedtime routine. Ordinary moments are the primary transfer points of legacy.

03 Diligence is the Requirement

The word "diligently" is not accidental. Legacy does not happen casually. It requires intention, repetition, and consistency over years and decades. The father who builds a legacy is not the most talented — he is the most faithful.

THE ILLUSTRATION

STERLING AND JEAN MILLER — TWO BUILDERS, ONE LEGACY

My father, Sterling Miller, was a builder of buildings. A visionary. He came to Lafayette, Louisiana with sixty dollars and a dream. No staff. No salary. No guarantee of any kind. Just 2.5 acres of ground, a God he trusted completely, and a decision to build something that would outlast him.

He drove stakes into the dirt when other people were still making excuses. He bought property when others said it was too soon. He built when others said it was too hard. He taught me that faith is not passive —faith picks up a shovel.

My mother, Jean Miller, was something different. She was a builder of people. I watched her love others — not when it was convenient, not when they deserved it — with patience and prayer and an unshakeable belief in what God could do with a willing heart. She sat with me at a kitchen table and taught me how to preach. How to serve. How to love the person in front of you like they were the most important person in the room — because to her, they were.

Together, they gave me the two things a father most needs to pass on: a vision for what God can build, and a model for how to treat the people He puts in your path. One built with his hands. The other built with her heart. Neither of them used the wordlegacy. Both of them lived it every single day.

I am standing on what two people built with faith, sweat, and sixty dollars. My sons are standing on what I built. Their children will stand on what they build. That chain did not happen by accident. It happened because someone decided to build deliberately.

APPLICATION FOR YOU

You may not have had parents like Sterling and Jean. Many men reading this page did not. But that does not disqualify you from building something remarkable — it simply meansthe chain starts with you.The man who decides to build deliberately in the middle of an ordinary life is doing exactly what my father did on 2.5 acres with sixty dollars. He is trusting that what God builds through a faithful man does not stop when that man does.

THIS MONTH'S IMPLEMENTATION

---

01 Write Your Legacy Statement

Before you can build a legacy, you have to know what legacy you are trying to build. Write a single paragraph — your personal Legacy Statement — answering three questions: What do I want my children to believe? How do I want them to live? What do I want them to say about me at my funeral? My father could not have articulated his in those words, but he lived it every day. That is even better. Name yours — then live it.

→ *Write your Legacy Statement this week. Keep it somewhere you will read it regularly.*

02 Audit Your Calendar

Your calendar is the most honest document in your life. It shows what you actually value, regardless of what you say you value. Pull up the last 30 days. Where did your time go? Does it match your stated priorities? My father's calendar was built around the church, the family, and the dream God gave him. Your calendar tells the same story about you — whether you like the story or not.

> → *Identify one time slot this week to give to one of your children that would not have happened otherwise.*

03 Have the Conversation

Most fathers have never told their children what they want to pass to them. This month, sit down with each of your children and tell them — specifically — what you believe about God, what you value in life, and what you hope for them. My mother sat with me and told me. Repeatedly. Those conversations are still shaping me. Do not assume your children know. Tell them.

> → *Schedule the conversation this week. Do not wait for the perfect moment. There is no perfect moment.*

04   Name Your Broken Patterns

Every family has patterns that should not survive another generation — anger, silence, addiction, emotional unavailability, fear of failure. Name them. Acknowledge them to yourself and to God. Make a decision: this stops with me. The chain you inherited is not the chain you have to pass on. My parents broke patterns from their own upbringing. You can break yours.

> → *Write down one pattern you are committed to ending in your family line. Share it with someone who will hold you accountable.*

05   Pray a Daily Blessing

Begin the practice of speaking a blessing over your children daily — by name, out loud, specifically. Not a formula. A real declaration of what you see in them and what you believe God is doing in them. My mother prayed like that. I knew it. And knowing she was going to God on my behalf gave me a confidence I could not have manufactured on my own. Your children need to hear your voice go to God for them.

> → *Start tonight. Speak it out loud. Do it every day this month.*

06   The Legacy Drive

Load the family in the car with no destination. Windows down, radio up. Drive through the neighborhood where you grew up, or the streets where your story started. Point things out. Tell them what it looked like when you were their age. Let them ask questions. Let the conversation go wherever it goes. You are not giving a history lesson — you are letting them inside your story.

→ *No phones. Just the road, the music, and your people.*

FAMILY EXPERIENCES THIS MONTH

Experience 01

The Legacy Letter

Write a letter to each of your children — to be opened at a time you choose — telling them what you want them to know about who you are, what you believe, and what you want for their lives. This is one of the most powerful things a father can do. Your children may not appreciate it now. They will not forget it later.

""What is one thing I never told you that I want you to know?""

""What do you want your children to know about our family?""

Experience 02

The Story Dinner

At dinner, tell your family the story of your life — the real one. Where you came from, what shaped you, what you believe, and why. Let them ask questions. Let them see the man behind the role of father. My sons know where I came from. They know the story of Sterling and Jean. That story is part of who they are now.

""What was the hardest moment of your life? What got you through it?""

""What do you wish someone had told you when you were my age?""

The Heritage Walk

Visit a place significant to your family's history or your own faith story — the church where you were saved, the place where God changed your direction, a mentor's home. Stand there. Tell the story. Let the geography become part of their memory. If possible, take them to the ground your parents or grandparents built on. Let them stand where it started.

""Why does this place matter to you?""

""What do you want me to remember about our family?""

The Values List

As a family, make a list together: "In our family, we believe..." Let every person contribute. Write it out. Frame it. Post it. This is your family's public declaration of its Legacy Code. It does not have to be eloquent. It has to be true.

""What's one thing you think is different about our family compared to most?""

""What's one thing you want our family to always be known for?""

DAILY BIBLE READING PLAN

WEEK ONE — WHO YOU ARE

Monday	**Psalm 78:1–7**	*Tell the Coming Generation*
Tuesday	**Deuteronomy 6:4–9**	*Love God — Teach Your Children*
Wednesday	**Proverbs 13:22**	*A Good Man Leaves an Inheritance*
Thursday	**Joshua 24:15**	*As for Me and My House*
Friday	**Psalm 112:1–2**	*His Children Will Be Mighty*

WEEK TWO — WHAT YOU CARRY

Monday	**Genesis 18:19**	*Abraham's Assignment*
Tuesday	**2 Timothy 1:5**	*Faith Passed Through Generations*
Wednesday	**Psalm 37:25–26**	*His Children Are a Blessing*
Thursday	**Proverbs 17:6**	*The Crown of Old Men*
Friday	**Isaiah 61:9**	*A People the Lord Has Blessed*

WEEK THREE — WHAT YOU BUILD

Monday	**Matthew 7:24–27**	*The Wise Builder*
Tuesday	**1 Corinthians 3:10–11**	*No Other Foundation*
Wednesday	**Proverbs 24:3–4**	*By Wisdom a House Is Built*
Thursday	**Psalm 127:1**	*Unless the Lord Builds*

Friday	**Nehemiah 2:17–18**	*Let Us Build*

WEEK FOUR — WHAT YOU LEAVE

Monday	**Hebrews 11:1–2**	*By Faith the Men of Old*
Tuesday	**2 Timothy 4:7**	*I Have Kept the Faith*
Wednesday	**Proverbs 20:7**	*The Righteous Who Walks in Integrity*
Thursday	**3 John 1:4**	*No Greater Joy*
Friday	**Revelation 14:13**	*Their Deeds Follow Them*

MONTHLY MEMORY VERSE

""We will not hide them from their children, but tell to the coming generation the glorious deeds of the Lord.""

Psalm 78:4 · ESV

LEGACY BUILDER REFLECTION

1.

When you think about Sterling and Jean Miller — a builder of buildings and a builder of people — which one more closely describes the legacy you are currently leaving? Which one do you want to leave?

____

____

____

2.

What is the single most important thing you want to pass to your children? Name it specifically. What are you actually doing — right now — to transfer it?

____

____

____

____

3.

What is one pattern in your family of origin that you do not want to repeat? What specific decision are you making today to end it?

____

____

____

____

4.

Have your children ever heard the full story of where you came from — the people who shaped you, the God who got hold of you, the decisions that changed your direction? If not, what is stopping you?

____

____

____

____

5.

If someone stood at your funeral and said what Sterling and Jean's
son said — "Everything I am, I learned from watching my father
live" — what would have to be true of the life you are living right
now?

____

____

____

____

Write Your Legacy Statement

This month, write your personal Legacy Statement — one paragraph that answers three questions: What do I want my children to believe? How do I want them to live? What do I want them to say about me? My father answered those questions with sixty dollars and a shovel. My mother answered them with a prayer life and a kitchen table. You answer them with the life you choose to live starting today. Share it with your spouse. Read it every week for the rest of this year.

I COMMIT TO THIS CHALLENGE BEGINNING:

____

WHAT I AM BELIEVING GOD FOR THIS MONTH:

____

____

____

Signature   Date

MONTH TWO

Chapter 2

02

The Generational Transfer

""You are not just raising children. You are shaping the family that will exist long after you are gone.""

— J.S.M.

THE CORE PRINCIPLE

Every man is a link in a chain.

Behind you stands every person who shaped you — for better or worse.

In front of you stand the men and women your children will become.

You are the hinge.

What passes through you — or stops with you — is the most consequential decision of your life.

Generations do not transfer automatically. They transfer intentionally — through men who decide, with full awareness of what is at stake, to pass something worth keeping. The Bible is not silent on this. From Abraham to Isaac to Jacob to Joseph, Scripture traces the deliberate passing of faith, character, and covenant from one generation to the next. It was never accidental. It was always intentional. And it always required a man who understood what he was carrying and took responsibility for where it landed.

""Generational transfer does not wait until your children are old enough to understand it. It begins the moment they are placed in your arms.""

Here is what most men get wrong:they assume that because they are present in the home, transfer is happening. It is not. Presence is not the same as intentionality. You can be in the same house for eighteen years and transfer almost nothing of lasting value — if you are not being deliberate about what you are passing. Presence without purpose produces proximity, not legacy.

> *""What you fail to pass on intentionally*
> *will be replaced by whatever the world*
> *passes on by default.""*

There are two kinds of transfer happening in your home right now whether you are aware of it or not. The first ispassive transfer— what your children absorb by simply watching you live. Your unguarded moments. Your default reactions. The way you talk about people you disagree with. What you do with your Sunday mornings. This transfer is always happening. You cannot turn it off.

The second isintentional transfer— what you deliberately speak, model, and create space for in your children's lives. The convictions you name out loud. The faith you practice visibly. The character you require and celebrate. The future you call out in them before they can see it themselves.This is the transfer that changes a family line.

The man who understands this does not wait for a teachable moment. He creates one. He does not wait until his son asks a spiritual question. He raises a son who knows where to bring his spiritual questions. He does not wait until his daughter is in crisis to tell her who she is. He has been telling her since she was an infant — so that when the crisis comes, she already knows the answer.

What you fail to pass on intentionally will be replaced by whatever the world passes on by default. The culture is not neutral. It has its own transfer system — its own values, its own vision of manhood, its own definition of success. And it is working around the clock. The only thing that counters it is a father who is more deliberate than the culture is persistent.

Psalm 78:1–7 · ESV

> *""Give ear, O my people, to my teaching… I will open my mouth in a parable; I will utter dark sayings from of old, things that we have heard and known, that our fathers have told us. We will not hide them from their children, but tell to the coming generation the glorious deeds of the Lord, and his might, and the wonders that he has done… so that they should set their hope in God and not forget the works of God, but keep his commandments.""*

God's Expectation Has Always Been Generational, Not Individual

01 We Do Not Hide It — We Tell It

The text says "we will not hide them from their children." The default for too many fathers is silence — about faith, about failure, about what they believe and why. God's instruction is the opposite. Open your mouth. Tell them. When I called out my sons' names over them as infants, I was not hiding it. I was declaring it. Your story is not just yours. It belongs to the next generation.

02 Hope is a Transferable Asset

The goal of the transfer is that they "should set their hope in God." You are not just passing down rules or religion. You are passing down a place to put their hope when life gets hard. The man who gives his children a God to run to has given them something money cannot buy and death cannot take. I wanted my sons to know — from the earliest moment of their lives — that there was a God who knew their name before I did.

03 The Transfer Goes Beyond Your Children

Psalm 78 speaks of telling "the coming generation" — not just your children but their children. What I prayed over my sons as infants is now something they are carrying into their own homes, their own marriages, their own children. You are not parenting one generation. You are shaping a lineage.

THE ILLUSTRATION

1996 — THE MILLER BOYZ BEGIN

In early 1996, a doctor confirmed what Tessy and I had been believing God for. We were pregnant with our first child. Our family, which had begun on July 15th, 1994, was now expanding beyond the two of us. What we did not know in 1996 was that over the next ten years, God would expand that family to seven. Five sons. The Miller Boyz.

I remember holding each of them as infants and doing something I could not have explained theologically at the time. I would call their names out to the Lord. Speak over them. Declare God's plan and purpose over their lives. I even called out their future wives — women they had not yet met, in some cases not yet born. I prayed over their callings. Their character. The men they would become.

I did not have a name for what I was doing. I had not read a book about it. I had not attended a conference on the subject. But looking back now, I know exactly what it was.I was practicing generational transfer.Deliberately. Intentionally. Before I had words for it. I was passing something into my sons — faith, identity, a sense of divine purpose — before they could even ask for it.

Today, all five of my sons are in faith. All five are serving. All three who are married, married women of God. The Miller Boyz did not happen by accident. They happened because a father decided — early, deliberately, and consistently — to transfer something worth keeping.

I did not know what to call it in 1996. I know what to call it now. Generational transfer. And it works.

> **APPLICATION FOR YOU**
>
> You do not have to wait until your children are teenagers to begin the transfer. You do not have to wait until you have the right words or the right moment.Start now. Speak over them. Call their names to God. Declare their futures.You may not see the full fruit of it for twenty years. But twenty years from now, you will be grateful you started today.

1 Map Your Generational Chain

Sit down and write out what you know about your father, your grandfather, and as far back as you can trace. What did they believe? What did they value? What did they pass down — good and broken? You cannot navigate where you are going without understanding where you came from.

> → *Write it out this week. Identify three things you want to keep and two things that stop with you.*

2 Name Your Transfer Goals

What are the three most important things you want to deliberately transfer to your children? Faith? Character? A work ethic? A love for Scripture? A covenant approach to marriage? Name them specifically. What does not get named does not get transferred.

> → *Write them down. Share them with your spouse. Post them somewhere visible.*

3   **Tell Your Story — Out Loud**

This month, sit your children down and tell them the story of how you came to faith. Not a sanitized version. The real one — including the detours. Your testimony is one of the most powerful transfer tools you have, and most children have never heard it fully told.

> → *Schedule a night this month. Tell the story. Let them ask questions.*

---

4   **Break One Generational Pattern This Month**

Every family has patterns that should not survive another generation. Identify one — anger, silence, addiction, workaholism, emotional unavailability — and make one concrete move toward breaking it this month. Name it to someone you trust. Get help if you need it.

> → *Name it. Speak it out loud. Take one step toward ending it today.*

---

5   **Create a Family Faith Ritual**

Choose one consistent practice that will become the rhythm of your home — a weekly blessing at the dinner table, a monthly family prayer night, a yearly tradition that declares who you are. Rituals become memories. Memories become identity. Identity becomes legacy.

> → *Choose one. Start it this week. Do not wait for the perfect moment.*

06 Find a Hole-in-the-Wall

Pick a small town within an hour of home that your family has never visited. Drive there with no reservations and no plan. Find a diner, a barbecue shack, or a family restaurant you have never heard of. Order the special. Talk to the owner. Let the kids pick the dessert. The whole point is going somewhere new together — because families that explore together build memories that last.

→ *No GPS recommendations. Just drive until something looks good.*

FAMILY EXPERIENCES THIS MONTH

Experience 01

The Family History Night

Pull out old photos, home videos, or whatever artifacts you have. Walk your children through the story of your family — where you came from, what shaped you, what you are proud of and what you have had to overcome. Let them see they are part of a story bigger than themselves.

""What do you know about your great-grandparents?""

""What's one thing you want our family to always be known for?""

Experience 02

The Blessing Dinner

At dinner, go around the table and have Dad speak a specific, personal blessing over each person — including his wife. Not generic. Specific. Name what you see, what you believe, what you are declaring over them. Then invite each person to bless someone else.

"A character quality you see developing in them"

"A future you are believing God for over their life"

Visit a Place That Shaped You

Take your children to a place that was significant in your spiritual formation — the church where you were saved, the camp where God got hold of you, a mentor's home. Stand there. Tell the story. Let the geography become part of their story too.

""What did God do in your life here?""

""What do you want God to do in mine?""

Write Letters to Future Grandchildren

Have every family member write a letter to a grandchild or great-grandchild they may never meet. What do you want them to know? What do you want to pass to them? Seal the letters. Keep them somewhere safe. This is generational transfer in its purest form.

""What I want you to know about our family is…""

""The thing I hope you never forget is…""

DAILY BIBLE READING PLAN

WEEK ONE — WHAT WAS PASSED TO YOU

Monday	**Psalm 78:1–7**	*The Command to Tell*
Tuesday	**Exodus 20:5–6**	*Generational Patterns*
Wednesday	**2 Timothy 1:5**	*Faith Passed Through Generations*
Thursday	**Proverbs 17:6**	*The Crown of Old Men*
Friday	**Deuteronomy 4:9**	*Do Not Forget — Teach Your Children*

WEEK TWO — WHAT YOU CHOOSE TO PASS ON

Monday	**Genesis 18:19**	*Abraham's Assignment*
Tuesday	**Deuteronomy 11:18–21**	*Write It on Your Heart — Then Your Home*
Wednesday	**Joel 1:3**	*Tell Your Children's Children*
Thursday	**Proverbs 22:6**	*Train Up a Child*
Friday	**Joshua 4:6–7**	*When Your Children Ask*

WEEK THREE — BREAKING WHAT SHOULD NOT CONTINUE

Monday	**Ezekiel 18:14–17**	*The Son Who Does Not Follow His Father's Sin*
Tuesday	**Romans 12:2**	*Be Transformed — Not Conformed*

Wednesday	**Galatians 5:1**	*Freedom — Not Slavery to the Past*
Thursday	**2 Corinthians 5:17**	*New Creation — New Patterns*
Friday	**Isaiah 43:18–19**	*Behold, I Am Doing a New Thing*

WEEK FOUR — THE LINEAGE YOU ARE BUILDING

Monday	**Psalm 112:1–2**	*His Children Will Be Mighty*
Tuesday	**Proverbs 13:22**	*A Good Man Leaves an Inheritance*
Wednesday	**Acts 2:39**	*The Promise Is for You and Your Children*
Thursday	**3 John 1:4**	*No Greater Joy*
Friday	**Psalm 127:3–5**	*Children Are a Heritage*

MONTHLY MEMORY VERSE

""We will not hide them from their children, but tell to the coming generation the glorious deeds of the Lord.""

Psalm 78:4 · ESV

1.

What did your father pass to you — intentionally or unintentionally — that you are grateful for? What did he fail to pass that you are still paying for?

____

____

____

____

2.

Name three things you are deliberately trying to transfer to your children. Are you actually transferring them — or just assuming you are?

____

____

____

____

3.

What is one generational pattern in your family line that must stop with you? What is one concrete step you will take this month toward ending it?

____

____

____

____

4.

Have your children ever heard the full story of how you came to faith? If not — what is stopping you from telling it?

____

____

____

____

5.

If your grandchildren were asked "What did your grandfather believe and how did he live?" — what would they say? What do you want them to say?

____

____

____

____

MONTHLY CHALLENGE

The Transfer Decision

This month, write a one-page document titled "What Passes Through Me." Name every conviction, value, and faith marker you are committing to transfer deliberately to your children. Sign it. Date it. Read it every month for the rest of this year. What you name, you can transfer. What you never name, you will likely lose.

I COMMIT TO THIS CHALLENGE BEGINNING:

____

WHAT I AM BELIEVING GOD FOR THIS MONTH:

____

____

________________________   ________________________

Signature   Date

MONTH THREE

Chapter 3

03

Raising Kings

---

*""You are not trying to raise a happy child.
You are trying to raise a man of God. Those
are not the same assignment.""*

— J.S.M.

Somewhere along the way, fatherhood got redefined.

The goal became: keep them happy. Keep them safe. Keep them comfortable.

And fathers began measuring their success by how little their children suffered — instead of how well their children were prepared.

We started feeding boys when we should have been shaping men.

And now we are living with the results of that trade.

Look around. The culture is drowning in men who never became men — boys in adult bodies, with adult responsibilities they were never trained to carry. Men who crumble under pressure because no one ever let them experience pressure. Men who have no convictions because no one ever modeled the cost of holding one. Men who cannot lead their families because they were never taught what leadership actually requires.

""You are not trying to raise a happy child. You are trying to raise a man of God. Those are not the same assignment.""

This did not happen by accident. It happened because a generation of fathers decided that their primary job was to be their son's friend, their daughter's protector from all pain, and the provider of maximum comfort. And in doing so, they failed to do the one thing their children actually needed: prepare them.

The most dangerous thing you can do for your son is remove every obstacle from his path. You are not protecting him — you are disabling him. You are raising a boy who has never learned what he is made of because you have never given him the opportunity to find out. Difficulty is not the enemy of your child's development. It is the instrument of it.

Raising kings means raising children who know who they are, what they believe, and what they are willing to pay to stand for it. It means raising sons who know their purpose and daughters who know their worth. It means that when the storm comes — and it will come — your children do not fold. They hold. Because someone prepared them for exactly this.

A king is not born comfortable. A king is forged. He is shaped by a father who refuses to let ease become the highest value in the home — who understands that what does not challenge a child does not change a child. The man who raises his son to handle difficulty is giving him a gift that no amount of money, protection, or convenience can replace.

And there is one more thing that raises kings — something that has nothing to do with physical toughness and everything to do with what your sons watch every single day. Your boys are learning how to treat a woman by watching how you treat their mother. What they see in your marriage is the standard they will carry into their own. Raise kings by being one — not just in how you face difficulty, but in how you love.

SCRIPTURE DEEP DIVE

1 Kings 2:1–3 · ESV

> *""When David's time to die drew near, he commanded Solomon his son, saying, 'I am about to go the way of all the earth. Be strong, and show yourself a man, and keep the charge of the Lord your God, walking in his ways and keeping his statutes, his commandments, his rules, and his testimonies… that you may prosper in all that you do and wherever you turn.'""*

A Father's Job Is to Produce a Man, Not Protect a Boy

01 The First Command is Character, Not Comfort

David's dying words to Solomon were not "be happy" or "be successful." They were "be strong and show yourself a man." The first thing a father is responsible for is the formation of character — the kind that holds when everything around it is shaking.

02 Obedience to God is the Foundation of Prosperity

David connects keeping God's commands directly to prospering in all you do. He is not promising ease — he is promising foundation. A child who is trained in obedience to God has been given the most durable infrastructure a human life can have.

03 A Father Passes the Charge, Not Just the Crown

David gave Solomon the charge of the Lord — not just the throne of Israel. The position without the conviction is just power with no compass. A father who raises his children for success without raising them for righteousness has raised them for danger.

THE MILLER BOYZ — RAISED, NOT JUST FED

My boys earned scars. I mean that literally.

Stitches. Dirt bikes going through fences. Lost teeth on handlebars. Flipped four-wheelers. We killed, cleaned, and ate fresh kill on camping trips. We stared death in the face every time we got on that boat in the Atchafalaya Basin — five-person rafts being pulled at forty miles per hour through one of the most treacherous waterways in Louisiana.

Was it intentional? Completely. I intentionally limited screen time. I limited the outside voices trying to direct my sons toward a softer version of manhood. I needed them to know what it felt like when everything is moving fast, the stakes are real, and the only thing between you and disaster is your preparation, your courage, and the man next to you. I needed them to learn that lesson before life taught it to them in a way I could not control.

In every one of those moments, I was teaching — about courage, about responsibility, about protecting the person next to you, about what men do when things get hard. Looking out for each other. Respecting others. Protecting the weak. These were not speeches. They were lived in the mud, on the water, around a fire.

But there was something else happening the whole time — something quieter and just as deliberate. All five of my boys had a front-row seat watching how I treated their mother. Every day. I spoke kind words to her. I lifted her up. I loved on her in front of them — not as a performance, but as a way of life. I was giving my sons a curriculum in marriage that no school in the world could teach.

> *Today, three of my sons are married. And I watch how they treat their wives. How they love them, honor them, lead them. Nobody taught them that in a classroom. They learned it at home, watching their father.*

APPLICATION FOR YOU

Your son needs to earn a few scars. Let him face difficulty that is real. Let him feel the weight of responsibility. Let him fail at things that will not kill him — and watch what it builds in him. And while you are doing all of that, let him watch how you treat his mother. Both things together — that is how you raise a king.

THIS MONTH'S IMPLEMENTATION

1 Raise the Standard in Your Home

This month, identify one area where you have let the standard slip — in behavior, responsibility, integrity, or effort — and raise it. Not harshly. But clearly. Name the standard. Explain why it matters. Then hold it consistently, regardless of pushback.

> → *Name the standard this week. Hold it without negotiating it away the first time it is tested.*

2 **Give Your Son Real Responsibility**

Assign your son something that is genuinely his to own —
a project, a responsibility in the home, a role in the family.
Something he can succeed or fail at. Something that
matters. Boys become men by being trusted with things that
are real.

> → *Assign it this week. Do not rescue him when it gets hard.*
> *Coach him through it.*

3 **Have the Vision Conversation**

Sit with each of your children and speak specifically about
who you believe they are becoming. Not performance —
identity. "I see in you a man who will..." Tell them what
you see. Tell them what you believe God has put in them.
Vision spoken by a father becomes a target a child spends
their life aiming for.

> → *Have this conversation individually with each child this*
> *month.*

4   Model What You Are Asking For

You cannot raise men of integrity if you cut corners. You cannot raise daughters who respect themselves if they watch you disrespect their mother. You cannot raise sons who keep their word if you don't keep yours. This month, audit the gap between what you require of your children and what you require of yourself.

→ Identify one area where your standard for yourself is lower than what you require of them. Fix it.

5   Introduce Your Children to Difficulty on Purpose

Choose one hard thing for your family to do together this month — a physically demanding activity, a service project, a fast, a difficult conversation. Difficulty faced together builds a kind of bond and resilience that ease cannot produce. Kings are forged, not found.

→ Plan it. Do it together. Debrief it around the table afterward.

06 The Sonic Run

Pile everybody in the car and head to Sonic. Everyone orders what they want — no budget conversation, no healthy alternatives tonight. Roll the windows down. Eat in the parking lot. Put on a playlist that everyone argues about. This is not about the food. It is about showing your family that you enjoy being with them. That they are not an obligation — they are your people. Sometimes the most powerful thing a father can do is just have fun.

→ *You pay. Everyone picks. No rushing.*

FAMILY EXPERIENCES THIS MONTH

Experience 01

The Hard Thing Day

Pick one hard physical challenge and do it as a family. A long hike, a manual project, something that requires sustained effort. No complaining allowed. Dad leads from the front. Debrief over a meal afterward: what did it feel like to push through?

""What was the hardest moment? What did you learn about yourself?""

""When do you want to quit in real life? What helps you push through?""

Experience 02

Serve Someone Harder Than You

Find a family in your church or community going through something genuinely difficult and serve them as a family. Cook a meal, do yard work, spend time with them. Let your children see need up close and respond to it. Compassion is caught, not taught.

""How did it feel to give something without getting anything back?""

""What do you have that others don't? What does that require of you?""

Experience 03

The Man-to-Man Walk

Take your son on a walk — just the two of you. No destination required. Tell him what a man is. Tell him what you expect him to become. Tell him what you are proud of in him already. Then ask him what he thinks it means to be a man. Listen without correcting.

"What you believe a man's first responsibility is"

"What you wish someone had told you at his age"

Experience 04

Introduce a Mentor

Identify a man in your community whose character you deeply respect, and intentionally introduce him to your son. Have them over for dinner. Let your son hear another man of God speak. A wise father knows his son needs more than one voice shaping him.

"A man whose marriage you respect"

"A man whose faith has survived real pressure"

DAILY BIBLE READING PLAN

WEEK ONE — WHAT A MAN IS		
Monday	**1 Kings 2:1–4**	*David's Final Words to Solomon*
Tuesday	**1 Corinthians 16:13**	*Act Like Men*
Wednesday	**Proverbs 27:17**	*Iron Sharpens Iron*
Thursday	**Micah 6:8**	*What God Requires*
Friday	**Joshua 1:6–9**	*Be Strong and Courageous*

WEEK TWO — THE COST OF CONVICTION		
Monday	**Daniel 1:8**	*Daniel Resolved*
Tuesday	**Daniel 3:17–18**	*Even If He Does Not*
Wednesday	**Romans 5:3–5**	*Suffering Produces Character*
Thursday	**James 1:2–4**	*The Testing of Your Faith*
Friday	**Hebrews 12:7–11**	*Discipline Produces a Harvest*

WEEK THREE — THE FATHER WHO PREPARES		
Monday	**Proverbs 22:6**	*Train Up a Child*
Tuesday	**Ephesians 6:4**	*Bring Them Up in the Discipline*
Wednesday	**Proverbs 29:17**	*Discipline Your Son*
Thursday	**Proverbs 13:24**	*He Who Loves His Son is Diligent to Discipline*

Friday	**Psalm 144:12**	*May Our Sons Be Like Plants Grown Up*

WEEK FOUR — IDENTITY BEFORE ACHIEVEMENT		
Monday	**Psalm 139:13–16**	*Fearfully and Wonderfully Made*
Tuesday	**Jeremiah 1:5**	*Before I Formed You*
Wednesday	**Ephesians 2:10**	*His Workmanship*
Thursday	**Romans 8:14–16**	*Sons of God*
Friday	**1 John 3:1**	*What Manner of Love*

MONTHLY MEMORY VERSE

""Be watchful, stand firm in the faith, act like men, be strong.""

1 Corinthians 16:13 · ESV

LEGACY BUILDER REFLECTION

1.

Are you raising your children to be comfortable or to be capable? Where in your parenting has comfort become the highest value?

____

____

____

____

2.

What have you required of your son recently that was genuinely
hard for him? If the answer is nothing — what does that tell you?

____

____

____

____

3.

What is the gap between what you require of your children and
what you require of yourself? Be honest.

____

____

____

____

4.

What specific vision have you spoken over each of your children
recently? Not praise for performance — a declaration of who they
are becoming.

____

____

____

5.

When your children face the hardest moments of their adult lives, what do you want them to reach for? Are you giving them that now?

____

____

____

____

30 Days of Standards

For 30 days, hold one higher standard in your home without negotiating it away. Pick one — integrity, effort, language, respect, responsibility. Name it. Explain why it matters. Then hold it every single day. A man who won't hold a standard in his home has surrendered the most important leadership position he will ever hold.

I COMMIT TO THIS CHALLENGE BEGINNING:

____

WHAT I AM BELIEVING GOD FOR THIS MONTH:

____

____

_____________________________   ______________

Signature   Date

MONTH FOUR

Chapter 4

04

The Quiet Marriage Killer Nobody Talks About

""Your marriage is either the greatest gift or the greatest wound you give your children.""

— J.S.M.

THE CORE PRINCIPLE

I want to start by asking you a question. And I want you to actually think about it — don't just let it fly past you.

When you hear the phrase "marriage killer" — what comes to mind?

Affairs. Pornography. Money fights. Neglect. Anger. Addiction.

Those things are real. Every one of them. And every one of them gets talked about — in books, in counseling, in church. We have sermons on all of it.

But what I want to talk about doesn't show up on most lists.

It's quieter than all of those. It doesn't announce itself. Nobody gets caught. Nobody blows up. There's no dramatic moment.

And I've watched it do more damage — slowly, quietly, invisibly — than almost anything else combined.

We call it disengagement. Not with a bang. Not with a crisis. With a slow, quiet fade. It does not announce itself. It does not arrive with a confrontation or a confession. It happens in the margins —

in the moments you were too tired to engage, the conversations you chose not to have, the emotional territory you quietly stopped showing up for.

""A husband who is physically present but emotionally and spiritually gone.""

Most men who disengage from their marriages never meant to. It happened in the in-between — in small moments of disconnection that went unaddressed, in needs that were never named, in the slow replacement of intimacy with routine. Before long, two people are living parallel lives under the same roof, and neither one can point to the moment it started.

""Your marriage may have sections of wall that have been broken down for years. That is not the end of the story. That is the beginning of the rebuild.""

The dangerous thing about disengagement is that it does not feel like failure. It feels like survival. You are providing. You are present physically. You are not doing anything wrong in the ways that would show up on a list. And so you tell yourself the marriage is fine — while your wife is quietly starving for a husband who is actually there.

I want to show you a man who understood what to do when he found himself looking at broken walls. Nehemiah. When he arrived in Jerusalem and surveyed the damage, he did not minimize what he saw. He did not tell himself the wall was fine. He went out at night, section by section, and made himself look at the full extent of the destruction. Then he called the people together and told them the truth: "The wall is broken down, the gates are burned — and we are in distress."

That is the first act of a rebuilder. Name the damage honestly. Not what you wish it were. What it actually is. Then Nehemiah did something that every disengaged husband must do. He did not organize a committee. He did not announce his intentions before he did the work. He got up. He went out. He picked up a stone and started building. Quietly. Humbly. Without fanfare. Section by section. Gate by gate. Day by day.

The man who names the damage and picks up a stone is already further along than the man still pretending the wall is fine. Disengagement is not the end of your marriage. It is a warning. And a warning, if you respond to it, becomes the beginning of the deepest season of covenant your marriage has ever known.

Your marriage is the primary curriculum your children are enrolled in right now. They are learning what love looks like, what conflict looks like, what covenant looks like — from watching the two of you every single day. The question is not whether you are teaching them. The question is what you are teaching them.

SCRIPTURE DEEP DIVE

Ephesians 5:25–28 · ESV

""Husbands, love your wives, as Christ loved the church and gave himself up for her… In the same way husbands should love their wives as their own bodies. He who loves his wife loves himself.""

WHAT THIS PASSAGE TEACHES THE LEGACY BUILDER

God Did Not Give Us a Feeling — He Gave Us a Command

01 Love is a Decision, Not a Destination

The word "love" in this passage is not a feeling — it is an action verb. Christ did not wait until He felt like going to the cross. He went because of covenant. Legacy Builders love their wives the same way: by decision, by discipline, and by daily recommitment regardless of how the season feels.

02 The Standard is Sacrifice, Not Comfort

Christ "gave himself up for her." The standard God sets for husbands is not a comfortable partnership — it is self-giving sacrifice. Your wife's flourishing matters more than your convenience. Her needs matter more than your schedule. Her security matters more than your comfort zone.

03 What You Do to Her You Do to Yourself

Scripture says "he who loves his wife loves himself." You and your wife are one. When she is diminished by your neglect, you are diminished. When she flourishes under your love and leadership, the whole family rises. A healthy marriage is the engine of a healthy legacy.

THE ILLUSTRATION

2015 — THE YEAR THE SLOW LEAK BECAME VISIBLE

By 2015, our house was buzzing twenty-four hours a day. Four teenage sons. One preteen. All five playing football — game once a week, practice four times a week, per son, per team. Throw in the occasional speeding ticket from a teenage driver, a fender-bender in a parking lot, the quarterly report card stress, and feeding five growing boys — five gallons of milk a week, four loaves of bread, what I can only describe as a fifty-five-gallon drum of cereal. Throw in the fast-paced ministry of a growing church and school, and the rising cost of car insurance for five teenage drivers coming down the pipeline.

What did that season produce in me? Tired. Exhausted. Under financial pressure. And the one word I did not see coming: disengaged. Not from the church. Not from the boys. From Tessy.

It was not anything dramatic. No blowup. No crisis. No moment anyone would have pointed to from the outside. Just a slow leak — the kind that happens when two people are both running at full speed in the same direction but no longer running together. Over time that slow leak left us emotionally flat toward one another. Physically present. Everywhere else — gone.

Then it broke open. And that was the grace. Because when it broke open, we did not walk away. We sat down. We had the conversations we had been avoiding. We looked at each other — really looked — and chose to fight for what we had built together. We regrouped. We realigned. We forgave each other for the ways we had both contributed to the drift. And we started the journey back — together.

> *Twelve years later, I would not trade that season of our marriage for anything in the world. Not because of what it cost us — because of what it built in us.*

APPLICATION FOR YOU

Disengagement is not the end of your marriage. It is a warning. And if you are honest enough to name it and brave enough to address it, that warning becomes the beginning of the deepest season of covenant your marriage has ever known. Do not wait for the break. Name the slow leak now. Pick up a stone and start rebuilding. The path back exists. I know — because I walked it.

THIS MONTH'S IMPLEMENTATION

01   Name the Drift

Before you can fix what is broken you have to name it honestly. This week, sit with a journal and answer: In what area has our marriage drifted most in the last 12 months? Emotionally? Spiritually? Physically? In friendship? Naming it is the first act of leadership.

> → *Share your honest answer with your wife this week — not as an accusation, but as a confession and an invitation.*

02 Pursue Her Again

Do you remember how you pursued her before the ring? The texts, the plans, the attention, the effort? She still needs to be pursued — maybe more now than then. This month, plan one intentional date that has nothing to do with the kids, the budget, or logistics. Just her. Just you.

> → *Plan and execute one real date this month. No phones. No agenda except her.*

03 Love Her Out Loud in Front of Your Kids

Your children need to see you choose their mother — publicly, consistently, and without embarrassment. Kiss her when you come home. Compliment her at the dinner table. Let your children see that their father is still in love with their mother. This is one of the greatest gifts you can give them.

> → *This week, say something specific and genuine about your wife in front of your children at least three times.*

04 Have the Conversation You've Been Avoiding

Every couple has one. The conversation that keeps getting postponed because the timing is never right or the topic feels too heavy. Unaddressed tension does not dissolve — it compounds. This month, have that conversation. Bring it in love, with humility, and with the goal of connection — not winning.

→ Identify the conversation. Schedule a time. Show up ready to listen more than you speak.

05 Pray Together — Out Loud

Couples who pray together are spiritually unified in a way no other practice can replicate. If you are not praying together, start tonight. Even 60 seconds. Even if it feels awkward. A man who leads his wife to the throne of God is doing something that reverberates for generations.

→ Begin praying out loud with your wife tonight. Start with: "God, thank you for this woman."

06 Date Night in the Driveway

After the kids are in bed — or with your older children watching the younger ones — pull two chairs into the driveway. Bring something cold to drink. No phones on the table. Just you and your wife, outside, under the sky, talking about whatever comes up. Not about schedules. Not about problems. About your life together. This costs nothing and it rebuilds something that busyness quietly steals.

→ *One hour. Two chairs. No agenda.*

FAMILY EXPERIENCES THIS MONTH

Date Night — Kids Watch You Leave

Let your kids see you get dressed up and take their mom on a real date. Tell them where you're going. Come home and tell them one thing you love about their mother. Make pursuit visible.

"That marriage is worth investing in"

"That mom is a priority — not just a parent"

Family Love Story Night

Pull out the wedding album or old photos. Tell your kids the story of how you met, how you fell in love, how you knew. Let them hear the romance. Let them see that their parents have a story worth telling.

""What made you fall in love with Mom?""

""What's your favorite memory together?""

Cook Dinner Together as a Family

Pick a meal. Assign every family member a job. Cook it together. Sit down together. No phones. Dad leads a toast honoring Mom. Let the dinner table be a place where family culture is built one meal at a time.

""What's one word that describes our family right now?""

""What's one way we can love each other better this month?""

Write Your Wife a Letter — Read It Aloud

Write your wife a genuine letter about what she means to you and your family. Then read it aloud to her in front of your children. Watch what it does to your kids when they see their father honor their mother with his words.

"A specific memory that shows who she is"

"What you see in her that your kids should notice too"

DAILY BIBLE READING PLAN

WEEK ONE — THE COVENANT

Monday	**Genesis 2:18–25**	*The Original Design*
Tuesday	**Malachi 2:13–16**	*God Hates Covenant Breaking*
Wednesday	**Proverbs 5:18–19**	*Rejoice in Your Wife*
Thursday	**Matthew 19:4–6**	*What God Has Joined*
Friday	**Hebrews 13:4**	*Marriage Held in Honor*

WEEK TWO — THE PURSUIT

Monday	**Song of Solomon 2:3–7**	*The Language of Pursuit*
Tuesday	**Ephesians 5:25–33**	*The Husband's Call*
Wednesday	**1 Corinthians 13:4–7**	*Love Defined*
Thursday	**Colossians 3:19**	*Love and Do Not Embitter*
Friday	**1 Peter 3:7**	*Live with Your Wife in Understanding*

WEEK THREE — THE BATTLE

Monday	**Proverbs 14:1**	*Building or Tearing Down*
Tuesday	**James 4:1–3**	*Where Conflict Comes From*
Wednesday	**Ephesians 4:26–27**	*Don't Let the Sun Go Down*
Thursday	**Proverbs 15:1**	*A Soft Answer*

| Friday | **Romans 12:10** | *Outdo One Another in Honor* |

Monday	**Ruth 1:16–17**	*Covenant Loyalty*
Tuesday	**Proverbs 31:28–29**	*Her Children Rise Up*
Wednesday	**Ecclesiastes 9:9**	*Enjoy Life With Your Wife*
Thursday	**1 John 4:19**	*We Love Because He Loved First*
Friday	**Revelation 19:7**	*The Marriage That Points to Heaven*

MONTHLY MEMORY VERSE

""Husbands, love your wives, as Christ loved the church and gave himself up for her.""

Ephesians 5:25 · ESV

LEGACY BUILDER REFLECTION

1.

In what specific area has your marriage drifted most in the past 12 months? Be honest.

____

____

2.

What is your wife's primary love language — and when is the last time you served her in it intentionally?

____

____

____

____

3.

What are your children learning about marriage by watching yours right now?

____

____

____

____

4.

What is one conversation you have been avoiding with your wife? What is stopping you from having it?

____

____

____

5.

Write three specific things you love and admire about your wife that you have never told her clearly.

The 30-Day Pursuit

For 30 days, do one intentional, specific act of love for your wife every single day. Not grand gestures — daily faithfulness. A note. A text. A prayer out loud. A chore she didn't ask you to do. A moment of full attention. Thirty days of pursuit. Watch what happens to your home.

I COMMIT TO THIS CHALLENGE BEGINNING:

____

WHAT I AM BELIEVING GOD FOR THIS MONTH:

____

____

_________________________   _________________________
Signature   Date

MONTH FIVE

Chapter 5

05

5 Areas Every Father Must Protect

""If you do not stand for something in your home, something will stand in your place — and you will not like what it is.""

— J.S.M.

THE CORE PRINCIPLE

Your family is under attack.

I am not being dramatic. I am being precise.

The culture, the enemy, and the natural drift of an undisciplined life are all working in the same direction — and that direction is away from everything you are trying to build.

A man who is not actively protecting his family is passively surrendering it.

There is no neutral ground. You are either holding ground or losing it.

Protection is not primarily physical. Most of the threats your family faces today will never require you to throw a punch. They will require you to have a conversation you don't want to have. To draw a line that invites conflict. To say no to something your children desperately want — or something the world is telling you they desperately need. That kind of protection requires more courage than most men realize, and more consistency than most men sustain.

> *""If you do not stand for something in your home, something will stand in your place — and you will not like what it is.""*

The enemy does not knock on your front door and announce himself. He comes in through the screens, through the slow drift of unguarded time, through the voices you never vetted and the influences you never evaluated. He does not need a dramatic entrance. He just needs you to be passive long enough for the ground to shift beneath your family's feet — and for you not to notice until it is already gone.

There are five areas where every father must plant a flag and hold it. Not occasionally. Not when it is convenient. Consistently, visibly, and without apology. Because the people who need you to hold those lines are watching every single day — not to catch you failing, but because they need to know that someone is actually standing guard.

Area 1 — The Spiritual Atmosphere of Your Home. Someone is setting the spiritual temperature of your home. If it is not you, it is something else — and that something else is not neutral. You protect this by establishing prayer, Scripture, and worship as normal rhythms. Not performance. Normal. The spiritual atmosphere of a home is never an accident. It is always the overflow of the man leading it.

Area 2 — What Comes Through Your Screens. Every device in your home is a portal. What comes through that portal is shaping the minds, desires, and identity of your children. A man who gives his family unlimited, unmonitored access and calls himself a protector is deceiving himself. Know what your children are watching, playing, listening to. This is not control. This is stewardship.

Area 3 — The Relationships Influencing Your Children. You do not get to choose every voice that speaks into your children's lives. But you get to know what those voices are saying. A wise father is not paranoid about this — he is informed. He stays close enough to know who is in the room and what they are saying.

Area 4 — The Culture of Your Marriage in Front of Your Kids. Your children are watching how you treat your wife every single day. This is not a private matter. It is a public curriculum. Protect the dignity of your marriage by never letting your children see you disrespect the woman you asked them to call Mother.

Area 5 — Your Own Soul. You cannot protect what you are. If you are drifting spiritually, your home will drift. If you are consumed by something secret, it will eventually reach everyone under your roof. The most strategic protective move you can make is to ruthlessly guard your own walk with God. A man who keeps his soul in order keeps his home in order.

SCRIPTURE DEEP DIVE

Nehemiah 4:14 · ESV

> *""Do not be afraid of them. Remember the Lord, who is great and awesome, and fight for your brothers, your sons, your daughters, your wives, and your homes.""*

A Man Who Will Not Fight for His Family Has Already Surrendered It

01 Fear is the Enemy of Protection

Nehemiah's first word is "Do not be afraid." Fear is what causes fathers to look away when they should look directly at the threat. Fear is what makes men avoid the hard conversation, ignore the warning sign, and hope the problem resolves itself. A protecting father does not have the luxury of fear.

02 Your Motivation is Specific People, Not Abstract Principles

Nehemiah does not say fight for justice or fight for principles. He says fight for your brothers, your sons, your daughters, your wives, your homes. Protection is personal. The faces of the people in your home are your motivation. Look at them. Then hold the line.

03 Remembering God is What Makes You Immovable

Before he names who to fight for, Nehemiah says "remember the Lord, who is great and awesome." The foundation of a protecting father is not his own strength — it is his clarity about who God is. A man who knows what God is like does not have to be afraid of what the world is like.

THE ILLUSTRATION

THE SUNDAY DECISION — AND WHAT IT PRODUCED

All five of my boys were athletes. Not just good — they excelled at every sport they touched. And when you excel, the invitations start coming. Travel teams. Elite showcases. Weekend tournaments. And the pitch that came with every one of them was the same: "This is where the college coaches are. This is where scholarships get awarded. If your son isn't here, he won't get seen."

Every one of those tournaments was on Sunday.

I want to be honest about what that decision cost us. There were coaches who raised their eyebrows. Parents who thought we were handicapping our sons. Boys who watched teammates leave on Saturday mornings for tournaments while they stayed home. The pressure was real. The voice that said "you're going to cost them their future" was genuinely loud.

But I had decided something before the pressure arrived. The spiritual formation of my sons was not a bargaining chip. Sunday was not a preference — it was a conviction. And a conviction, by definition, is something you hold even when holding it costs you something. So we stayed. Week after week, season after season — we stayed. Church. Family. The non-negotiable.

Four of my five boys pursued college athletics after high school. Every one of them was awarded a scholarship in their sport.

The very thing we were told we would lose by protecting Sunday — God provided anyway. You cannot out-give God. And you cannot out-protect what He has already decided to cover.

APPLICATION FOR YOU

What is the Sunday in your home? What territory is the world telling you to surrender for the sake of opportunity — while God is calling you to protect it? Hold it. Not because you have a guarantee of the outcome. Because the One who called you to protect it is faithful to cover what you cannot. A man who holds the line on what God told him to hold will always have a testimony on the other side of it.

THIS MONTH'S IMPLEMENTATION

01   **Audit What Comes Through Your Screens**

This week, sit down and inventory every device in your home. What are your children watching, playing, and listening to? What are you consuming? You cannot protect what you have not examined. Pull back the curtain on the digital world operating inside your home and make deliberate decisions about what stays and what goes.

→ Set one new screen boundary this week — for your children and for yourself.

02 Protect the Sabbath in Your Home

The enemy's most effective strategy is not dramatic assault — it is the slow erosion of margin. A family that never rests never reconnects. This month, establish one day where the pace slows, screens are limited, and the family is together without an agenda. You are not just resting. You are resisting the culture of relentless motion that is slowly consuming your family's soul.

> → *Pick a day. Protect it. Refuse to let anything take it this month.*

03 Know Who Is Speaking Into Your Children

You cannot be the only voice, but you can know what the other voices are saying. This month, get informed about your children's friendships, their influencers, their online world, and the messages they are absorbing. Not as a spy — as a father who is paying attention. A man who knows what his children are hearing is a man who can counter the lies before they take root.

> → *Have one conversation with each child this month about who or what is influencing them most right now.*

04 Guard Your Own Soul First

You cannot protect what you are not. A man whose soul is drifting — from God, from his wife, from his own convictions — is a man whose family is already exposed. This month, take an honest inventory of your spiritual life. Are you in the Word? Are you in prayer? Are you accountable to someone? The most strategic protective act you can take is to ruthlessly guard your own walk with God.

→ *Identify one area of your personal spiritual life that has drifted. Address it this week.*

05 Draw a Line and Hold It

Every father has a line he needs to draw in his home — a boundary that protects what matters most. For some it is Sunday. For some it is what their children watch. For some it is who they spend time with. Whatever that line is for your family — draw it clearly, communicate it honestly, and hold it without apology. A line you do not hold is not a line at all.

→ *Identify the one boundary your family most needs right now. State it out loud this week. Then hold it.*

06 The Unplugged Evening

One evening this month — announce a no-screen night. Every device goes in a basket by the door. Then just see what happens. Play a board game. Tell stories. Go for a walk around the block. Sit on the porch. Let the silence be a little uncomfortable at first — that is normal. Then watch how quickly your family finds each other again. What you protect grows. What you neglect dies.

> → *Two hours minimum. No exceptions for anyone — including you.*

FAMILY EXPERIENCES THIS MONTH

Experience 01

The Screen Audit Night

Gather the whole family and do a screen inventory together. Every device on the table. What apps are on them? What are they watching? What does your family's digital diet actually look like? Make it honest, not punitive. Then together, set one new screen agreement that everyone commits to this month.

> *"What is one thing on your phone or screen that is pulling you away from what matters most?"*

> *"What would change in our family if we protected one evening a week from all screens?"*

Experience 02

The Boundary Walk

Take a walk around your neighborhood or property with your family. As you walk, talk about what you are protecting — your home, your peace, your family's faith. Stop at the front door and pray together before you go back in. This is not a formal exercise — it is a physical picture of a spiritual reality. You are a man who guards the gate. Let your family see it.

> *"What is one thing trying to get into our home right now that we need to guard against?"*

> *"What does it mean to you to know that Dad is paying attention to what comes through our door?"*

Experience 03

The Influence Conversation

Take each child on a one-on-one walk or drive this month and ask them honestly: Who are the five people that influence you most right now? Listen without reacting. You are not interrogating — you are paying attention. This conversation will tell you more about your child's world than a month of observation.

> *"Who do you want to be like when you grow up — and why that person?"*

> *"Is there anyone in your life right now who makes it harder to be who God made you to be?"*

Experience 04

The Family Prayer of Protection

Gather your family and pray specifically over your home. Name the gates — the screens, the friendships, the culture coming through the door — and ask God to guard them. Let your children hear their father pray with authority over their lives.

"What is one area of our home or family that you want us to pray for specifically this month?"

"What does it mean to you when you hear your father pray for you by name?"

WEEK ONE — WHAT YOUR HOME SAYS

Monday	**Deuteronomy 6:6–9**	*Write It on Your Doorposts*
Tuesday	**Proverbs 15:17**	*Better a Meal of Herbs*
Wednesday	**Psalm 101:2–3**	*I Will Walk in Integrity in My House*
Thursday	**Joshua 24:15**	*Choose This Day*
Friday	**Proverbs 14:1**	*The Wise Woman Builds Her House*

WEEK TWO — THE TONE OF THE HOME

Monday	**Ephesians 4:29–32**	*Let No Corrupting Talk Come Out*
Tuesday	**Colossians 3:12–15**	*Put On Compassion, Kindness, Humility*
Wednesday	**Proverbs 17:1**	*Better a Dry Morsel with Quiet*
Thursday	**Romans 15:5–7**	*Live in Harmony*
Friday	**1 Peter 3:8**	*Have Unity of Mind*

WEEK THREE — WHAT GETS CELEBRATED

Monday	**Proverbs 31:28–31**	*Her Children Rise and Call Her Blessed*
Tuesday	**1 Thessalonians 5:11**	*Encourage One Another and Build Up*

Wednesday	**Hebrews 10:24**	*Stir Up One Another to Love and Good Works*
Thursday	**Romans 12:15**	*Rejoice with Those Who Rejoice*
Friday	**Philippians 4:8**	*Think on These Things*

WEEK FOUR — BUILDING ON PURPOSE

Monday	**Matthew 7:24–27**	*The House Built on Rock*
Tuesday	**Psalm 127:1**	*Unless the Lord Builds the House*
Wednesday	**Proverbs 24:3–4**	*By Wisdom a House Is Built*
Thursday	**Nehemiah 2:17–18**	*Let Us Build*
Friday	**Haggai 1:7–8**	*Consider Your Ways — Build the House*

MONTHLY MEMORY VERSE

""Unless the Lord builds the house, those
who build it labor in vain.""

Psalm 127:1 · ESV

LEGACY BUILDER REFLECTION

1.

If your children were asked to describe in three words what it feels like to live in your home, what would they say? What do you wish they would say?

____

____

____

____

2.

What does your home's calendar say about what your family actually values? Does it match what you say you value?

____

____

____

____

3.

What do you celebrate most frequently in your home? What does that tell your children about what matters most to you?

____

____

____

4.

What is the emotional temperature of your home right now? What role do you play in setting that temperature?

5.

Write a one-sentence description of the culture you are intentionally trying to build in your home. Then ask: does the way I actually live match that sentence?

MONTHLY CHALLENGE

The 30-Day Protection Plan

For 30 days, stand guard over one specific gate in your home that has been left unprotected. It may be the screens. It may be the Sabbath. It may be your own soul. Choose the one area where the enemy has had the most access — and close it. Tell your family what you are doing and why. Do not negotiate with the drift. Hold the line every single day for thirty days and watch what God does with a man who refuses to surrender what matters most.

I COMMIT TO THIS CHALLENGE BEGINNING:

____

WHAT I AM BELIEVING GOD FOR THIS MONTH:

____

____

_________________________________   _______________

Signature   Date

MONTH SIX

Chapter 6

06

The Culture of Your Home

""Culture is invisible — but its effects are undeniable. You set it whether you mean to or not.""

— J.S.M.

Every home has a culture.

Most fathers did not choose it. They inherited it, stumbled into it, or let it form while they were busy with other things.

Culture is what happens in your home when no one is performing. It is the default. The normal. The atmosphere everybody breathes without noticing.

It is the tone in the car. The way conflict gets handled at dinner. What gets celebrated and what gets ignored.

Someone set that culture. In your home, that someone is you.

The culture of a home is not set by the rules on the refrigerator. It is set by the man who lives in it. Your children are not primarily shaped by what you tell them. They are shaped by what they observe — the emotional temperature, the spiritual tone, the way people in your home treat each other when things get hard. That atmosphere is the most powerful formation tool available to you. And it is either working for you or against you right now.

> *""Your children will not primarily remember what you said. They will*

remember what it felt like to live in your house.""

Culture is not created in the big moments. It is created in the repeated ones. The dinner table that is either a gathering or a pit stop. The way you greet your family when you walk through the door. What you laugh at. What you stop to pray over. What you make time for and what you let fall away. Every repeated behavior is a brick. Lay enough of them in the same direction and you have either built a cathedral or a wall.

Here is the hard truth most men avoid: the culture of your home is an accurate reflection of who you actually are — not who you intend to be, not who you are at church on Sunday, but who you are at 6pm on a Tuesday when you are tired and nobody is watching. That man sets the culture. And your family has been absorbing that culture every day, whether you have been deliberate about it or not.

The good news is that culture can be changed. Not by a single dramatic gesture, but by a sustained, deliberate series of small ones. A man who decides today to be present at the dinner table, to set the emotional tone before he walks through the door, to celebrate what matters and protect what is sacred — that man is building a new culture. It will not happen overnight. It will happen consistently. Culture always moves toward what is most repeatedly honored.

The most powerful cultural act a father can perform is to create a tradition. Not a rule. Not a policy. A tradition — something the family chooses and anticipates and builds memory around. Traditions become the skeleton of a family's identity. They are the answer to the question every child eventually asks: "Who are we?" When a family has traditions, the answer is not abstract. It is specific. It is lived. It is something they will carry into their own homes and pass to their own children long after you are gone.

SCRIPTURE DEEP DIVE

Deuteronomy 6:6–9 · ESV

> *""And these words that I command you today shall be on your heart. You shall teach them diligently to your children, and shall talk of them when you sit in your house, and when you walk by the way, and when you lie down, and when you rise. You shall bind them as a sign on your hand, and they shall be as frontlets between your eyes. You shall write them on the doorposts of your house and on your gates.""*

Faith is Not a Program — It is a Culture

01 Culture Starts with What is in Your Own Heart

God does not begin with "teach your children." He begins with "on your heart." The culture of your home flows from the inside out — from who you actually are when no one is watching, from what you actually love, from what genuinely moves you. You cannot produce a culture of faith from a heart that is not full of it.

02 Culture is Built in Ordinary Moments, Not Special Events

God describes culture-forming moments as sitting, walking, lying down, rising up. Not retreats or conferences or special services. The ordinary rhythm of a day. The culture of your home is built in the mundane moments — and whether those moments are saturated with faith or emptied of it is entirely up to you.

03 Make It Visible — Not Just Felt

Write it on the doorposts. Bind it as a sign. God tells His people to make their culture tangible, physical, and visible. What is visible in your home? What do your walls say? What does your calendar say? The visible things in a home declare what the family actually values — whether they intended that declaration or not.

THE ILLUSTRATION

> **THE MILLER STAYCATION — CULTURE MADE VISIBLE**
>
> *In 2020, we started a new tradition in the Miller family. We simply called it the Staycation.*
>
> *The weekend of Father's Day. At the time, three of my boys were married. On Thursday around 5pm, all the kids would arrive back at our house — sons, daughters-in-law, grandchildren. For the next seventy-two hours or so, we were all together under one roof. We ate every meal together. Sat at the same table three times a day. Played games together. Laughed together. Prayed together. Created memories together.*
>
> *I would rent a fifteen-passenger van so we could travel together for special meals or events. Not because it was efficient. Because it was us — loud, together, taking up space, doing life as a unit. There is something that happens when a family piles into a van together that cannot happen any other way.*
>
> *We did not post an itinerary or plan it weeks in advance. We just showed up. We ate. We talked. We sat with each other long after the plates were cleared, because nobody was in a hurry to leave. That table — full, loud, unhurried — that was the culture of our home made visible in a single weekend.*
>
> *The Staycation is now a tradition we all still look forward to, even as the families continue to grow. More spouses. More grandchildren. More chairs pulled up to the table. More noise. More laughter. More of exactly what we built it to be.*

We did not build it on a grand budget or a perfect plan. We built it on a decision — that being together mattered enough to protect a weekend on the calendar every year, no matter what else was happening.

APPLICATION FOR YOU

You do not need a tradition as elaborate as a seventy-two hour Staycation. You need something — some repeated, anticipated, protected practice that says to your family: this is who we are and this is what we value. Start small. Be consistent. Let it grow. Twenty years from now, your children will gather their own families around that same tradition — and tell their children where it came from.

THIS MONTH'S IMPLEMENTATION

1   Name Your Culture

Before you can build the culture you want, you have to honestly assess the culture you have. This week, ask yourself: if a stranger lived in my home for one week without knowing anything about us, what would they conclude we actually value? What would they say our home feels like? Honest diagnosis is the first step.

> → *Write down three words that describe your home's current culture. Then write three words that describe the culture you want. Work from the gap.*

2

Set the Emotional Tone

The emotional temperature of your home follows your emotional temperature. If you come home carrying unresolved anger, your family absorbs it. If you come home present and engaged, your family rises to it. This month, make a decision before you walk in the door: I am going to set a tone of warmth, engagement, and stability — regardless of what my day was like.

> → *Create a transition ritual between work and home. Five minutes in the car. A walk around the block. Something that helps you shift before you walk through the door.*

3

Create Family Vocabulary

Every family with a strong culture has language that belongs to them — phrases, words, sayings that carry meaning. "In this family, we…" Create words that become the internal language of your family's identity. Language shapes culture. Culture shapes behavior. Behavior shapes legacy.

> → *Come up with three phrases that belong to your family. Use them consistently until they become automatic.*

---

4 Make the Dinner Table Sacred

The dinner table is the most underused culture-forming tool in the modern home. Phones off. Everyone present. Dad leads a question — not a lecture, a question. Let everyone speak. Let there be laughter. Let there be honesty. A family that eats together, talks together, and listens to each other at the table is building something most families never build.

→ *Commit to four phone-free family dinners per week this month. Lead a question each time.*

5 Celebrate What You Want More Of

Culture follows celebration. What gets celebrated gets repeated. If you only notice your children's academic performance and never celebrate their character, you are building an achievement culture. Celebrate courage. Celebrate honesty. Celebrate faith. What you cheer for becomes what your family chases.

→ *This month, catch your children doing something right in character — not performance — and make a big deal of it.*

06 Build the Playlist Together

Sit down together and build a Miller family playlist — one song chosen by each person in the family. No vetoes. No judgment. Everyone picks one song that means something to them right now. Then put it on shuffle during dinner or on a family drive. Let each person explain why they picked theirs. You will learn things about your kids you did not know. And they will learn something about you.

> → *Save the playlist. Add to it every year. It will become a time capsule.*

FAMILY EXPERIENCES THIS MONTH

Experience 01

Create Your Family Crest

Sit together and design a family crest — a symbol, a motto, and three values that define who you are as a family. It does not have to be artistically brilliant. It has to be genuinely yours. Frame it. Post it. Let it become a visible declaration of your family's culture and identity.

"A symbol that represents your family's story"

"A motto that captures your family's mission"

Experience 02

The Culture Assessment Dinner

At dinner, ask each family member to answer honestly: "What three words would you use to describe the feeling of our home?" Write down every answer. No defensiveness. Just listening. Then ask: "What's one thing we could change that would make our home feel even better?"

"Dad goes last — and takes every answer seriously"

"No defensiveness. Only questions and listening."

Experience 03

Phone-Free Weekend

From Friday evening to Sunday evening, the phones go in a basket. Replace the time with presence — board games, walks, conversations, cooking together, reading. Let your family experience what it feels like when the biggest competitor for their attention is removed. Then talk about what you all noticed.

""What did you miss? What did you not miss at all?""

""What did we do this weekend that we should do more often?""

Experience 04

Celebrate a Character Win

This month, watch for a moment when one of your children demonstrates real character — honesty that cost them something, courage that surprised you, kindness that was not required. When you see it, stop and make a big deal of it. Take them out. Call it out publicly in the family. Let them feel what it is like when character gets celebrated.

"A culture where character matters more than performance"

"Children who know what you are actually watching for"

WEEK ONE — WHAT YOUR HOME SAYS

Monday	**Deuteronomy 6:6–9**	*Write It on Your Doorposts*
Tuesday	**Proverbs 15:17**	*Better a Meal of Herbs*
Wednesday	**Psalm 101:2–3**	*I Will Walk in Integrity in My House*
Thursday	**Joshua 24:15**	*Choose This Day*
Friday	**Proverbs 14:1**	*The Wise Woman Builds Her House*

WEEK TWO — THE TONE OF THE HOME

Monday	**Ephesians 4:29–32**	*Let No Corrupting Talk Come Out*
Tuesday	**Colossians 3:12–15**	*Put On Compassion, Kindness, Humility*
Wednesday	**Proverbs 17:1**	*Better a Dry Morsel with Quiet*
Thursday	**Romans 15:5–7**	*Live in Harmony*
Friday	**1 Peter 3:8**	*Have Unity of Mind*

WEEK THREE — WHAT GETS CELEBRATED

Monday	**Proverbs 31:28–31**	*Her Children Rise and Call Her Blessed*
Tuesday	**1 Thessalonians 5:11**	*Encourage One Another and Build Up*

Wednesday	**Hebrews 10:24**	*Stir Up One Another to Love and Good Works*
Thursday	**Romans 12:15**	*Rejoice with Those Who Rejoice*
Friday	**Philippians 4:8**	*Think on These Things*

WEEK FOUR — BUILDING ON PURPOSE

Monday	**Matthew 7:24–27**	*The House Built on Rock*
Tuesday	**Psalm 127:1**	*Unless the Lord Builds the House*
Wednesday	**Proverbs 24:3–4**	*By Wisdom a House Is Built*
Thursday	**Nehemiah 2:17–18**	*Let Us Build*
Friday	**Haggai 1:7–8**	*Consider Your Ways — Build the House*

MONTHLY MEMORY VERSE

""Unless the Lord builds the house, those who build it labor in vain.""

Psalm 127:1 · ESV

1.

If your children were asked to describe in three words what it feels like to live in your home, what would they say? What do you wish they would say?

____

____

____

____

2.

What does your home's calendar say about what your family actually values? Does it match what you say you value?

____

____

____

____

3.

What do you celebrate most frequently in your home? What does that tell your children about what matters most to you?

____

____

____

4.

What is the emotional temperature of your home right now? What role do you play in setting that temperature?

5.

Write a one-sentence description of the culture you are intentionally trying to build in your home. Then ask: does the way I actually live match that sentence?

30 Days of Intentional Culture

For 30 days, make one deliberate culture-setting decision every single day. One question at the dinner table. One moment of celebration. One time you set the tone before walking through the door. One intentional act of warmth. Culture is not built in grand gestures. It is built in small, repeated decisions. Make 30 of them.

I COMMIT TO THIS CHALLENGE BEGINNING:

____

WHAT I AM BELIEVING GOD FOR THIS MONTH:

____

____

________________________________   ________________

Signature   Date

07
Men Who Leave Marks

""God is not looking for famous men. IIe is looking for faithful ones. The world remembers the famous — eternity honors the faithful.""

— J.S.M.

THE CORE PRINCIPLE

We have confused influence with impact.

We have confused followers with fruit.

We have decided that a man's worth is measured by how many people know his name — and in doing so, we have undervalued the most consequential work any man can do.

The man who raises children who walk in integrity will outlast any platform.

The man who loves his wife faithfully for fifty years will leave a mark that no viral moment can touch.

The men who leave the deepest marks rarely appear on stages. They appear at dinner tables. They show up in the stands. They answer the phone at midnight. They stay when leaving would be easier. They keep their word when keeping it is costly. They build quietly, invisibly, stubbornly — in the private places where no one is filming and no one is measuring their reach.

> *""God is not looking for famous men. He is looking for faithful ones. The world remembers the famous — eternity honors the faithful.""*

The world has sold us a counterfeit version of significance. It tells us that what matters is what is visible — your platform, your following, your highlight reel. But the things that outlast a man are almost never the things that made him famous. They are the things that made him faithful. The prayers nobody heard. The conversations that never made it onto social media. The miles logged in ordinary places with ordinary people who happened to be his children.

A mark is not what you leave on a stage. A mark is what you leave in a person. It is the conviction that takes root in a child's heart because a father spoke it over them enough times that it became their own. It is the standard that a son holds himself to — not because anyone is watching, but because someone showed him what it looked like to hold a standard when no one was watching. That is the mark. And it does not wash off.

The most powerful marks are left in the most ordinary places. A pickup truck. A back porch. A fishing boat. A gravel road. The men who leave marks understand that significance is not found in the size of the moment — it is found in the intention behind it. Every ordinary moment with your child is either an investment or a missed opportunity. The Legacy Builder sees the investment. The drifting father misses the moment.

You do not need a platform to leave a mark. You need a family. You need a handful of people who are better because you showed up. A spouse who feels pursued and honored. Children who carry your convictions into their own homes. Grandchildren who grow up hearing stories about a grandfather who understood the assignment. That is not a small life. That is the most consequential life imaginable.

SCRIPTURE DEEP DIVE

Luke 16:10 · ESV

""One who is faithful in a very little thing is also faithful in much, and one who is dishonest in a very little thing is also dishonest in much.""

Legacy is Built in the Small Things Nobody Sees

01 Character is Consistent Across Scales

Jesus says the man who is faithful in little is faithful in much. This works in both directions. The man who cuts corners on small commitments will cut corners on large ones. The man who keeps his word in small things will keep it in large ones. Your character is not what you aspire to — it is what you consistently do in the small moments nobody's watching.

02 The Small Things Are the Test for the Large Ones

God does not give large responsibilities to men who have not been faithful with small ones. Before you pray for greater influence, examine what you are doing with the influence you already have. Are you faithful to your wife right now? To your children right now? To your word right now? That faithfulness is the test — and the training.

03 Dishonesty Compounds Downward

The reverse is equally true. Small dishonesty — with your finances, with your time, with your word — produces a man who cannot be trusted with anything that truly matters. The cracks always start small. And a man who does not take small cracks seriously is one day shocked by a collapse that everyone else saw coming.

THE ILLUSTRATION

14 MILES OF GRAVEL ROAD

Fourteen miles. That was the distance from the paved blacktop to the home of my grandfather, Mathius Miller — my dad's dad. Fourteen miles of gravel road, dust billowing behind the truck the whole way.

Those fourteen miles are forever etched in my mind. It was on that road that I sat in my dad's lap as he taught me to drive before I could reach the pedals. It was on that road that I held my first shotgun and he taught me to hunt. At the end of those fourteen miles was a pond where he taught me to swim. And during every one of those miles, we talked. We dreamed. He spoke into me.

He was not delivering a curriculum. He was not checking boxes on a fatherhood program. He was just driving to his father's house — and he made every mile count. The conversation, the lessons, the vision he spoke over me — none of it happened on a stage. All of it happened in a truck cab, on a dirt road, with dust on the windshield and nowhere particular to be.

Now, some fifty years later, I still find an excuse to go and drive that same stretch of gravel. Not because anything significant is waiting at the end of it. Because everything significant already happened on it. Those fourteen miles marked me in ways I am still discovering.

Grateful that my father understood the assignment. He did not need a platform. He had a pickup truck and fourteen miles — and he made it enough.

APPLICATION FOR YOU

What is your fourteen miles? What is the ordinary, unremarkable context where you have the most access to your child — the car ride, the dinner table, the back porch, the Saturday morning errand? That place is your platform. The mark you leave there will outlast anything you ever accomplish anywhere else. Do not wait for a significant moment. Make the ordinary one significant — by showing up with intention in the middle of it.

THIS MONTH'S IMPLEMENTATION

1 Be Faithful to One Small Thing Every Day

Choose one daily practice that costs you something — morning prayer, reading Scripture before your phone, calling your child just to tell them you love them, coming home at the time you said you would. Do it every day this month without exception. Faithfulness in small things is not the training ground for legacy. It is the legacy itself.

→ *Name the one daily practice. Track it. Do not miss a day this month.*

2 Keep a Promise You Have Been Postponing

Every man has a promise he has been meaning to keep —
to his children, his wife, a friend, himself. Identify one. Not
a comfortable one. A real one. And keep it this month. The
accumulated weight of unkept promises is one of the most
underestimated forms of integrity erosion in a father's life.

> → *Name the promise. Set a date to fulfill it. Do not let this
> month pass without keeping it.*

3 Invest in One Man

The men who leave marks are almost always men who
poured themselves into other men. This month, identify one
younger man — a son, a nephew, a young man in your
church — and invest in him. Have coffee. Share your story.
Offer your hard-won perspective. The influence you pour
into one man compounds for generations.

> → *Reach out this week. Set the first meeting. Show up with
> intention.*

4   Do One Anonymous Good

Serve someone this month in a way they will never know was you. Pay a bill. Leave a note. Meet a need. Do it with no social media post, no mention, no credit. Then sit with how it feels to give without receiving recognition. This is the character formation that platforms will never produce in you — and that God rewards in ways no audience can.

> → *Choose one. Do it. Tell no one.*

5   Write Your Personal Mission Statement

A man who leaves a mark is a man who knows what he is building and why. This month, write a one-paragraph personal mission statement — not a career mission, a life mission. Who are you trying to become? Who are you trying to impact? What mark are you deliberately choosing to leave? Put it somewhere you will read it regularly.

> → *Draft it this week. Refine it. Commit to it. Review it every month.*

06 Find a Piece of History

Drive to an old cemetery, a historic neighborhood, or a landmark in your area that has been around longer than you have. Walk around. Read names. Look at dates. Let the weight of other people's lives land on your family for a few minutes. Then ask your kids: what do you want people to remember about you? Let the conversation go. History has a way of making the important things clear.

→ *Bring nothing. Just your family and the quiet.*

FAMILY EXPERIENCES THIS MONTH

Experience 01

Visit a Legacy Maker

Take your family to visit an older man whose life they should observe — a godly grandfather, a senior pastor, a man from your church who has lived with integrity for decades. Let your children ask him questions. Let them hear from someone whose long obedience has produced something beautiful.

""What is the best decision you ever made in your marriage?""

""What would you tell your younger self about what actually matters?""

Experience 02

Serve Anonymously as a Family

Find a need in your community and meet it — anonymously, as a family. Rake a neighbor's yard without being asked. Leave groceries at someone's door. Stock a pantry. Let your children experience what it feels like to give without receiving credit. Then talk about it together.

""How did it feel to give without anyone knowing?""

""Do you think God noticed? How does that make you feel?""

The Faithfulness Dinner

At dinner, have each family member share the name of one person who has left a mark on their life — someone faithful, not famous. Tell the story of what that person did and why it mattered. Let the table fill with stories of ordinary faithfulness. Then ask: who will tell a story like that about us someday?

""What did that person do that made such a difference?""

""What mark do you want to leave on someone's life?""

Keep a Family Promise

As a family, identify one promise you have made to someone — a neighbor, a friend, a community — that has not been fulfilled. Fulfill it together this month. Let your children experience what it feels like when a family follows through. Then talk about why integrity matters, even when no one would have known the difference.

"A family culture where a promise means something"

"Children who understand that your word is your bond"

WEEK ONE — THE SMALL THINGS

Monday	**Luke 16:10**	*Faithful in Little — Faithful in Much*
Tuesday	**Matthew 25:21**	*Well Done, Good and Faithful Servant*
Wednesday	**Proverbs 20:6**	*A Faithful Man — Who Can Find?*
Thursday	**1 Corinthians 4:2**	*Required of Stewards — Be Faithful*
Friday	**Revelation 2:10**	*Be Faithful Unto Death*

WEEK TWO — INTEGRITY WHEN NO ONE IS WATCHING

Monday	**Proverbs 10:9**	*Whoever Walks in Integrity Walks Securely*
Tuesday	**Psalm 15:1–5**	*Who Shall Dwell on Your Holy Hill*
Wednesday	**Daniel 6:4**	*No Error or Fault Found in Daniel*
Thursday	**Proverbs 11:3**	*The Integrity of the Upright*
Friday	**Luke 6:31**	*Do to Others as You Would Have Them Do*

WEEK THREE — THE LONG OBEDIENCE

Monday	**Galatians 6:9**	*Do Not Grow Weary in Doing Good*

Tuesday	**Hebrews 12:1**	*Run with Endurance*
Wednesday	**Psalm 37:3–4**	*Trust in the Lord and Do Good*
Thursday	**2 Timothy 4:7**	*I Have Kept the Faith*
Friday	**James 1:12**	*Blessed Is the Man Who Remains Steadfast*

WEEK FOUR — WHAT LASTING LOOKS LIKE

Monday	**Hebrews 11:39–40**	*These All Died in Faith*
Tuesday	**Psalm 37:37**	*Mark the Blameless — His Future is Peace*
Wednesday	**Proverbs 22:1**	*A Good Name Rather than Great Riches*
Thursday	**Ecclesiastes 7:1**	*A Good Name is Better than Fine Perfume*
Friday	**Revelation 14:13**	*Their Deeds Follow Them*

MONTHLY MEMORY VERSE

""His master said to him, 'Well done, good and faithful servant.""

Matthew 25:21 · ESV

1.

Who is the most faithful man you have ever known personally? What did his faithfulness look like in practice? What mark did he leave on you?

____

____

____

____

2.

Where in your life right now are you being faithful in the small things? Where are you cutting corners in the small things? Be specific and honest.

____

____

____

____

3.

What promise have you been postponing — to your wife, your children, a friend, God? What has kept you from keeping it?

____

____

____

____

4.

If your children are asked at your funeral to describe the mark you left — not your accomplishments, but your mark — what do you want them to say?

____

____

____

____

5.

Write the one-sentence mark you want to leave. Not what you want to achieve — what you want to leave behind in people. Read it every morning this month.

____

____

____

____

30 Days of Faithfulness

Choose one area — one relationship, one commitment, one practice — and be ruthlessly faithful to it for 30 days. No exceptions. No negotiations. No days off. A man who cannot be faithful to one thing for thirty days is not yet ready to be trusted with a legacy. Build the muscle. Hold the line.

I COMMIT TO THIS CHALLENGE BEGINNING:

____

WHAT I AM BELIEVING GOD FOR THIS MONTH:

____

____

_________________________   _____________

Signature   Date

MONTH EIGHT

Chapter 8

08

Building a Family That Stands

""The storm does not reveal the quality of the man. It reveals the quality of the foundation he built when no storm was coming.""

— J.S.M.

THE CORE PRINCIPLE

A storm is coming to your family.

I am not being pessimistic. I am being biblical.

Jesus did not say "if the storms come." He said "when the rains fall and the floods come and the winds blow." He assumed the storm. The only variable in His story was the foundation.

Two houses. Same storm. Completely different outcomes.

The difference was not what the storm did to them. It was what the builder had done before the storm arrived.

Most fathers are so busy managing the present that they never think seriously about building for the future. They are managing behavior when they should be laying foundations. They are solving today's crisis when they should be building the infrastructure that will handle tomorrow's. The crisis is not the problem. The foundation is the issue — or the solution.

> *""You do not build a foundation after the storm arrives. You build it in the ordinary days when nothing is wrong and nobody thinks you need it.""*

A family that stands when everything falls apart was built by a man who paid the price of foundation-laying in the quiet seasons. He was faithful when it was boring. He was present when it was inconvenient. He built the spiritual infrastructure of his home when no one would have noticed if he had not. And when the storm came — and it came — his family stood.Not because they were exceptional. Because they were built on something that does not move.

The foundation is not built in a crisis. It is built in the ordinary — in the Tuesday evenings when you open the Word with your children, in the Sunday mornings when you lead your family to worship even when you don't feel like it, in the conversations you initiate about God when no one is asking. Every one of those moments is a stone laid in the foundation. And when the storm finally comes — and it will come — your family will stand or fall based on what you did in the quiet seasons before it arrived.

There are two kinds of fathers when the storm hits. The first kind is surprised. He has been managing the surface of his family's life — schedules, grades, activities, appearances — but he has never gone deep. He has been a good provider and a decent man, but he has never been a builder of foundations. When the storm comes, there is nothing underneath to hold. The second kind of father is steady. Not because his family is perfect. Not because the storm does not hurt. But because he built something real underneath, and real things hold.

Legacy Builders build foundations before they are needed. They do not wait for a crisis to establish family prayer. They do not wait for a prodigal to start speaking faith over their children. They do not wait for a broken marriage to begin pursuing their wife. They build in the ordinary days, trusting that what is built faithfully in secret will hold publicly when it matters most.

Matthew 7:24–27 · ESV

> *""Everyone then who hears these words of mine and does them will be like a wise man who built his house on the rock. And the rain fell, and the floods came, and the winds blew and beat on that house, but it did not fall, because it had been founded on the rock. And everyone who hears these words of mine and does not do them will be like a foolish man who built his house on the sand. And the rain fell, and the floods came, and the winds blew and beat against that house, and it fell, and great was the fall of it.""*

Hearing is Not Enough. Building Requires Doing.

01 Both Men Heard the Same Words

The wise man and the foolish man both heard Jesus' words. The difference was not information — it was application. This is the most convicting reality for men who sit under great preaching, read great books, and attend great conferences: hearing changes nothing. Doing is where foundations get built.

02 The Storm Hit Both Houses

Notice that Jesus does not say the storm avoided the wise man's house. The same rain fell. The same floods came. The same winds blew. A godly foundation does not spare you from storms. It gives you something to stand on when the storms arrive. Stop trying to prevent the storm. Start building the foundation.

03 The Fall of the Second House Was Great

Jesus says "great was the fall of it." A foundation built on sand does not just produce a small failure. It produces a collapse — and the collapse is proportional to what was built on top of it. The bigger the life you are building, the more catastrophic the collapse if the foundation is wrong. Do not build on sand and hope for the best.

THE ILLUSTRATION

A STORY THAT DRIVES IT HOME

I have sat with two families in the same kind of crisis — a prodigal child, the same age, from similar backgrounds, making similar destructive choices.

In the first family, the crisis nearly destroyed them. The marriage buckled under the weight of it. The other children felt abandoned as all attention went to the crisis. The father spiraled into guilt and anger. The family, which had seemed solid from the outside, came apart at the seams because the seams were never that deep.

In the second family, the crisis was devastating — but they held. The marriage got stronger in it. The other children watched their parents pray together, fight together, and refuse to give up together. The family's faith, which had been built into their normal daily rhythms for years, became the thing that carried them through the unimaginable.

Same storm. Completely different outcomes. The foundation was built long before the crisis arrived.

APPLICATION FOR YOU

You do not know what storm is coming for your family. But you can decide right now what kind of foundation it will land on. Build today. Build in the ordinary. Build without waiting for a crisis to make it urgent.

1 Establish a Daily Point of Contact with God

A family's foundation is built on the father's personal walk with God. Not performance — actual relationship. This month, establish or recommit to a daily time of Scripture and prayer that is non-negotiable. Not when you feel like it. Every morning. This is the foundation beneath the foundation.

> → *Set a specific time. Put it on your calendar. Guard it like a meeting you cannot miss.*

2 Build a Family Prayer Life

Pray out loud with your family. Not just a blessing before meals — real prayer. Pray together about real things. Name struggles. Name fears. Name hopes. Let your children hear their father pray with authority and vulnerability. A family that prays together is building something the storm cannot easily reach.

> → *Pray out loud with your family at least five times this week. Make it real, not religious.*

3 Stress-Test Your Foundation

Ask yourself honestly: if a significant crisis hit my family in the next six months — a health crisis, a financial collapse, a prodigal child, a marriage crisis — what would reveal itself about the strength of our foundation? Where are the weaknesses? Address them now, not later.

→ *Name one specific weakness in your family's foundation. Make one concrete move toward strengthening it this month.*

4 Build a Crisis Response Plan

Wise builders think about worst-case scenarios before they happen. This month, have a conversation with your spouse about how you would handle a major crisis together. Who would you call? What would anchor you? What would you protect? A couple who has talked about the crisis before the crisis arrives is far better equipped to survive it.

→ *Have this conversation with your spouse this month. Not to create fear — to build readiness.*

5 Build Margin Into Your Family

An overcommitted, overextended family has no buffer when the storm comes. Build margin — financial, relational, physical, spiritual. Say no to one thing this month to create space for what matters most. Families that stand under pressure are families that were not already stretched to their limit before the pressure arrived.

→ *Identify one commitment to eliminate or reduce. Create margin deliberately. Protect it.*

06 Build Something Together

Pick a simple project you can complete in one evening — a birdhouse kit, a small garden box, a piece of furniture from a kit, even just a massive puzzle. Work on it together. Let it be imperfect. Let everyone contribute something. At the end, step back and look at what your family made. Then say out loud: that is what we do. We build things together. The project does not matter. The lesson does.

→ *Whatever you build, keep it somewhere visible for the rest of the month.*

Experience 01

Family Prayer Night

Designate one evening for a real family prayer night. Not a casual blessing. Actual time on your knees together, praying for each other, praying for your home, praying for your future. Let your children hear you intercede for them by name. This is one of the most powerful foundation-building experiences a family can have.

"Each family member by name — their specific needs"

"Your home, your marriage, your family's future"

Experience 02

Tell a Storm Story

Share with your family a time when a significant storm hit your life — a crisis, a loss, a failure — and what got you through it. Let them see that storms come, and that faith, family, and foundation are what make the difference. Your testimony of surviving a storm is one of the most powerful investments you can make in their future ability to survive theirs.

"What the storm felt like from the inside"

"What specifically held you when everything else was shaking"

Experience 03

Build Something Physical Together

Build something with your hands as a family this month — a garden bed, a piece of furniture, a birdhouse, a bookshelf. It does not matter what it is. What matters is the metaphor of building together, the satisfaction of something made to last, and the conversation it creates about what it means to build things worth keeping.

""What made this hard? What made it worth it?""

""What are we building in our family that we want to last?""

Experience 04

Interview a Family That Has Survived

Identify a couple in your church or community that has survived something significant — a health crisis, financial ruin, the loss of a child, a prodigal — and invite them to dinner. Ask them to tell your family what held them together. Let your children hear from people whose foundation was tested and held. This is education money cannot buy.

""What was the hardest moment? What did you reach for?""

""What would you tell our family to build now, while everything is okay?""

DAILY BIBLE READING PLAN

WEEK ONE — THE FOUNDATION

Monday	**Matthew 7:24–27**	*The Wise and Foolish Builders*
Tuesday	**Psalm 127:1**	*Unless the Lord Builds*
Wednesday	**1 Corinthians 3:10–11**	*No Other Foundation*
Thursday	**Proverbs 24:3–4**	*By Wisdom a House Is Built*
Friday	**Isaiah 28:16**	*A Cornerstone That Will Not Shift*

WEEK TWO — WHEN THE STORM COMES

Monday	**James 1:2–4**	*Count It All Joy*
Tuesday	**Romans 5:3–5**	*Suffering Produces Hope*
Wednesday	**2 Corinthians 4:8–9**	*Pressed But Not Crushed*
Thursday	**Psalm 46:1–3**	*God Is Our Refuge and Strength*
Friday	**Isaiah 43:2**	*When You Pass Through the Waters*

WEEK THREE — STANDING FIRM

Monday	**Ephesians 6:13**	*Having Done All — Stand*
Tuesday	**1 Corinthians 15:58**	*Be Steadfast, Immovable*
Wednesday	**Hebrews 10:36**	*You Have Need of Endurance*
Thursday	**Galatians 6:9**	*You Will Reap in Due Season*

| Friday | **Philippians 4:13** | *I Can Do All Things* |

WEEK FOUR — THE GOD WHO HOLDS

Monday	**Isaiah 41:10**	*Do Not Fear — I Am With You*
Tuesday	**Deuteronomy 31:6**	*He Will Not Leave You or Forsake You*
Wednesday	**Psalm 23:4**	*Even Though I Walk Through the Valley*
Thursday	**John 16:33**	*I Have Overcome the World*
Friday	**Romans 8:38–39**	*Nothing Can Separate Us*

MONTHLY MEMORY VERSE

""Everyone who hears these words of mine and does them will be like a wise man who built his house on the rock.""

Matthew 7:24 · ESV

LEGACY BUILDER REFLECTION

1.

If a major storm hit your family in the next six months, what would it reveal about the strength of your foundation? Be brutally honest.

____

____

____

2.

What is the current state of your personal daily walk with God? Is it a strong foundation — or is it something you are managing from a distance?

____

____

____

____

3.

What storm has your family already survived? What did it reveal about your foundation — for better or worse?

____

____

____

____

4.

Where is your family overextended right now? What margin needs to be created before the next season of pressure arrives?

____

5.

What is one thing you are going to build into your family's foundation this month that was not there last month?

Build Before the Storm

This month, identify the single weakest point in your family's foundation and take a deliberate, sustained action to strengthen it. Not a gesture — a structural change. One new practice. One repaired relationship. One addressed issue. The best time to build the foundation was ten years ago. The second-best time is today.

I COMMIT TO THIS CHALLENGE BEGINNING:

____

WHAT I AM BELIEVING GOD FOR THIS MONTH:

____

____

______________________   ________________

Signature   Date

MONTH NINE

Chapter 9

09

The Priest of Your Home

""Someone is setting the spiritual atmosphere of your home. The only question is whether it is you — or whether you have abdicated that assignment to something else.""

— J.S.M.

THE CORE PRINCIPLE

In the Old Testament, the priest stood between God and the people.

He interceded. He represented. He covered.

He did not wait until the people asked for prayer. He went to God on their behalf — consistently, routinely, as his primary assignment.

That is your assignment in your home.

And most men have never been told that — or have been told and have not taken it seriously.

You are the priest of your home. Not because you are perfect. Not because you have all the theological answers. Not because you are the most spiritually mature person in the house. You are the priest because God assigned the spiritual responsibility of the home to the father— and He did not revise that assignment based on your comfort level with it.

> *""A home with a praying father is one of the most supernaturally protected environments a child can grow up in. And most children have never lived in one.""*

The spiritual atmosphere of your home is not created by what church you attend. It is created by what happens in your home between Sundays. It is created by whether your children see you open your Bible — not just carry it. Whether they hear you pray — not just say grace. Whether they know you wrestle with God — not just perform religion.The priest of a home does not outsource the spiritual formation of his family to the church. He partners with the church from a position of leadership that begins in his own house.

Most men have been told to provide for their families. Few have been told to cover them. There is a difference. Provision is what you put on the table. Coverage is what you bring into the room when you walk through the door. It is the spiritual atmosphere you create — or fail to create — by the posture of your own soul. A father who is walking closely with God brings something into his home that money cannot buy and performance cannot manufacture. His children feel it. His wife feels it. The enemy feels it.

Job did not wait for his children to ask for prayer. He rose early and offered sacrifices for each of them —regularly,consistently, as a matter of routine. He did not know what his children had done. He covered them anyway. That is the posture of a priest. He does not wait for evidence of need. He intercedes because he understands the assignment. Your children do not need to ask you to pray for them. They need a father who prays whether they ask or not.

You set the spiritual temperature of your home. Not your church. Not your children's youth group. Not the worship music you play on Sunday morning.You.The question is not whether you are setting it. You are always setting it. The question is whether you are setting it deliberately or by default. A home where the father prays is a home where children learn that God is real. A home where the father reads Scripture is a home where children learn that the Word has authority. A home where the father confesses and repents is a home where children learn that grace is available. Every spiritual habit you practice is a sermon your family hears without words.

You do not have to be a theologian to be the priest of your home. Job was a man, not a Levite. He was a father, not a professional clergy. What qualified him was not his theological credentials but his consistent intercession. God called him blameless and upright — a man who feared God and turned from evil. That is the qualification for the priesthood of your home. Not perfection. Consistent, humble, God-fearing faithfulness.

SCRIPTURE DEEP DIVE

Job 1:4–5 · ESV

> *""His sons used to go and hold a feast in the house of each one on his day, and they would send and invite their three sisters to eat and drink with them. And when the days of the feast had run their course, Job would send and consecrate them, and he would rise early in the morning and offer burnt offerings according to the number of them all. For Job said, 'It may be that my children have sinned, and cursed God in their hearts.' Thus Job did*

continually." "

The Priestly Father Does Not Wait for a Crisis to Pray

01 Job Prayed for His Children Preemptively

Job did not wait until one of his children fell into sin. He prayed for them continually — as a precaution, as an act of priestly covering. "It may be that my children have sinned." He did not know. He prayed anyway. A father who prays for his children before problems arrive is doing priestly work that most men never start until it is too late.

02 He Did It Continually — Not Occasionally

The text says "thus Job did continually." Not when he felt spiritual. Not during a crisis. Not after church on Sunday. Continually. The priestly covering of a home is not a one-time event — it is a sustained, consistent practice that becomes as automatic as breathing for a man who understands his assignment.

03 He Rose Early to Do It

Job "would rise early in the morning." He prioritized the priestly work above his own comfort and convenience. The man who will pray for his children when it is easy but not when it requires sacrifice has not yet understood the weight of his assignment. The priest of a home rises before the demands of the day and goes to God first.

THE ILLUSTRATION

A STORY THAT DRIVES IT HOME

A man in his fifties came to me after a service. He was weeping. His son had just walked away from faith, his marriage, and his children — all in the same year.

He said: "I never prayed for my children. I mean I said prayers. Before meals. At church. But I never really interceded for them. I never went to war for them in prayer. I thought church would take care of it."

And then he said something I have never forgotten: "I outsourced my priesthood and I didn't even know that's what I was doing."

He was not a bad man. He was a faithful churchgoer, a decent provider, a generally present father. But he had never understood that the spiritual covering of his home was his responsibility — not his pastor's, not his children's youth leader's, not the Christian school's.

His. It was his. And he had never picked it up.

APPLICATION FOR YOU

The church is a partner in the spiritual formation of your family. It is not the primary agent. You are. Pick up your priesthood. Cover your children in prayer. Set the spiritual atmosphere of your home. Do it today — not after a crisis makes you regret waiting.

1

Pray Over Your Children by Name — Every Day

This month, begin the practice of praying over each of your children by name, out loud, every single day. Not a generic "bless my kids" prayer. Specific intercession — for what they are facing, what they are afraid of, what they are being tempted by, what God is doing in them. A father who prays for his children this way is doing the most consequential thing he can do for their future.

> → *Start tonight. Pray over each child by name. Be specific. Do it every day this month.*

2

Lead a Family Devotional

Once a week this month, lead your family in a short time of Scripture and prayer. It does not have to be polished or long. Five to ten minutes. Read a passage. Ask one question. Pray together. What matters is not the production value — it is the message it sends: the man of this house leads us to God.

> → *Choose a day. Put it on the calendar. Lead it — even if you feel unqualified. Especially if you feel unqualified.*

3 **Consecrate Your Home**

Walk through every room of your home and pray out loud over each space. Over the bedrooms for purity and peace. Over the kitchen for provision and health. Over the living room for connection over distraction. Over the front door for what goes out and what comes in. This is your home. Pray over every square foot of it like you mean it.

→ *Do this walk-through prayer this week. Invite your family to join you if they are willing.*

4 **Fast on Behalf of Your Family**

This month, choose one day to fast on behalf of your family — specifically, intentionally, sacrificially. Fast for a prodigal child. Fast for a struggling marriage. Fast for a child who is walking through something hard. Fast for the spiritual atmosphere of your home. Fasting is one of the most powerful priestly acts available to a father, and most men have never done it specifically for their family.

→ *Choose a day. Name what you are fasting for. Spend the time you would have eaten in prayer.*

5   Let Your Family See You in the Word

Let your children catch you reading your Bible — not for show, but because it is a genuine practice. Leave your Bible open. Let them see you journaling. Let them hear you reference something you read that morning. A father whose children have seen him in the Word knows that his example is more powerful than any sermon they will ever hear.

→ *Read your Bible in a visible place this month. Let it be seen. Let it be normal.*

---

06   Sunrise Together

Set one alarm this month — early, before the rest of the world is moving. Wake up your family. Drive somewhere you can watch the sunrise together. A hilltop, a field, a lake, a bridge — anywhere with a view of the eastern sky. Bring coffee for the adults and donuts for the kids. Watch the sun come up in silence for at least five minutes. Then pray together before the day starts. A family that seeks God together in the early morning is a family that stands.

→ *No explanation needed. Just show up and let the sunrise do the talking.*

FAMILY EXPERIENCES THIS MONTH

Experience 01

Family Fast Day

Designate one day where the whole family fasts something together — a meal, screens, social media — and replaces that time with prayer, Scripture, and conversation about God. Let your children experience spiritual discipline practiced together. Explain what fasting is and why it matters. This is one of the most formative experiences a family can share.

> *""Why do you think God calls us to fast?""*

> *""What did you notice when you chose to say no to one thing today?""*

Experience 02

The Prayer Walk

Walk through your home together and pray out loud over each room and each family member. Dad leads. Let each person pray for the next. Let children hear each other intercede. Let them hear their father cover them with authority and tenderness. This is the priestly work — visible, normal, and unforgettable.

> *"Every bedroom — purity, peace, rest, protection"*

> *"The front door — what goes out and what comes in"*

Experience 03

Tell Your Testimony

Set aside an evening and tell your children — in full, unedited detail — the story of how God got hold of your life. The before. The moment. The after. Let them hear the real version, not the clean one. Your testimony of God's faithfulness in your own life is one of the most powerful spiritual gifts you can give your children.

"The moment everything changed for you"

"What you know now that you wish you had known then"

Experience 04

The Blessing Ceremony

Create a formal moment — at a meal, at a special gathering — where Dad places his hands on each family member and speaks a specific, Scripture-based blessing over them out loud. This is one of the most ancient and powerful acts of priestly fatherhood. Your words spoken over your children in this context carry a weight that ordinary moments rarely produce.

"A Scripture that speaks to who they are"

"A declaration of what you see God doing in them"

DAILY BIBLE READING PLAN

WEEK ONE — THE PRIESTLY ASSIGNMENT		
Monday	**Job 1:4–5**	*Job's Continual Intercession*
Tuesday	**Exodus 28:29**	*Bear the Names Before the Lord*
Wednesday	**1 Timothy 2:1**	*First of All — Supplications and Prayers*
Thursday	**Ephesians 6:18**	*Praying at All Times in the Spirit*
Friday	**Colossians 1:9**	*We Have Not Ceased to Pray for You*

WEEK TWO — THE POWER OF A FATHER'S PRAYER		
Monday	**James 5:16**	*The Prayer of a Righteous Man*
Tuesday	**Matthew 7:7–11**	*Ask, Seek, Knock*
Wednesday	**Psalm 34:17**	*The Righteous Cry Out — He Hears*
Thursday	**Philippians 4:6**	*Do Not Be Anxious — Pray*
Friday	**1 John 5:14–15**	*The Confidence We Have*

WEEK THREE — THE SPIRITUAL ATMOSPHERE		
Monday	**Deuteronomy 6:6–9**	*In Your House — When You Sit*
Tuesday	**Psalm 101:2**	*I Will Walk in Integrity in My House*

Wednesday	**Acts 10:2**	*A Devout Man Who Feared God with All His Household*
Thursday	**Joshua 24:15**	*As for Me and My House*
Friday	**Psalm 122:1**	*I Was Glad When They Said — Let Us Go*

WEEK FOUR — INTERCEDING FOR THE NEXT GENERATION

Monday	**Isaiah 44:3**	*I Will Pour My Spirit on Your Offspring*
Tuesday	**Acts 16:31**	*You Will Be Saved — You and Your Household*
Wednesday	**Psalm 102:28**	*The Children of Your Servants Shall Dwell Secure*
Thursday	**Isaiah 54:13**	*All Your Children Shall Be Taught by the Lord*
Friday	**Proverbs 15:29**	*He Hears the Prayer of the Righteous*

MONTHLY MEMORY VERSE

""The prayer of a righteous person has great power as it is working.""

James 5:16 · ESV

1.

When did you last pray specifically, by name, for each of your children about something specific they are facing? If the answer is "I don't remember" — what does that tell you?

____

____

____

____

2.

Who is setting the spiritual atmosphere of your home right now? If you are honest — is it you, or have you outsourced that to the church, a school, or no one?

____

____

____

____

3.

Have your children ever heard you pray with full authenticity — not a polished prayer, but a real one? What would it mean to them if they did?

____

____

____

____

4.

What spiritual practice do you engage in privately that your
children have never seen? Is there any reason it needs to remain
invisible?

____

____

____

____

5.

Write out a prayer for each of your children. Specific. Honest. Not
a formula — your actual heart for each of them. Then pray it every
morning this month.

____

____

____

____

30 Days of Priestly Intercession

For 30 days, pray over each member of your family by name —
out loud, every single day. Not a formula. A real prayer. Cover
them. Intercede for them. A father who prays for his children
every day for thirty days will have built something in his family
that no program, no conference, and no curriculum can produce.
The priest of a home is its most powerful resource.

I COMMIT TO THIS CHALLENGE BEGINNING:

____

WHAT I AM BELIEVING GOD FOR THIS MONTH:

____

____

_________________________   _______________

Signature   Date

MONTH TEN

Chapter 10

10

Words That Build or Break

""Your children are keeping records you don't know exist — not in notebooks, but in their nervous systems.""

— J.S.M.

THE CORE PRINCIPLE

Your children are keeping a record.

Not in a notebook. In their nervous systems.

Every word you have spoken over them — in anger, in love, in passing, in their most vulnerable moments — has been filed and stored.

And they are using that record right now to decide who they are.

The question is not whether you are writing on them. You are. The question is what you are writing.

A father's words do not just enter the ear. They enter the identity. They land in the place where a child decides what is true about themselves — and they stay there, playing on repeat, long after the moment they were spoken has been forgotten by everyone in the room except the child who received them.

""Death and life are in the power of the tongue, and those who love it will eat its fruits." — Proverbs 18:21"

This is not metaphor. This is how human beings are formed. A child who hears "you are smart" from a father they trust will attempt hard things. A child who hears "you'll never amount to anything" from that same father will spend decades either proving it right or fighting to prove it wrong — neither outcome being the one God designed for them. The most powerful voice in a child's world is a father's voice. And it is either building something or tearing something down. There is no neutral.

The verse does not say death and life are in the power of the dramatic moment. It says the tongue. The everyday instrument. The thing you use before you are fully awake, under pressure, in the car, at the dinner table, in the argument you did not plan to have. That ordinary, unremarkable instrument carries the power of life and death over the people in your home. Most men have never stopped to feel the full weight of that.

Here is what the research confirms and what Scripture declared thousands of years ago: negative words are remembered longer, felt more deeply, and believed more quickly than positive ones. Your child will forget a hundred encouragements before they forget one cutting remark spoken in anger. Which means a father who is careless with his words when he is tired, frustrated, or under pressure is doing damage that a thousand good days cannot fully undo.

But here is the other side — and this is where the Legacy Builder leans in: words spoken deliberately over a child, repeated consistently over time, become the architecture of that child's identity. A father who decides what he wants his child to believe about themselves — and then speaks it, week after week, year after year — is doing something that school, church, and culture combined cannot replicate. He is writing on the deepest wall of a human soul.

You do not need to be eloquent. You do not need a ceremony. You need to be intentional. Decide what is true about your child — what God put in them, what you see emerging, what their future holds. Then open your mouth and say it. Directly. By name. Repeatedly. The words you speak over your children today are still speaking twenty years from now.

SCRIPTURE DEEP DIVE

Proverbs 18:21 · ESV

> *""Death and life are in the power of the tongue, and those who love it will eat its fruits.""*

You Are Speaking Life or Death — There Is No Neutral

01 There Is No Such Thing as a Careless Word

Scripture says death AND life are in the power of the tongue. Not just the big moments — the small ones too. The throwaway comment. The sigh of disappointment. The dismissive response. The comparison to a sibling. Every word either builds or breaks. There is no neutral ground.

02 You Will Eat the Fruit of Your Words

Proverbs says those who love the tongue "will eat its fruits." This is a long-game warning. The words you speak over your children today are seeds. Some will bear fruit in five years. Some in twenty. Some in the grandchildren you haven't met yet. What harvest are you planting right now?

03 The Blessing is Your Assignment

Throughout Scripture, fathers blessed their children — intentionally, specifically, and out loud. Isaac blessed Jacob. Jacob blessed his twelve sons. The fathers who marked generations were fathers who opened their mouths and called destiny into their children. This is your assignment. Not just to avoid cursing — but to actively bless.

THE ILLUSTRATION

"SON, YOU ARE A BLESSING TO MY LIFE"

In 1990, I was twenty years old and newly installed as the junior high youth pastor at my church. One Wednesday night before service, an elderly grandmother walked up to me with her grandson. She looked me in the eye and said seven words I was not prepared for: "He needs a father figure. He's yours."

At first I thought she was joking. Then I realized she meant every word.

This boy was being raised in an area of town where the statistical chances of making it out alive were slim. He had no father in the home. He needed someone to show up — not occasionally, not when it was convenient, but consistently and deliberately. So I did. I went to his games. I made sure he was in church. I spoke into his life.

And I told him the same thing, over and over, for six years: "Son, you are a blessing to my life." I meant every word. Not because he was always easy. Not because everything was going well. Because I had decided what was true about him — and I was not going to stop saying it until it became what he believed about himself.

Six years. Every week. The same words. Until he graduated from high school and walked into his own life carrying a record that said: I am a blessing. Someone saw it. Someone said so. And he meant it.

That young man is now 46 years old. Married. Two beautiful children. College graduate. Master's degree in Education. Working toward his doctorate. And this whole time — thirty-six years later — he is still by my side. Still a vital part of our family and the lives of my own children.

I am grateful for that old grandmother who believed a twenty-year-old youth pastor would have the right words for her grandson. She was right. The words were simple. The consistency was the miracle.

APPLICATION FOR YOU

You do not have to be perfect to speak life. You have to be deliberate. Pick one thing that is true about each of your children — something God-given, something you see emerging, something their future requires — and begin saying it. By name. Out loud. Repeatedly. A child who hears the right words from the right person enough times will eventually stop arguing with them. They will simply begin to believe them. And then they will begin to become them.

01 Conduct a Word Audit

For one week, pay attention to the words you are most frequently speaking over each child. Not the big conversations — the small, daily ones. What do you say when they fail? When they succeed? When they frustrate you? Write down what you observe without judgment. Awareness is the first step.

> → *At the end of the week, ask: Is the pattern I observed building my child — or breaking them?*

02 Speak a Specific Blessing Over Each Child

This month, pull each child aside individually and speak a specific, personal blessing over them. Not generic praise. Specific destiny language. "I see in you a man who will…" "God has put something in you that…" "I want you to know that I believe you are…" Speak it. Mean it. Watch them receive it.

> → *Do this before the month is over. Write out what you will say beforehand. Don't wing it — this matters too much.*

03 Replace the Verdict with a Vision

Every father has said something that became a verdict in a child's mind. This month, identify one negative label that may be operating in one of your children's lives, and intentionally replace it with a vision statement. Instead of reacting to what they are, start speaking to who they can become.

→ *Write the new vision statement. Speak it to them this week — and keep speaking it.*

04 Create a Family Declaration

Write a family declaration — a set of statements your family speaks about who you are and who you are becoming. "In this family, we are…" Post it on the wall. Say it together. Let your children grow up speaking identity over themselves every time they read it. Words repeated become beliefs. Beliefs become identity. Identity becomes legacy.

→ *Write your family declaration this week. Frame it. Put it somewhere visible in your home.*

05 Write Each Child a Letter of Blessing

This month, handwrite a letter to each of your children. Tell them what you see in them. Tell them what you believe God has placed in them. Tell them you are proud of who they are — not just what they do. Seal it. Give it to them now, or save it for a significant moment. Some of the most life-changing words a child ever receives come from a father who put it on paper.

> → *Begin the first letter tonight. Start with: "What I want you to know about who you are…"*

---

06 The Encouragement Table

Before dinner one night this month, put a stack of index cards and pens in the middle of the table. Every person — including you — writes one encouraging sentence about every other person at the table. Then read them out loud. No sarcasm. No jokes. Just truth. Watch what happens in that room when your children hear their father speak specific, written, chosen words about who they are. Keep the cards. They will be read again.

> → *You go first. Set the tone. Make it specific, not generic.*

The Encouragement Dinner

At dinner, go around the table and have every family member say one specific thing they admire about every other person. Dad goes first — and sets the bar for specificity and sincerity. This one dinner can change the atmosphere of your home for weeks.

"Be specific — not "you're nice" but "I love how you…""

"No phones. Full presence. Dad leads."

Write Your Family Declaration Together

Sit down as a family and co-author your Family Declaration. Ask everyone: "What do we want to be known for? What do we believe about ourselves?" Write it together. Let every voice be in it. Then frame it and put it on the wall.

""In this family, we always…""

""We are the kind of people who…""

Speak Over Your Kids Night

Set aside one evening where each child sits in a chair and every family member speaks something specific and encouraging over them. Dad closes with a blessing. This is one of the most powerful things you can do as a family — and your children will remember it forever.

"A gift or strength you see in them"

"A destiny statement: "I believe you will…""

One-on-One Walk with Each Child

Take each child on a solo walk this month — just the two of you. No destination required. Walk and talk. Let them lead the conversation. And before you come back, speak something specific and meaningful over them. Just you and them and words that will outlast the walk.

""What's something you've been thinking about lately?""

""Here's what I see in you that I want you to know...""

DAILY BIBLE READING PLAN

WEEK ONE — THE POWER OF THE TONGUE

Monday	**Proverbs 18:21**	*Death and Life*
Tuesday	**James 3:1–12**	*The Untameable Tongue*
Wednesday	**Proverbs 12:18**	*Reckless Words Pierce*
Thursday	**Matthew 12:36–37**	*Careless Words Accountable*
Friday	**Psalm 141:3**	*Set a Guard Over My Mouth*

WEEK TWO — THE BLESSING

Monday	**Genesis 27:27–29**	*Isaac Blesses Jacob*
Tuesday	**Genesis 48:14–16**	*Jacob Blesses His Grandsons*
Wednesday	**Numbers 6:24–26**	*The Priestly Blessing*
Thursday	**Luke 3:21–22**	*The Father Speaks Over His Son*
Friday	**Hebrews 11:20–21**	*Blessing as an Act of Faith*

WEEK THREE — SPEAKING LIFE

Monday	**Ephesians 4:29**	*Words That Build Up*
Tuesday	**Proverbs 15:4**	*The Healing Tongue*
Wednesday	**Isaiah 50:4**	*A Word to Sustain the Weary*
Thursday	**1 Thessalonians 5:11**	*Encourage One Another*
Friday	**Colossians 4:6**	*Seasoned with Salt*

WEEK FOUR — IDENTITY AND DESTINY		
Monday	**Jeremiah 1:4–5**	*Known Before You Were Born*
Tuesday	**Psalm 139:13–16**	*Fearfully and Wonderfully Made*
Wednesday	**Romans 8:16–17**	*Children of God*
Thursday	**Ephesians 2:10**	*God's Workmanship*
Friday	**Proverbs 31:28**	*Her Children Rise and Call Her Blessed*

MONTHLY MEMORY VERSE

""Death and life are in the power of the tongue, and those who love it will eat its fruits.""

Proverbs 18:21 · ESV

LEGACY BUILDER REFLECTION

1.

What words from your own father — positive or negative — are still shaping how you see yourself today?

2.

When your children hear a voice in their head at age 40, what do you want it to sound like? What does it currently sound like?

____

____

____

____

3.

Is there a negative label — spoken or unspoken — operating in one of your children's lives that originated with you?

____

____

____

____

4.

Write a specific blessing for each of your children — what destiny, gift, or calling do you see in them?

____

____

____

5.

What is one thing you have never said to one of your children that they need to hear from you — and when will you say it?

____

____

____

____

Speak Life for 30 Days

For 30 days, speak one specific word of affirmation, blessing, or encouragement over each of your children — every single day. Not generic. Not habitual. Specific and intentional. Thirty days of deliberate, life-giving words. Watch what happens to your children. Watch what happens to you.

I COMMIT TO THIS CHALLENGE BEGINNING:

____

WHAT I AM BELIEVING GOD FOR THIS MONTH:

____

____

_________________________   _______________
Signature   Date

MONTH ELEVEN

Chapter 11

11

Building on Purpose

""Drift is not neutral. Drift has a destination — and you will not like where it takes you.""

— J.S.M.

THE CORE PRINCIPLE

Most men don't choose a bad legacy.

They drift into one.

They never decided to be distant. They just kept choosing convenience over presence — one small decision at a time — until distance became the default.

They never decided to let their marriage go cold. They just kept choosing distraction over pursuit — one missed moment at a time — until cold became normal.

Drift is one of the most dangerous forces in a family — precisely because it never feels urgent until it is a crisis.

Intentional fatherhood is the direct antidote to drift. It is not complicated. It is not primarily a program or a system or a methodology. It is a man who wakes up every morning and makes a choice — about where his attention will go, what he will protect, who he will pursue, and what he is building. He does not wait for the right season. He does not wait until the kids are older or the schedule opens up or the finances improve.He decides that today is a day of building, and he builds.

> *""The difference between a deliberate
> father and a drifting one is not talent or
> time. It is the daily decision to show up
> with intention when showing up without
> intention would be so much easier.""*

Intentional fatherhood requires that you count the cost — and pay it willingly. It will cost you time you could spend on other things. Opportunities you could pursue. Comfort you could indulge. It will require you to be present when you are exhausted, engaged when you are distracted, and steady when you are falling apart on the inside. That is the price of a deliberate legacy. And every man who has paid it will tell you — without exception — that it was worth every sacrifice it demanded.

The decision to build on purpose begins with a single honest question: Where am I drifting? Not where you have failed spectacularly. Most men have not failed spectacularly. They have drifted quietly. Drifted from their wife. Drifted from their children. Drifted from the Word. Drifted from the man they once believed they could be. The Legacy Builder names the drift before it becomes a direction. He does not wait for a crisis to diagnose the problem. He evaluates regularly, honestly, and without self-protection.

Building on purpose means establishing rhythms that outlast your moods. A man who only leads his family when he feels spiritually motivated will lead them inconsistently. A man who has built rhythms — daily prayer, weekly family time, monthly evaluation, annual intentionality — will lead them regardless of how he feels on any given Tuesday. The rhythm carries the mission when the motivation is low.Legacy is built in the rhythms, not in the moments of inspiration.

The man who builds on purpose also builds with the end in mind. He asks himself regularly: What do I want my children to say about me at my funeral? What do I want my grandchildren to know about the man I was? What will my marriage look like in thirty years if I continue on my current trajectory? These are not morbid questions. They are clarifying ones. They help a man see past the noise of the urgent into the weight of the important. A man with a clear picture of where he is going makes very different daily decisions than a man who has never thought past next week.

SCRIPTURE DEEP DIVE

Ephesians 5:15–17 · ESV

> *""Look carefully then how you walk, not as unwise but as wise, making the best use of the time, because the days are evil. Therefore do not be foolish, but understand what the will of the Lord is.""*

Wisdom Looks Carefully — Foolishness Drifts

01 Look Carefully — Not Casually

Paul says "look carefully" — not glance occasionally, not check in when things seem off. Carefully. The deliberate father pays close attention to his walk. He evaluates regularly. He asks hard questions of himself. He does not assume that because things feel fine, everything is fine. He inspects the foundation while there is still time to strengthen it.

02 Redeeming Time Is an Act of Warfare

"Making the best use of the time, because the days are evil." Paul connects the intentional use of time directly to the nature of the world his readers live in. The culture is not neutral — it is actively working to steal your time, your attention, and your family. A father who redeems his time is not just being efficient. He is fighting for his family.

03 Knowing God's Will Is the Foundation of Purpose

"Understand what the will of the Lord is." Intentional fatherhood must be rooted in something larger than your own good intentions. A man who builds his family according to God's design — covenant marriage, deliberate formation, spiritual leadership, generational transfer — is building toward a target that does not move. That is the only intentionality that produces legacy.

A STORY THAT DRIVES IT HOME

A man came to me at 58. His youngest had just left for college. His house was quiet in a way he had not anticipated, and the silence was forcing him to look at what he had actually built during the eighteen years his children were home.

He did not like what he saw. His oldest rarely called. His relationship with his daughter was polite but distant. His son in the middle had chosen a path he could not endorse and seemed to barely tolerate his father's presence at holidays.

"I was there," he said. "I was in the house. I provided everything they needed. I just — I never stopped to build anything. I was managing, not building. And now I'm looking at what I managed to produce — and it's not what I wanted."

Presence without purpose produces managed children, not formed ones. You do not have to be absent to miss the assignment. You can be physically present and still drift through fatherhood.

APPLICATION FOR YOU

Your children are in your house right now. The window is open. When it closes, it does not fully reopen. Build with intention — today, not eventually. The man who says "I'll be more intentional when things slow down" is making a promise he will never be able to keep.

THIS MONTH'S IMPLEMENTATION

1 Create a Family Mission Statement

A family that does not know its mission cannot build toward it. This month, craft a one to two sentence Family Mission Statement — what your family exists for, what you are building together, and what you will be known for. Then make decisions through that filter. Does this activity, commitment, or relationship move us toward our mission or away from it?

> → *Draft it this week. Refine it with your spouse. Post it somewhere visible. Use it as a decision-making filter this month.*

2 Audit Your Calendar Against Your Values

Look at your calendar for the past 30 days. Then look at your stated values. Do they match? What got the most of your time? What got the least? Your calendar is the most honest document in your life — it shows what you actually value, regardless of what you say you value. An intentional father closes the gap between the two.

> → *Do the audit this week. Identify one thing to eliminate and one thing to protect.*

3 Schedule What Matters Before Something Else Takes the Slot

Date nights do not happen accidentally in a busy life. One-on-one time with each child does not happen accidentally. Family devotions do not happen accidentally. Whatever you do not schedule will be displaced by whatever is loudest. This month, put the most important things on your calendar first — and defend them like appointments you cannot cancel.

> → *Schedule one date night and one one-on-one with each child this month. Put them on the calendar now.*

4 Name Your Drift

Every man has an area where he has been drifting — a relationship going quiet, a practice he has let slip, a child he has been meaning to pursue, a conversation he has been postponing. Name it. Do not generalize it. Name it specifically. Then take one intentional step back toward it this week. The antidote to drift is always the same: one deliberate decision in the right direction.

> → *Name it out loud. Write it down. Take one step today.*

5   End Every Day with One Intentional Question

Before you fall asleep tonight — and every night this month — ask yourself one question: "Did I build anything today that will outlast me?" Not every day will produce a dramatic answer. Some days it will be a conversation. Some days a moment of patience. Some days a prayer. But the man who asks the question every night will live differently during the day.

> → *Ask the question tonight. Write what comes to mind. Do it every night this month.*

---

06   The Dream Drive

Take your family on a drive through the part of your city or town that represents what you are all working toward — a neighborhood you admire, a business district, a campus, a piece of land. Tell your family what you are dreaming about for your next five years. Ask them what they are dreaming about for theirs. Let the conversation be big. Men who build on purpose give their families permission to dream. Be that man tonight.

> → *Ask more questions than you answer. Listen more than you talk.*

Experience 01

The Family Mission Night

Gather your family and spend an evening crafting your Family Mission Statement together. Ask each person: "What do you think our family is here to do? What do you want us to be known for?" Write down every idea. Refine it together. Frame it. This is one of the most clarifying and unifying things a family can do.

> *""If someone studied our family for one year, what would they say we're about?""*

> *""What do we want to be different in the world because our family existed?""*

Experience 02

One-on-One Month

This month, take each of your children on a one-on-one experience — just the two of you. It does not have to be expensive. A drive, a meal, a walk. The point is undivided attention. Ask them about their life. Listen more than you talk. The child who gets one-on-one time with their father regularly is one of the most secure children you will ever meet.

> *""What's been hard for you lately that I don't know about?""*

> *""What's one thing you wish was different about our relationship?""*

Experience 03

The Drift Conversation

Have an honest family conversation about drift. "What are some ways we've drifted as a family this year from what we said we value?" No blame — just honest assessment. Then ask: "What's one thing we want to be more intentional about together in the next three months?" Let everyone have a voice. Let Dad commit to something specific in front of the family.

> *"No defensiveness. Only honesty and forward motion."*

> *"Dad goes last — and commits to something specific."*

A Legacy Project

Choose a project your family will build together this month that is designed to outlast the month — a garden, a piece of furniture, a charitable initiative, a gift for someone in need. Let the physical act of building something together become a metaphor for the spiritual building you are doing. Debrief it: "What did we make? What did we learn? What does it take to build things that last?"

> *""What was the hardest part of building this?""*

> *""What are we building in our family that we want to last even longer?""*

DAILY BIBLE READING PLAN

WEEK ONE — THE DANGER OF DRIFT

Monday	**Ephesians 5:15–17**	*Walk Carefully — Not as Unwise*
Tuesday	**Hebrews 2:1**	*Lest We Drift Away*
Wednesday	**Proverbs 14:23**	*In All Toil There Is Profit*
Thursday	**Proverbs 6:6–8**	*Go to the Ant — Consider Its Ways*
Friday	**Ecclesiastes 3:1–8**	*A Time for Every Matter Under Heaven*

WEEK TWO — REDEEMING THE TIME

Monday	**Psalm 90:12**	*Teach Us to Number Our Days*
Tuesday	**Colossians 4:5**	*Making the Best Use of the Time*
Wednesday	**James 4:13–14**	*You Do Not Know What Tomorrow Will Bring*
Thursday	**Proverbs 27:1**	*Do Not Boast About Tomorrow*
Friday	**Isaiah 55:6**	*Seek the Lord While He May Be Found*

WEEK THREE — THE PURPOSEFUL MAN

| Monday | **Philippians 3:13–14** | *Forgetting What Lies Behind — Pressing On* |

Tuesday	**1 Corinthians 9:26**	*I Do Not Run Aimlessly*
Wednesday	**Proverbs 21:5**	*Plans of the Diligent Lead to Abundance*
Thursday	**Romans 8:28**	*Called According to His Purpose*
Friday	**Jeremiah 29:11**	*Plans for a Future and a Hope*

WEEK FOUR — FINISHING WHAT YOU STARTED

Monday	**Philippians 1:6**	*He Who Began a Good Work Will Complete It*
Tuesday	**2 Timothy 4:7**	*I Have Finished the Race*
Wednesday	**John 17:4**	*I Glorified You — Having Accomplished the Work*
Thursday	**Hebrews 12:1–2**	*Run with Endurance — Looking to Jesus*
Friday	**Revelation 3:11**	*Hold Fast What You Have*

MONTHLY MEMORY VERSE

""Look carefully then how you walk, not as unwise but as wise, making the best use of the time.""

Ephesians 5:15–16 · ESV

1.

In what area of your fatherhood have you been drifting? What has that drift cost you — or will cost you if it continues?

____

____

____

____

2.

Look at your calendar for the last month. What did you actually build that will outlast you? What did you spend time on that will not?

____

____

____

____

3.

What is your family's mission? If you cannot answer that clearly, what does it tell you about how intentionally you have been building?

____

____

4.

What relationship in your family has been drifting toward distance rather than closeness? What one step will you take toward it this week?

5.

If you found out today that you had five more years with your family — five more years of full presence and health — how would you spend them differently than you are spending today?

---

30 Days of Intentional Building

For 30 days, end every evening with this question: "Did I build anything today that will outlast me?" Write your answer — even if it is just one sentence. At the end of the month, read what you built. A man who accounts for his days builds more deliberately in them. The question is what focuses the building. Ask it every night.

I COMMIT TO THIS CHALLENGE BEGINNING:

____

WHAT I AM BELIEVING GOD FOR THIS MONTH:

____

____

_____________________________   _____________

Signature   Date

MONTH TWELVE

Chapter 12

12

The Man in the Mirror

""Legacy is not written at the end. It is written daily — in the ordinary moments most men overlook and most families never forget.""

— J.S.M.

You have come a long way in twelve months.

But I want to end this workbook where every good thing begins and ends — with the man in the mirror.

Not the man you perform for church. Not the man your colleagues see.

Not the man you are when the room is full and the lights are on.

The man you are when no one is watching. The man your family actually lives with. That man writes your legacy.

The hardest work in this entire workbook is not the outings or the challenges or the implementation steps. The hardest work is the interior work — the honest, relentless, uncomfortable examination of the gap between who you say you are and who you actually are when the pressure is on and no one is grading you. That gap is where legacy is either built or quietly lost.

> *""The Legacy Builder is not the man who never fails. He is the man who refuses to stop. He gets back up. He makes the adjustment. And he keeps building.""*

Most men are willing to work on their behavior. Far fewer are willing to work on their character. Behavior is what you do when someone is watching. Character is what you do when no one is. And it is character — not behavior — that your family absorbs. Your children are not primarily learning from your best moments. They are learning from your default ones. The man you are at 6pm on a Tuesday when you are tired and the day was hard — that man is writing the chapter they will remember.

Finishing well is not a destination you arrive at. It is a daily decision you make. The man who finishes well is not the man who was always strong — he is the man who, when he was weak, chose to be honest about it. Who looked in the mirror and named what he saw without flinching. Who asked for forgiveness from the people he let down. Who made the adjustment and kept going. That man — the one who refuses to stop — is the man his children will rise and call blessed.

This is not about perfection. Every man in this workbook has failed. The question is not whether you will fail — it is what you do with the failure. Do you minimize it, justify it, and move on unchanged? Or do you bring it into the light, sit with it, learn from it, and use it to build something better? The men who leave the deepest marks are almost never the men who had the fewest failures. They are the men who let their failures make them more honest, more humble, and more dependent on God.

Three declarations from the apostle Paul — a man who had every reason to quit and chose every single day not to. Three sentences that every Legacy Builder must be building toward: I have fought the good fight. I have finished the race. I have kept the faith. Not I was perfect. Not I never stumbled. I fought. I finished. I kept. That is the bar. And it is not a bar you clear once — it is a bar you choose to reach for every morning you wake up.

SCRIPTURE DEEP DIVE

2 Timothy 4:6–8 · ESV

> *""For I am already being poured out as a drink offering, and the time of my departure has come. I have fought the good fight, I have finished the race, I have kept the faith. Henceforth there is laid up for me the crown of righteousness, which the Lord, the righteous judge, will award to me on that Day, and not only to me but also to all who have loved his appearing.""*

Three Declarations Every Legacy Builder Must Be Able to Make

01 I Have Fought the Good Fight

Not the easy fight. Not the comfortable one. The good one — the fight for your marriage when it would have been easier to let it die, the fight for your children's souls when the culture was fighting harder than you were, the fight to remain the man you said you would be when no one was holding you accountable. Legacy is built by men who were willing to fight for what mattered, regardless of the cost.

02 I Have Finished the Race

Not started it. Not run it well for the first half. Finished it. The most devastating failures in legacy-building are not the men who never started — they are the men who started well and stopped. The men who were intentional fathers to young children and disconnected fathers to teenagers. The men who built strong marriages for twenty years and then stopped pursuing. Finishing matters more than starting.

03 I Have Kept the Faith

Everything in this workbook — every principle, every practice, every challenge — is built on the assumption that the faith is worth keeping. That God is real, His Word is true, and the man who builds his home on that foundation is building on the only thing that cannot be shaken. Keep the faith. In the dark years. In the prodigal years. In the years when nothing seems to be working. Keep it.

THE ILLUSTRATION

THE MAN IN THE MIRROR — STILL UNDER CONSTRUCTION

I am fifty-five years old. Married for over thirty years. Five sons. Three of them married to women of God. Three grandchildren and counting. A church I have pastored for more than two decades. A school. A podcast. A family that has stuck together through some of the hardest seasons any family can face.

And I still have to look in the mirror. It is not always fun.

Even now — after everything God has built in and through our family — I see things in that mirror that I do not like. Habits that have not fully been broken. Tendencies I recognize from seasons I thought I had moved past. A lack of motivation some mornings that surprises me. Mindsets that creep back in when I am tired or under pressure. Ways of thinking that are more like the old man than the new one.

I want to be honest with you about something. It would be very easy to end this book with a triumphant summary of everything God has done. The boys are walking in faith. The grandchildren are being raised in homes filled with the presence of God. The marriage has survived and is stronger than it has ever been. All of that is true — and I am deeply, profoundly grateful for every bit of it.

But I am not finished. And neither are you.

Legacy is not written at the end of a man's life. It is written daily — in the ordinary decisions, the private moments, the mirror no one else sees. The season of life changes. The responsibilities shift. The children grow up and move out and start their own homes. But the work of becoming who God called you to be does not stop until you draw your last breath. I still have things to address. Habits to break. Mindsets to surrender. A greater likeness to Christ to pursue. That is not discouraging to me. It is clarifying. Because it means that today still matters. This morning still matters. The man I choose to be today is still adding to — or subtracting from — the legacy my grandchildren will one day describe.

No matter how much has been built, the mirror is still the most important room in the house. Because the man in that mirror is still the man who sets the temperature of everything else.

APPLICATION FOR YOU

Do not close this workbook and assume the work is done. The work is never done. But that is not a burden — it is a gift. It means you still have today. You still have the ability to look your child in the eye and tell them who they are. You still have the chance to choose your wife deliberately instead of taking her for granted. You still have a mirror. Use it. Be honest in front of it. And then walk out of that room and build something that lasts.

1 Do a 12-Month Legacy Audit

Go back through this workbook. Read what you wrote. Read what you committed to. Honestly assess: Where did you grow? Where did you fall short? What principles changed you? What challenges did you keep? This audit is not for guilt — it is for course-correction. The man who honestly examines his own life is the man who can improve it.

→ *Do the audit this week. Write a one-page summary of what this year built in you.*

2 Ask for an Honest Assessment

This month, ask the people who know you best — your spouse, your children, a trusted friend — to tell you honestly: Where have you grown this year? Where do they still wish you would grow? A man who can receive honest feedback from the people closest to him is a man who will never stop improving. This is one of the bravest things you will do in this workbook.

→ *Ask your spouse first. Listen without defending. Thank them. Then act on what you hear.*

3 ### Write Your Legacy Letter

Write a letter to your family — to be read at a time of your choosing, or after you are gone — that captures who you tried to be, what you believed, what you wanted most for them, and what you want them to know about the man behind the role of father. This letter is one of the most powerful things you will ever give them. Do not leave it unwritten.

→ *Begin the letter this week. It does not have to be perfect. It has to be real.*

4 ### Celebrate What God Built This Year

Do not finish this workbook without celebrating what happened. Call your family together. Tell them what you set out to build at the beginning of this year and what God helped you build. Let them participate in the acknowledgment. A family that celebrates growth together is a family that will pursue more of it.

→ *Plan a celebration this month. Invite your family into it. Let them know what this year meant to you.*

5   Commit to Year Two

The work of a Legacy Builder does not fit in twelve months. It fits in a lifetime. Decide now — before the momentum of this year fades — what you will do next. Find a group of men to pursue with. Find an accountability partner. Start the workbook over with fresh eyes. Whatever it takes — do not let the year end without committing to continuing. The best thing about finishing well is that you do not have to stop finishing.

> → *Make the commitment now. Name who you will build with. Do not let this be the end.*

06   The Gratitude Tour

Drive to three places that have mattered in your family's story — the hospital where a child was born, the church where you got married, the house you first lived in, the school that shaped someone, the field where something important happened. At each stop, get out. Stand there for a minute. Tell your family what that place means to you. Thank God out loud for what He built in those places. A man who shows his family where they came from gives them something to stand on.

> → *End the drive at home. Walk in the front door and say: this is what we are building. This matters.*

FAMILY EXPERIENCES THIS MONTH

Experience 01

The Legacy Celebration Dinner

Host a dinner where Dad shares with the family what this year of intentional building meant to him. What he tried to build. What God helped him build. What he still wants to build. Let each family member share one way they noticed growth in Dad this year. Let the table become a celebration of what a year of intentional fatherhood produces.

> *""What's one way Dad is different than he was a year ago?""*

> *""What's one thing you want to build together as a family in the next year?""*

Experience 02

Read the Legacy Letters

If you wrote letters to your children during this workbook year, choose one to read aloud this month — to the child it was written for, in front of the family if appropriate. Or simply give each child the letter you wrote for them. Let the written word do what the spoken word cannot always do: outlast the moment it was created in.

> *"Your children receive something tangible from this year"*

> *"They see that their father thought about them specifically"*

Experience 03

The Family Declaration of Year Two

As a family, write a one-paragraph declaration of what you are building together in the year ahead. Make it specific. Make it ambitious. Make it anchored in your faith. Frame it. Put it next to your Family Mission Statement. Let your children see that the building never stops — it just deepens.

""In the year ahead, we are building…""

""We believe God is doing… in our family, and we commit to…""

A Gratitude Ceremony

Close the year with a simple ceremony of gratitude. Go around the table and have each family member complete two sentences: "This year, I am most grateful for..." and "Next year, I am believing God for..." Let Dad pray over the family to close — a long, specific, grateful, expectant prayer that seals the year and launches the next one.

"A family culture of faith-filled expectation"

"Children who learn to mark time with gratitude and vision"

DAILY BIBLE READING PLAN

WEEK ONE — THE MAN YOU ARE

Monday	**Psalm 139:23–24**	*Search Me, O God — Know My Heart*
Tuesday	**James 1:23–25**	*The Man Who Looks and Forgets*
Wednesday	**Lamentations 3:40**	*Let Us Test and Examine Our Ways*
Thursday	**1 Corinthians 11:28**	*Let a Person Examine Himself*
Friday	**Proverbs 4:23**	*Keep Your Heart with All Vigilance*

WEEK TWO — FINISHING THE RACE

Monday	**2 Timothy 4:6–8**	*I Have Finished the Race*
Tuesday	**Hebrews 12:1–3**	*Run with Endurance — Looking to Jesus*
Wednesday	**Galatians 6:9**	*Do Not Grow Weary*
Thursday	**1 Corinthians 9:24–27**	*Run to Obtain the Prize*
Friday	**Philippians 3:12–14**	*Press On Toward the Goal*

WEEK THREE — THE LEGACY YOU ARE LEAVING

| Monday | **Psalm 71:17–18** | *Even to Old Age — Declare Your Power* |
| Tuesday | **Proverbs 20:7** | *The Righteous Who Walks in Integrity* |

Wednesday	**Joshua 23:14**	*Not One Word Has Failed*
Thursday	**Psalm 78:4–7**	*Tell to the Coming Generation*
Friday	**3 John 1:4**	*No Greater Joy*

WEEK FOUR — THE BEGINNING OF WHAT NEVER ENDS

Monday	**Matthew 25:21**	*Well Done, Good and Faithful Servant*
Tuesday	**Revelation 14:13**	*Their Deeds Follow Them*
Wednesday	**2 Corinthians 5:10**	*We Must All Appear Before the Judgment Seat*
Thursday	**1 Thessalonians 2:19**	*Our Hope and Joy and Crown*
Friday	**Psalm 23:6**	*Goodness and Mercy Shall Follow Me*

MONTHLY MEMORY VERSE

""I have fought the good fight, I have finished the race, I have kept the faith.""

2 Timothy 4:7 · ESV

LEGACY BUILDER REFLECTION

1.

What is the most significant change that happened in you during this workbook year? Not what you did — who you became.

2.

Where is the largest remaining gap between the man you said you
wanted to be at the beginning of this year and the man you actually
are today?

3.

If your family were asked to describe the difference in you from
twelve months ago — what do you hope they would say? What do
you think they would actually say?

4.

Write Paul's three declarations — "I have fought the good fight, I
have finished the race, I have kept the faith" — and honestly
assess: how close are you to being able to say each one today?

____

____

____

____

5.

Write a letter to yourself — to be read one year from today. What do you want to be able to say you built? What kind of man do you want to have become? What do you want your family to say about the year ahead?

____

____

____

____

Don't Stop Building

You have reached the end of twelve months of intentional fatherhood. But there is no finish line for a Legacy Builder — only a deepening. Commit today to what comes next. Who will you build with? What will you build toward? How will you ensure that what was started in this workbook does not stop when you close it? The best legacy builders are the ones who never stopped building. Finish well — and keep going.

I COMMIT TO THIS CHALLENGE BEGINNING:

____

WHAT I AM BELIEVING GOD FOR THIS MONTH:

____

____

______________________________   ________________

Signature   Date

You Were Built for This

The men God uses most powerfully are rarely the most talented or the most gifted. They are the most faithful. They are the men who showed up — in the ordinary, in the inconvenient, in the unseen — and kept building long after everyone else stopped watching.

"Legacy is not what you leave for others — it is what you leave in others."

Now go build something that lasts.

Jay S. Miller

Legacy Builder · Husband · Father · Grandfather · Pastor

www.jaysmiller.com · Legacy Builders Podcast

CONNECT WITH JAY S. MILLER

WEBSITE	www.jaysmiller.com
PODCAST	Legacy Builders Podcast
YOUTUBE	youtube.com/@pastorjaymiller
THE FAMILY CHURCH	thefamilychurch.com
LAFAYETTE CHRISTIAN ACADEMY	www.lafayettechristianacademy.com
EMAIL	Pastor@thefamilychurch.org
BULK ORDERS & SPEAKING INQUIRIES	Pastor@thefamilychurch.org

If MARKED has impacted your life, your marriage, or your family — Jay would love to hear from you.

USING MARKED IN A GROUP SETTING

MARKED was written for individual fathers. But it works powerfully in community.

Men's groups, small groups, Sunday school classes, and father-son cohorts have used this workbook as a twelve-month guided journey. Each chapter's reflection questions are designed for honest conversation, and the monthly challenges create shared accountability that accelerates growth.

Here is a simple framework for group use:

Meet monthly	Gather once per chapter — twelve meetings over twelve months. Keep the group to six to twelve men.
Read independently	Each man reads the chapter and completes the reflection questions before the meeting.
Open with the core principle	Begin each gathering with a brief review of the month's teaching. Allow ten to fifteen minutes.
Work through two or three reflection questions	Choose the questions that generated the most conviction for the group. Protect honesty.
Share your monthly challenge	Each man reports on his commitment from the previous month before receiving a new one.
Pray together	Close each session by praying specifically over one another's families by name.

For bulk orders, group pricing, or to inquire about Jay S. Miller speaking to your men's group or church, contact Pastor@thefamilychurch.org · jaysmiller.com

SCRIPTURE INDEX

Key passages referenced throughout MARKED.

STELLAR URGES

ALIEN GLADIATOR KINGS, BOOK FIVE

Jove Chambers

Punk Rawk Books

STELLAR URGES

ALIEN GLADIATOR KINGS, BOOK FIVE

Jove Chambers

ONE

eventh

"Harder," I grunted. I was on my hands and knees on the bed in the university dorm room, my legs spread, speared and filled by the guy behind me, who was some kind of species from the planet Blirn, but I couldn't remember what they were called or what his name was. His cock had a ridge in the underside, a bony protrusion that rubbed my insides raw. It hurt. "Harder," I repeated.

He was panting behind me, and there was another guy—this one a half human and half gerren, the native species on the planet Kalion, lying next to me, his gaze honed in on where I was joined to the other guy. He should have been down for the count, because I'd already fucked him, but his cock looked like it was perking up.

I grunted again, moving my hips backwards, trying to get more friction, more length, more pain—*something.*

It was never enough, that was the thing.

People judged me.

These guys were judging me even as they enjoyed me, took advantage of what I offered them, *used* me.

My roommate here at the university, she judged me, and I knew it, which was why I'd stopped bringing guys back to my own room. She could have asked if she wanted to know why I did it, why I slept with so many different guys, why I always wanted it rough, why I was insatiable and would fuck my way through a party of hoverball players if I was in the mood.

She could have asked, but she didn't. She just judged.

Of course, maybe I was lying to myself to think that it was justified. Maybe I was only incredibly screwed up in the head. It didn't matter. I wasn't going to stop.

Behind me, the nameless Blirn guy's rhythm missed a few strokes and he dug his fingers into my hips.

"You are not going to come already, are you?" I snarled at him over my shoulder.

"Fuck… you are one crazy slut, aren't you?" he wheezed, eyes half-lidded as he slammed into me again and again.

"Don't you dare." I looked back at the other guy, gauging the status of his erection. "Can you get hard again?"

He guffawed. "Is this girl for real?"

"Come on, you're halfway there. Touch your fucking dick and—"

I never finished, because I was interrupted by blaster fire.

Except I didn't register immediately what the sound was, because blaster fire was incongruous with the situation where I was. I had heard blaster fire before, back on the planet Bravren where I'd grown up. People used blasters there to hunt for food sometimes. And I'd heard blaster fire on action holovids, but not…

Not in a dorm room, not while I had a ridged cock in me, not while I was naked.

The guy inside me slammed into me, hard, and we

both collapsed into the bed.

The guy beside me, the half human? There was a spray of blood on his face and he let out a high-pitched shriek, looking over the body of the guy on top of me at the door to the dorm.

Body.

I registered that, somehow, that there was a dead man on top of me, a dead man's cock inside me, and I would have thought that *I* would have screamed, but I didn't. I went oddly calm and efficient, and I slithered out beneath the dead weight on top of me and dove for the floor.

Just in time, because there was more blaster fire and the scream of the half gerren cut off.

Fuck.

The door to the dorm room had a big hole burned through it, which was smoking. The barrel of a blaster poked through the hole, followed by a djiss, a species from the planet Nevis 4. This one was huge. His head came through the hole, but he couldn't get his shoulders through. He had wide set eyes, big and globelike on either side of his head, and a gaping teeth-lined mouth — three rows of sharp teeth.

I rolled under the bed.

Great plan, Eventh, I thought to myself, and I was stunned that my inner voice was amused and rueful like that. This was the time to panic, right? But no, panicking would be stupid. I needed to be calm because I needed to get out of this. I had gone into some odd, detached auto-admii I hadn't even known I was capable of.

Funny the things you find out about yourself in moments of extreme stress, said my internal voice. *Now get to the fucking window, bitch.*

Hey, did I need to be insulted?

If it works to keep us alive.

Wonderful, now there was an 'us,' apparently. Probably, I was having a psychotic break, but this really wasn't the time to worry about it. I dragged my bare skin over the floor, glancing through the sheets and blankets that hung haphazardly over the side of the bed at the djiss as he struggled into the room.

The window was on the other side of the room, and I could crawl under the bed, roll out, stand up, open the window, and hurl myself out of it. It was a two-story drop, and I might break a limb, but it would be better than blaster fire. Of course—

The window shattered, busting apart in a million pieces of plasglass as someone dove through it and into the room.

The figure was furry and large—not nearly as large as the djiss, but muscled and tall, striped—it looked like a wvorn, actually, the native species on the planet I'd grown up on. It looked like—

It *was.*

Sevren, high chieftain of the Chavrax clan, looked mostly the same—well, notably wider with larger muscles in his arms—which—were they shaved? Maybe I knew that. Maybe they made gladiators do that?

I hadn't seen him in nine gecycles, but he looked mostly the same.

He had a blaster and he opened fire on the djiss in the door.

The djiss howled, retreating.

Sevren's gaze swept the room, taking in the bodies of the naked men. "Eventh?"

I rolled out from under the bed and looked up at

him.

He looked me over, my nakedness, and his gaze jerked up *real* fast. He shouldered the blaster — it was one of those rifles that holds a big plas-cartridge — and focused on the doorway, talking to me. "Find some clothes."

"What's going on?" I gasped.

"That djiss hates me. He knows about you. Figures killing you is the best way to hurt me." He headed toward the door with his blaster. "Where the fuck is he? Izar? Did you run like a fucking coward?"

Another beam of blaster fire came through the door, missing Sevren by a finger's width.

He yelped.

I snatched up a pair of shorts from the floor underneath the bed. They weren't mine. They belonged to the guy who'd been fucking me, but they had a drawstring waist. I yanked them on, tightening them.

Sevren was pumping blaster shot after shot out the door, screaming, "You'll never touch her, Izar," at the top of his lungs.

I covered my head with my hands.

Sevren opened the door and went out into the hall.

I waited, cringing, looking out between my fingers.

Sevren came back. "He's gone, I think."

"Why does he hate you?"

"I accidentally killed his brother in the ring. He's been doing to-the-death fights for over ten gecycles. It fucks with your head, and he's not exactly — you're still not dressed, baby girl."

Baby girl. The words felt like a punch to my chest, like he'd just shattered my ribs. I glared up at him. "Should you still call me that?"

He cringed. "Maybe not," he breathed, looking

away.

I spied a shirt—also not mine, but possibly belonging to the half human. I shrugged into it and got to my feet. Shoes. I needed—

Aha. There were my shoes. I yanked those on, too.

"Let's go," he said.

"Go? Where are we going?"

"I'm getting you somewhere safe," he said. He reached out and one of his big, furred hands closed around my upper arm. Then he let go immediately, as if touching me burned.

I had to admit some odd jolt had gone through me at his touch too, and I felt it everywhere, especially in my pussy, especially in my clit.

Stars.

I had never felt anything like that in my *life*.

"Come with me," he growled, his voice all strangled and weird, reminding me of that time when I'd been in his lap, that time right before he'd gone away without saying goodbye. He left the room again.

I went after him. "Where are we going?"

The hallway was a wreck. There were scorch marks everywhere, holes in the wall, the ceiling. "Stars," I breathed, looking around.

"The gladiator guild will clean up after him," muttered Sevren. "He's a draw. They want their credits. He can get away with literal murder. This way." He hurried down the hall.

Doors opened a crack, students in the dorm peering out, wide-eyed and frightened.

I kept pace with Sevren as we hurried through the hallway.

We got in a transroom and went down to the first level and out the front door.

A speeder was parked haphazardly—half on the walkway, half in a parking space. He touched his bracelet and the doors opened. "This is us. Get in."

I got in.

He got in to the driver's side. It was one of those two-person hoverspeeders. "Buckle up."

"Where are we going?"

"Buckle up, baby girl, come on."

I buckled myself in. "I'm not a baby," I said. "And I'm not—you and me—I haven't seen you in very long time."

"Well, this'll be a short trip and you hopefully won't ever see me again," he muttered.

"Where are we going?"

"We're going to a watervessel on the Dracian Sea, where you'll take a nice trip and be safely tucked away until I can deal with Izar fucking Fjass." He started the speeder.

"I can't go on a watervessel! I have school. I have time scheduled in the lab tomorrow."

The speeder roared to life and we took off.

"You'll make up your schoolwork later," he said, staring straight ahead. I looked him over. He looked… wow, he looked *good*.

Had he always looked this good? He was older now. How old would he be now? Thirty-five gecycles. I was twenty. Last time I'd seen him, he was twenty-six and I was eleven. I remembered burying my face in his chest and breathing in his scent, which was the only thing that made me feel good while my body felt like it was burning itself from the inside out.

I'd been in heat.

I was a human. I wasn't supposed to even go into heat.

He had been the reason it was happening, and the only balm for the agony.

I smelled him now. That scent washed into me, waking me up all over, burrowing into me in the strangest of ways. It was nice. He smelled like branciuth sap. Branciuths were a tree on Bravren. The sap was a sort of syrupy, earthy deep scent. And there were notes of coffee, too, something sharp but pleasant.

I let out a sigh.

"Don't do that," he muttered.

He was wearing a short-sleeved shirt, and his arms *were* shaved, because they shaved gladiators to show off their muscles and he was a gladiator now. He was also striped underneath, on his skin, dark stripes against his thickly-muscled forearms. His thighs were thick and muscled too, and he was—

Oh, stars.

He was hard. I could see the tent his cock was making of his pants. He was—wow, he had a big cock, didn't he? Huge fucking cock that would probably feel like…

Well, with him, I wouldn't need…

I let out another sigh, this one trembling, affected.

"Eventh," he growled.

"Sorry," I said. "Does it still do that around me?" Sitting in his lap all those years ago, my face in his shirt, feeling his erection, and him whispering to me not to worry. *I'd never hurt you, you know that, right? I can't help this, but you don't have to worry about this. This isn't coming near you.*

Except it *was* near me. Except I could *feel* his hard-on. Except I remembered the way it had pressed into me through our clothes, hard and pulsing and *impossibly* large back then, but…

What? Had I blocked that out? Is that why the sight of his size now seemed like a revelation?

I shuddered.

Well, it *had* been traumatic. I'd been a little girl.

"What are you talking about?" Sevren glanced at me and then back at the road.

"I-I meant your…" I looked away, out the window, at the lights of the city going by. "Nothing. Never mind." I let out another sigh, but this one wasn't affected, just a reaction to everything. I was overwhelmed and confused just then. Everything was insane.

"I guess you were interrupted in the middle of, uh, whatever that was, and that's why you're making those noises, but don't."

"Does it make your hard-on worse?" I asked the window.

"Spirits," he groaned. "Did you just *say* that?"

"Imagine if you'd come through the window a few hidosecs earlier. You could have seen the whole show."

The speeder jerked, swerving a bit.

I turned to him. "*Hey.*"

"Sorry," he breathed. "It's just… you… you're…"

"Are you jealous?"

"More like concerned," he said. "My cock might think of you that way, baby girl, but I don't, and you know that. You're like my…"

"What?" I said. "What is the relationship that we have? Especially since I haven't seen you since I was a kid?"

"That was for your own good," he said. "The heat suppressants have a lot of breakthrough incidents when a female is in the presence of her mate—"

"Yeah, they're not really great at suppressing it in

the best of circumstances. I get these... mini heats, and they're frequent. I need... but I can never..." I shook my head. I didn't have the words to even explain this.

It was quiet.

His voice was gruff. "You know, I hadn't really thought about that for some reason."

"Thought about what?"

"That you can't have orgasms either," he said.

I looked at him.

He glanced at me and then went back to the road.

Ahead, there was a traffic signal, and he pulled the speeder to a stop.

"Either," I said. "So, you..."

"I can't get *erect* when you're not around," he said, eyeing me. "So, no. Definitely none for me. But you've... you've *never* had one. And how old are you now? How could I not have thought of this?"

My brain was working overtime, trying to put this all together. "Wait a hisec, if you can't get an erection unless you're in my presence, then... were you getting them when I was a kid?"

"Nope. None at all for the first eleven years of your life."

"Being mated to me meant you couldn't..."

"It's fine," he said. "I can handle this. You, on the other hand, are a vibrant, beautiful young woman who's—"

He was cut off by the angry noise of a beep coming from another speeder behind us, telling us to get moving.

The signal had changed.

He gunned the speeder and it shot forward.

"I'm so sorry," he said.

"You can't have *sex*," I suddenly realized. "At *all*."

"I'm fine," he said, but his voice had gone weirdly growly.

I was re-examining everything, suddenly, going back over all of my memories of this man, this man who I hated, who I despised, who had betrayed me and left me alone and broken my heart and *abandoned* me.

And maybe I had been a little bit hard on him.

Because…

Stars.

"You were fifteen when I was born," I said. "When we bonded. Had you…?" My lips parted. "Are you a virgin?" I breathed.

"Why are we talking about this?" The speeder was going faster now. He touched the dashboard and a holoprojection popped up. "Maybe I could… like be a room over while you had… why can't you have a boyfriend, baby girl? Just *one* guy, who you like, who's age appropriate and who you're exploring your sexuality healthily with?" He manipulated the holoprojection until it lit up a map of the city and showed a route for the speeder to take. "Why are you getting *gang-banged* in a dorm room?"

"Two guys is not a gang bang," I said. "It's a threesome." Of course, it wasn't like there hadn't been things that could easily be termed gang bangs in my past, if we wanted to be really technical about it.

"Did I fuck up leaving you?" he said in a low voice. "Would you have been better off if I'd just…" He made a fist and punched it into the holoprojection. "No. No way."

"Maybe," I said. "Maybe you fucked up."

"Spirits," he said softly.

"Or maybe… maybe I see why you did it, did all of it, but you have to understand why *I* do it. Because I get... urges."

"The suppressants don't make those go away entirely," he said dully.

"And I can't ever get any kind of satisfaction, no matter what," I said.

"So, you need more," he said.

"Yes," I said, nodding.

"More than one partner, more than something healthy and simple."

"I just push for things, to try, to see if they could... like it's better if it hurts or if it's rough or if it's—"

"Stop." His voice broke.

"Look, you're being dumb about it. There's no reason that experimenting with multiple partners or some bondage or a little blood play has to be unhealthy if it's between consenting and adventurous adults."

"*Blood* play?" He turned on me, his face twisting.

I shrank from him.

"What the spirits is—"

Another speeder crashed into the side of our speeder, forcing us off the road and into the rail on the side of the road in a shower of bright purple sparks.

TWO

Sevren was the chieftain of the clan in the village where I grew up—the only human girl amongst a clan of wovrn—and he was my best friend.

It sounds weird to say, I guess.

I never remember a time when he wasn't around. He wasn't there all the time, but he was there every suncycle and usually for hihors at a time. When I was a toddler, I have these early memories of him carrying me around on his shoulders or helping me climb up into the tree house that was in the little play area for kids in the clan. It was always harder for me to climb than it was for the other kids because I didn't have claws like they did.

He loved me like no one loved me.

My parents, they loved me like parents, and they were great parents. My mom and dad are amazing. But Sevren was patient in a way they weren't. I was always the most interesting thing in the room to him. I was his most important person, and it was a heady thing to feel.

He'd do whatever I wanted to do, play any game I wanted, listen to any long and meandering little-girl story I wanted to tell. I remembered ordering him around, and him taking it with this ridiculous grin on his face, like I was the sun that lit up his sky or something.

He…

I loved him, too.

I adored him. He was my favorite person in the world.

It wasn't creepy, I swear.

I don't know, though. When I think back on it, knowing all the things I know now, I think it has to be creepy. I think that no matter what, even though there was no sexual element to it at all, it was too much for me, because I was too young for that kind of an emotional attachment.

I was too young to love like that, to *be* loved like that.

Usually people get time to grow into themselves.

Maybe that's why I was such a bratty teenager. Too much of my childhood had been spent in service of him, right? He wasn't the only person who bent himself in knots to please the other one of us. So, once he was gone, I went a little crazy and I got a little selfish. I needed it. I never had a chance before.

Sevren and I were mated.

I just didn't know that growing up.

Mating isn't supposed to work like that.

Obviously.

It happened when I was a baby. My parents ended up on the planet Bravren because they were brought there to be experimented on in a lab owned by the Toth. They were human, and they were, like, bred to each other. I don't… never asked a lot of questions about how that worked. They were both pretty young, though, both still teenagers.

Sevren got my parents out of there and brought them to live with his tribe.

And several moon-cycles later, I was born.

But the thing was, my parents had been given injections that had allowed them to survive on the planet, which had a substance called praxicc in its atmosphre. It was toxic to humans. It actually was a by-product of most of the plant-life on the planet, and it was released in gaseous form from their leaves. The substance was easily broken down by the lifeforms native to the planet, and humans could do it too if they were given a certain enzyme called miicc which would bond to certain receptors—

Sorry.

I get a little too technical with scientific explanations sometimes. Comes with the territory of being a biology nerd. The point is, I took my first breaths outside of my mother's body, and I started to die.

I don't know exactly how it was that Sevren came around to biting me, but they tried it, knowing that a mating bite had altered a human in another clan, one over the ridge and beyond the orange waterfalls in the forest, and they were desperate.

It worked. His saliva altered my body. It gave me miic, which created a chain reaction in my body and altered it so that I could break down praxicc. But it did something else too. It bonded me to *him*, mating us.

And then he was my everything and I was his.

I had a very happy childhood with my loving parents and with *him*.

And then, it all changed.

Amongst the wovrn clan, the women started to sexually mature a little later than humans do, and I started to mature pretty young for a human anyway. My mother said I could have waited until I was thirteen or even sixteen, but I was eleven.

Even when a wovrn woman was sexually mature, she would not go into heat until she was mated, and it was tradition for women of the clans to spend their youth trying different pairings out until they settled on someone right for them. Then they did the biting ceremony with their chosen mate—usually when they were in their early twenties or so. After that, their heats would start and they'd have babies.

I was way too young for all of that by the metrics of both humans and wovrn.

But I remembered the way things started changing. The budding barely-there breasts I had and the way my body started tingling whenever he was around.

And then there was the time we went swimming.

Sevren was always around with me, and he was the chieftain of the clan, because his father had been killed young, and Sevren had taken over. So, everyone trusted him, and they all understood the situation. It wasn't uncommon for Sevren to be the supervising adult with a big group of kids, including me. That sun-cycle, we'd all trekked out from the village into the forest to the swimming hole—which was fed by the orange waterfall—and we were out there swimming, and Sevren got weird.

I remembered his gaze on me. We all wore barely anything to swim, and the wovrn girls my age didn't have breasts, so a lot of them were just in little shorts, their chests bare. I knew, somehow, that I couldn't anymore, so I had a shirt on, but it was wet, and clinging to me, and a little see-through, and Sevren *stared* at me. There.

At my not-breasts.

He wouldn't get out of the water and sent us off through the forest without him.

Looking back on it, he must have gotten an erection. I can only assume that this might have been his first erection in eleven gecycles. No wonder he couldn't handle it.

At the time, I felt hurt and confused. Because after that, he stopped coming around. I went two days without seeing him, which was unheard of. I'd never gone that long without seeing him.

I threw a tantrum—even though I was too old to throw tantrums—and I remember my mother contacting him on his bracelet to ask him what was going on, and whatever he said back to her…

She told me that I wouldn't be seeing Sevren for a while, and that it was best for both of us.

And then he was just gone pretty much all the time.

He came by once or twice, but he always got immediately weird, put distance between us, and then left really fast.

I saw him one more time, when I went into heat for the first time, and then…

He left the *planet*.

He took a gladiator contract, left his entire clan in the hands of his sister, leaving her as the chieftess, and never came back. Ever again.

He didn't even say goodbye to me.

* * *

sevren

I popped off my seatbelt and wrapped my body around her, rolling to brace against the impact, so that I'd absorb it, and she'd be all right. I didn't think. I just did it, because I lived to protect her.

But.

I had not been this close to her in…

Oh, spirits only knew how many gecycles since I'd

touched her. She felt perfect in my arms. She belonged there, and even as the speeder crumpled and buckled around us, even as my shirt burned off my back and my body lit up in pain, the clearest sensation I had was of how *right* it was to touch her.

I was assailed by five different images of our bodies entwined—things we could do, things we *needed* to do, and my cock got somehow harder and bigger, even though I had previously thought it was so hard and big that it was going to explode.

The speeder stopped moving. I gasped, disentangling us, snatching up the blaster and pushing out of the mangled driver's side door of the speeder.

Izar's blaster was in my face, and I shot at him.

It was stupid, because he was right there, and he should have shot me, but somehow, luck was on my side, and the blast caught him in the arm.

He screamed, dropping his blaster, going down on one knee to clutch himself.

I reached back for Eventh. "Baby girl, come on. Quickly now."

She grasped onto me.

Keeping my gaze on Izar, I yanked her out of the speeder. I balanced the blaster with one arm, keeping it trained on him, and I kicked his blaster away from him.

"I should kill you," I told him.

"The guild would love that," he said, grinning up at me.

"With Griz, it was an accident," I said. "You know things happen in the ring. You know—"

"Fuck you," he growled.

I set the blaster to stun. I pulled the trigger.

The stun beam hit him and he slumped to the ground.

Eventh pressed into me. "Sevren," she gasped.

I wrapped my hand around her waist. Wow. She had a waist now. And hips. And breasts. Yeah, I'd seen everything in that dorm room, because she'd been entirely nude, but now, I could *feel* her, and she felt perfect.

I turned to her, my breath going erratic.

She looked up at me, tilting her head back, parting her lips, offering them to me. She was in my arms, and she wanted to be kissed, and I wanted to kiss her.

As if moving of its own volition, my head bent to hers.

She let out a noisy breath.

I rubbed my flat nose against her sharper, human one. I tickled her cheek with my whiskers. Our mouths were almost touching.

And somehow, I managed to pull away.

She let out a disappointed sound.

I extricated us, making sure she was upright before letting go of her entirely.

Ahead of us, a cop-bot was approaching. "Accidents happen, remain calm," it announced in an electronic voice. "Please state your names, addresses, and vehicle insurance information for public record."

I switched the blaster from stun to blast and blew up the cop-bot.

It erupted in a shower of sparks.

"W-why did you—?"

"Trust me, last thing we need is a report trail," I said. "guild's going to wipe this like it never happened, and if you're a casualty, they could give a fuck, but I will never let that happen." I eyed Izar's speeder, which had also been damaged in the crash. I wondered if he'd traced my bracelet. Grimly, I took it off and gestured for Eventh to give me hers.

"What?" she said.

"Give me your bracelet, baby girl," I said.

"No. What are you going to do with it?"

I reached over and unbuckled it. She gasped when my fingers made contact with her skin. I groaned.

I lost it. I straightened, seizing her by the back of the head and assaulting her mouth with mine. I parted her lips with my tongue and swept in there and she tasted like sweet nexberries and she clung to me, and my whole world went into a bright, hot explosion of —

"Fuck." I pushed her away.

She stumbled, letting out a cry.

"Bracelet," I ground out.

She gave it to me, her hands shaking.

I dropped them both on the ground and stomped on them.

"What the stars are you doing?" she demanded.

"I don't want him tracing us again," I said in a tight voice. "Get in." I pointed to Izar's speeder.

"It's wrecked."

"It will run."

"It's not going to —"

"Get in, Eventh," I snarled. "The stun blast will not last forever, especially not on a djiss." I glared at him. I *should* kill him. I should just…

Yeah, that'll be great, and when the guild comes to you and asks you to pay them back for how many credits they're going to lose without him, you'll have to sign another contract with them and in ten gecycles, you'll be too old to fight.

Spirits, I was too old now.

She got into the speeder.

I went around and got in the other side. All this time,

other speeders had been whooshing past us on the road, none of them giving us the a second glance beyond thinking it was just a regular accident. People were busy in the city.

I started the speeder.

"Repairs needed," said the speeder in an electronic voice.

"Override repair alarm," I said, pulling up the holodisplay and punching in a few commands. I set another course.

The speeder chirped and sent out several scolding beeps and alarms. Then I got it to shut up, and we were back on the road.

We sped past buildings, going through the city, and then I saw a ramp for a higher access lane, one that would take us out into a less-populated area, and I navigated the speeder onto that.

Once we were settled into one of the lanes where I could turn on the autodrive feature, I did that. I let go of the steering wheel and glanced at her. "I'm sorry I kissed you."

She wouldn't meet my gaze. "That was, um, that was…"

"Sorry," I said again. "Are you hurt? Did you get hurt in the crash?"

"Your shirt is half burned off," she said and now her fingers were on my back, against the tatters of my clothing there. Her touch made my eyes roll back in my head. I hissed. "Baby girl, don't do that," I breathed. I wanted to sound irritated, but I didn't. I sounded greedy for her touch.

"You've got *burns*."

"I'm hopped up on an injection my agent gets me for fights. I'll be fine," I said. "It'll heal up real fast." I cleared my throat. "You're okay? You didn't get hurt?"

"No, not at all. You, um, you took all the impact."

"Yeah, of course I did." I let out a long, shaking breath. "If I ever figure out how he found out about you, I'm going to kill whoever gave him that info."

"I don't see why he'd think you'd even care about me," I said.

"Yeah, well, that's because you're human, and humans don't mate," I muttered.

"Djiss don't either."

"Well, he knows about species who mate."

"I grew up watching mated wvorns," she said. "And I know how we are with each other—were. How we were." She sighed heavily. "Where are we going?"

"I'm getting you away from him. I'm getting you somewhere safe."

"The watervessel thing? How long is that going to last?"

"I don't know. I don't know what I'm going to do with him," I said. "Maybe I should let him kill me. You'd be free. That'd solve everything."

"No." She drew herself up. "No, no, no. Don't you dare. If you think I could handle it if you were dead, then you've lost your mind." Her eyes shone, tears springing to them. "I hate you so much, do you even know that?"

I shook my head at her. "Why do you hate me? Do you have any idea all the things I've done for you?"

"You do *nothing* for me."

"Everything I do is for you." My voice rumbled, a growl rising in my chest.

She rolled her eyes.

"It is," I said. "Why do you think I'm a gladiator?"

"I have no idea, because you just left and didn't

bother to say goodbye."

"Where do you think ten gecycles worth of suppressants came from?" I said. "You think, in our village, we had credits or capability to get that kind of thing?"

She blinked at me. "What are you saying?"

"I traded. Suppressants for the contract," I said. "Your mother didn't tell you."

She shook her head. "My dad really didn't like us to talk about you."

I let out a low, bitter laugh. "Oh, that figures. Fucking Dannor." He and I had never gotten along. Admittedly, my having a crush on the woman carrying his child was... awkward. But it was of course ten times *more* awkward when I was yanked immediately out of having any sort of feelings for Belini and into a mating bond with his infant daughter.

Or when his eleven-gecycles-old daughter was banging on the door of my bedchamber, in full-fledged heat, and then rubbing her barely pubescent body all over me and I was on my bracelet typing furiously at him, *Come get your daughter. I'm out of control.*

Yeah, well, maybe he had reasons not to like me.

"How long of a contract?" she said. "If you traded nine star-shined gecycles, you got a raw deal—"

"No, it's over. I'm not... I have an agent now. I set up my own jobs."

"So, you could have come home?" She glared at me.

"Well, no, I could not have. Because you were still there, I thought."

"I got this scholarship to Brakmills last gecycle," she said. Brakmills was a university on Kalion.

"No one told me," I said. "I don't really keep in touch with your father, and he gets weird if your mother gets in touch with me."

"Why is that?"

"You know, just because of history stuff."

"Wait, there's something with you and my mother?" She was appalled.

I groaned.

"Are you kidding me? So, you're not a virgin. You fucked my mom."

"No!" I shook my head vehemently. "No, your mom has it bad for your dad. It was very one sided. I was fifteen gecycles old. It was just a crush. It didn't mean anything."

"You *are* a virgin."

"Spirits." I sighed.

She folded her arms over her chest.

I looked her over. "Yes. Technically, yes. Okay? That what you wanted to hear?"

"Technically?"

"Eventh, my body has biologically determined that you're the only person I can be with, but that doesn't mean I haven't done... had experiences... I might not be able to... I can still... why are we talking about this?"

"Huh, I'm jealous," she said in a thoughtful voice. "Do you have a girlfriend?"

"No."

"Good," she said. "That's good."

I let out a helpless laugh. This was all so messed up. "Never had a girlfriend." *Don't say that out loud to her.*

"No?" she said. "Like, you're not sure if you could feel that for someone? That's how I always feel anyway. Like, there's this you-shaped hole in my heart somewhere—"

"You were a kid. There's no hole in your heart—"

"What the stars do you know about it?" And she now sounded like she was going to cry. "And that's why I hate you, because you acted like I was a kid—"

"You *were* a kid. You're *still* a kid."

"I am *not*."

"You are. You're twenty. That's nothing."

"Oh, it's always going to be nothing if you're as much older than me than you are—"

"Which is why it can never—"

"I love you." Her voice broke. "And *that's* why I hate you."

"That makes tons of sense," I mumbled. "Maybe we should talk about something else. I don't like getting you upset." Never had. I spoiled her when she was a kid, for instance. I was never in any position to be a disciplinarian, not even when she was a brat, taking other kids toys or cheating at playing games. I couldn't help but take her side. I was hers.

"Don't like getting me upset? What do you think happened to me after you left?"

"Okay, look, baby girl, it wasn't easy for me either, but it was either get away or… or…" *Fuck you.* Because I would have. I wanted her. I never wanted anything like I wanted… When she was in heat, the way she *smelled*, it drove me mad. "Let's drop this. Drop all of this." I sighed.

She sighed too. "Don't get me wrong. I was a kid. I was too young for…" Her voice dropped. "Sex. If you'd done that to me—"

"Never," I snapped, even though the only thing I knew right now was that I had to get away from her soon, because I wasn't strong enough to resist. She smelled good now. *Really* good. Her scent was like her taste. Nexberries and a hint of the breeze in springtime.

She was mine, and we were meant to be together, and I belonged with her.

"Never?" she said in a tiny voice. "Because, I don't know, I was thinking maybe, um, maybe just once or something?"

My heart lurched and my cock jerked. I looked at her mouth and remembered kissing her.

"Just to know what it's like?" she whispered.

I shook my head. "It'd be like fucking my kid sister."

"I don't know about that," she said softly.

"I'm going to drive," I said suddenly, turning to the dashboard to switch off the autodrive feature. I needed something to focus on.

"I'm old enough now," she said. "I am a grown woman by any metric that—"

"You're young enough to be my daughter."

"I'm not," she said. "Not really. My dad is way older than you."

He was three gecycles older than me. Belini, her mother, was one gecycle older than me. Admittedly, neither of them had chosen to become parents at such a young age. My understanding was that the Toth pumped them full of aphrodisiacs and threw them in a cell together, and that was how they met. It didn't actually sound super consensual to me, but then I guessed people bonded in shared trauma and that kind of thing.

And anyway, I wasn't bitter about it anymore. All those weird, tangled feelings of wishing that Belini could see me differently had gone out like a flame being extinguished the hidosec I'd put my teeth in Eventh's skin.

And when I was away from Eventh, my body was essentially sexless, although my mind wasn't exactly there. Which was why there were occasionally interludes with women. I could get them off, I could feel some closeness, the touch of skin on skin… without that, occasionally, I'd probably go insane.

Eventh was still talking. "I mean, since you think my sexuality is so unhealthy anyway, how much worse for me could you be than a gang bang, right?"

My mouth went dry. That was actually a good argument.

It was definitely possible that there were psychological ramifications of the mating bond that I hadn't considered, and maybe it would be for her own good if we, uh, just once… and I'd be good to her and take care of her and please her and treat her like she deserved. There would be no blood play, for spirits' sake, or anything else like that.

The thought of some idiotic university boy making her bleed and using his cock—

I wanted to punch something.

I let out a shaky breath. "I guess Izar must have found out why I can't do to-the-death fights, and that's maybe how he know I had a mate."

"What are you talking about?" she said.

"Whoever wins a deathmatch has to fuck a prize in the middle of the arena for the crowd. You know about this, right? Well, I can't do that, so I've never been able to take a deathmatch fight."

"You wouldn't," she said in a high-pitched voice. "You can't put yourself in danger like that, not—"

"I could die in the ring anyway," I said. "That's what happened to Izar's brother. He and I were in a regular match, not a deathmatch, and he went over the side of the ring. They're up on thrusters, you know, floating in the middle of the arena. They say, a fall like that, you're dead from fear before you hit the ground. I hope so. He fell a long way. I knocked him off on accident. I didn't mean for it to happen. Izar… I think his brother was the only thing keeping him together. The only thing in the world he still loved. Because, when you're a gladiator, it's easy for it all just to become a world of nothing but pain and fighting and injury and—"

"But you didn't quit when your contract was up," she said. "So, you must love it."

"I told you, I couldn't go back home, not if you were there."

"How long was the contract?"

"Five gecycles. You were sixteen when it was up. Still too young."

"Too young? I thought I was never going to be old enough."

I let out another sigh. I stared out into the darkness, at the distant lights of other speeders on the highway with us. "Baby girl, baby girl."

"You keep calling me that."

True. I'd called her that her whole life. And I'd held her in my arms when she was born. This was gross, and it was *always* going to be gross.

"Maybe once," I said. "Maybe just once."

"Really?" she breathed.

"I got to deal with Izar first," I said. "I'll get you on the watervessel, and figure out how to deal with him, and then we can… I don't know, but…" My whole body clenched.

You're sick and twisted, Sevren. I reached inside my pants to rearrange my stupidly hard cock. None of my blood was rushing toward my brain right now.

THREE

sevren

It wasn't gross when she was a kid, I swear. It sounds like it would be gross, but I swear to the spirits in all the sacred trees of the groves of the forest, she…

She was like my baby sister.

More than that maybe.

I don't know. She was a kid, and I loved her, but it wasn't like *that*.

That whole aspect of me turned off, and I didn't even really notice for probably gecycles, as weird as it sounds. I stopped masturbating, but I didn't *want* to masturbate, so I didn't care. When I did realize it, I was relieved, because she had become the most important thing to me—way more important than myself—and I was glad that there was no way I could hurt her.

I was really glad it couldn't be gross.

So glad, because I worshiped her. All I wanted to do was to go spend my afternoons pretending to have dinner parties for stuffed animals or braiding her dolls' hair. She was an imaginative child and so clever, and we'd spend hihors playing together, and it was effortlessly wonderful.

Her father hated it.

I would have been there more, but he put limits on it. He didn't like it to be more than a few hihors a day, and he also didn't like it when we were alone, but that happened. Dannor and Belini ended up knowing a lot of intimate details about me, like that I'd stopped functioning sexually.

I told them because I thought they would be relieved, and they were. We all were, because when I'd bitten her, to save her life, we hadn't had time to consider all the repercussions of a mating bond with an infant. It wasn't done. No one had ever done something like that, and no one knew what would happen.

The idea that the bond itself was altering me to protect her, it was really reassuring.

And then things changed.

When I started realizing that I was getting aroused around her, that I was developing an attraction to her, it kind of broke me. I loved her, and I knew that I was suddenly a danger to her, that there was no way that a little girl could cope with that from someone like me, basically a family member. That's what it felt like we were. I knew it would mess her up really bad.

I told Belini, but I asked her not to say anything to Dannor. I thought he might get a hunting blaster and blow my head off.

Eventh really was still a little *girl*.

And I kept my distance. Belini told me that she explained it to Eventh in a way a kid could understand it, which... turned out... no. She didn't really tell her much of anything, but then I didn't explain it either, because I didn't know what to say, didn't explain it until it was way too late.

That period of time—it was maybe a few mooncycles from when I first started getting aroused and when her heat came in—it was this horrible period of time when I felt as if I was struggling to breathe all the time, as if I was in freezing cold and that I couldn't warm up. She was my air. She was my warmth.

She was gone.

I had to stay away from her.

It kind of broke me.

But I've gotten use to it as the gecycles have passed. It's not so bad anymore.

Anyway, that night, the night of the heat, I was asleep in my bedchamber. It was the chieftain's bedchamber, and it was connected to the rest of the family hut, which was sprawling and huge. It had been built generations ago by my great-great-grandparents. My bedchamber had a door into the rest of the hut, but it also had its own entrance.

We were not entirely primitive on Bravren. We had plaslights and some plaspower for things like doors and heating and cooking and that kind of thing. We had bracelets and we could connect to the networks. We were backward, and we weren't what you might call modern, but it was something.

So, first there was a query at the door. She tried the technology first. When I didn't get there fast enough, there was just frantic banging, and she was sobbing.

Her crying tugged inside me somewhere, the way it always did, and I let her in.

I always thought, later, that I should have called someone, but I didn't. I should have called someone to get her and just talked to her through the door. That would have been better, if I'd only thought of it.

But I didn't think of it, and the door opened, and her smell was this wall of... spirits. I never scented something like that before. I never *knew* that kind of a scent. I was instantly and violently turned on, and she jumped on me, and I caught her.

She wrapped her legs around my hips and pushed her face into my chest, into the nightshirt I was wearing, and she was crying and rubbing her face there, and I wrapped my arms around her, and held her there.

She felt perfect.

I rubbed my forehead into the top of her head, scenting her, scenting her the way a mate does when he's marking a woman as his.

Not proud of that.

I put her down, gently, and I said to her in this weird, strange, scratchy voice I'd never even heard come out of my mouth, "Baby girl, you need to go." The door was open, wide open, and the scent of the night was coming in and so was the distant sound of the night birds in the forest.

"No," she said. "No, please, no. I *need* you." She came for me.

I backed up, holding up both of my hands. "You don't. You think you do, but I am the last person you need right now, I swear to you."

"What's happening to me, Sevren? My mom says I'm sick, that I have a fever, but I don't feel sick. When you're sick, you want to sleep, and all I want to do is… is…"

I collided with my bed and sat down hard on it.

She climbed on to the bed after me and straddled me — one of her small legs on either side of me. She pressed her pelvis into mine, into my cock, which was huge and straining and throbbing.

I gasped. "Baby girl, please."

"I don't know what I want to do, but it's something. And I can't stop thinking about you, and you *smell* good." She put her face in my chest again, rubbing her face all over me.

I sank a hand into her hair, groaning.

"What's happening to me?" she said. "What's happening?"

"You're in heat," I whispered.

She sat up straight, breaking contact with my chest, but jamming her pelvis tighter against me.

I grunted. "Can you not—"

"I'm too young to be in heat," she said.

"I know that," I said in a labored voice.

She eyed me, and I could see that she was thinking, she was making connections, working it out. "You're my mate," she said in realization.

I reached up and cupped her face with one hand.

"But you're too old to be my mate," she said. "I'm too young to have a mate. This isn't *right*, Sevren."

"I know, baby girl, I know." I feathered my thumb over her cheekbone.

"Did it happen when I was a baby?" she said. "My bite mark. It's a mating mark." She fingered it, touching the little scar on her shoulder. "You did it so that I could live on the planet and now we're…"

"Yeah," I whispered. We'd explained to her that the bite had altered her body so that she could survive on Bravren, but we'd never told her more. She knew about mating marks, because all the mated pairs in the village had them. But she'd never put it all together before.

She jammed her hips against me again.

I caught her with my other hand, digging my fingers into her small thigh. "Stop *moving*," I rumbled.

She seemed to register something about our pelvises now. She drew back, and there wasn't any contact with my cock anymore, which was a relief.

"If we're mates, then you use that to… to… I know

about this," she said, gesturing at my crotch. "I know about what sex is, and that's… way bigger than I thought they were. There's no *way*—"

"I'd never hurt you, you know that, right?" I whispered. "I can't help this, but you don't have to worry about this. This isn't coming near you."

She buried her face in my shirt. "Okay, but I need to sleep here."

"No," I said. "Absolutely not. You need to go home right now."

"I can't sleep otherwise." Now, she undulated, sliding her face up to my neck, pressing her chest into mine, sighing as *she* scented *me*.

I sighed too, and now her scent was exploding through me, lighting me up, mingling with my own scent in a perfect way, a very, very good way, and my body pulsed. My chest contracted and I let out a rumbling noise of satisfaction. "Baby girl, I cannot have you here."

"I've been burning *up*." Her voice was throaty now, too old for her little girl mouth. "You're the only thing giving me any relief. Around you, I don't feel so feverish." She pushed on me.

We went backwards onto the bed, and she curled up against my side, pillowing her head on my shoulder. It felt like a thing we'd done a thousand times before, because of course I'd cuddled her when she was small. It was only that now, I could feel her barely-developed breasts through her shirt, her rock-hard tiny nipples, and she had wound her thighs around one of mine, pressing herself into me there, rocking her hips a little.

"Eventh, no," I said.

She sighed, yawning, and fell right to sleep in my arms.

And I didn't get my bracelet and send a message right away. I lay there, holding onto her, enjoying the way she smelled and the way she felt close to me and thinking about… thinking thoughts I'm ashamed of.

But eventually, I did get my bracelet and I contacted Dannor.

I think I went to him first instead of Belini because I wanted him to be angry. Maybe I wanted him to blow my head off. I don't know. I felt soiled when I met them outside the bedchamber. Eventh was still in my bed, sleeping soundly. My scent was all over it, and I figured it was soothing her.

Dannor didn't bring a blaster, but he slammed me up into the outer wall of my hut, forearm at my throat. I'm bigger than he is—taller, broader, and, even then, before I was a gladiator, I had a lot more in the way of muscle mass.

But I didn't fight.

He bared his teeth at me, his face in my face. "I will *end* you," he whispered in a lethal voice.

"Stop it, Dannor," said Belini from behind him.

"What did you do to her?"

"Nothing, nothing," I said. I swallowed. "Well, I scented her. I didn't mean it. It h-happened, and I c-couldn't stop it. She's in heat, do you understand what that *means*, Dannor?"

"What does it mean? That you're going to rape my little girl? That's what it means? And you're going to pretend like you can't control yourself because of your mating bonds?"

"Dannor!" Belini pulled him off me.

I slumped against the wall. "You take her and lock her up. You do a better job of keeping her in. Don't let her get out. She'll come right to me. Keep her *away* from me."

"You fucking waste of air," said Dannor, shaking off Belini and coming for me.

Belini wedged herself between her husband and me, facing him. "Dannor, look at me. Without Sevren, we wouldn't *have* her. She would have *died*."

"You always say this, sweetheart, but the thing is, whatever damage he did by saving her life is unacceptable. He's been perving on my little girl her entire life—"

"Just take her away," I said, clenching my hands into fists. "Get her out of my bed."

"She's in your *bed?*" snarled Dannor. "How did *that* happen?"

I buried my face in my hands. My shoulders shook. I was on the verge of tears.

Belini touched me. "You'd never hurt her," she breathed. "I know you wouldn't."

I dragged my hands down, digging my fingers into my cheeks. "Take my sheets. My scent should help her sleep. Maybe help with the fever too."

"I didn't know," said Belini. "I thought she had a virus. If I'd suspected that she was... she's so young. I'm sorry. If I thought she was in heat, I would have stayed up to watch over her."

"It's not your fault," said Dannor to his wife.

"Well, it's not actually Sevren's fault either," said Belini.

"You always take up for him," muttered Dannor, pushing into my hut.

"I'm so sorry," said Belini, looking at me. "What are we going to do? This will be, what? Four days? Five?"

"Maybe only three," I said. "A first heat doesn't usually last as long, I don't think."

"But it'll be every moon cycle, won't it?"

I nodded.

"You can resist it," she said. "We'll keep her away from you. And you would never…" She licked her lips. "You wouldn't, would you?"

I couldn't meet her gaze.

Dannor came out the door, Eventh in his arms, wrapped up in my sheets and blankets. She looked snug and small sleeping against her father's chest, just a girl, just a *little* girl.

I clenched my hands into fists.

I had to fix this.

FOUR

eventh

"I think we should do it now," I said, pressing my legs together, feeling a strange tendril of want working its way through me, overwhelming and good. Sevren's scent was more intense now. It had been getting more potent the longer we were near each other.

"No," he said.

"I think you'll be able to concentrate better and think about how to get us out of this situation if we do it," I said. "You're distracted now. At least, I am. Your scent is overpowering right now."

He swallowed. "Yeah..." His voice was uncertain and rough. "Your scent is really intense, too."

"So?" I hated how eager I was for this. "So, take an exit."

He glanced at me, and then put the speeder into autodrive again and turned to me so that we could talk. "Take an exit? You want to just pull over on the side of the road and go at it?"

I nodded. "Yeah. I mean... maybe not *right* on the side of the road, but a little out of the way somewhere. I can't tell, but isn't it all basically grasslands out here? We're in the middle of nowhere, so pull out off into the darkness and..."

"Not like this," he said, looking around the inside of

the speeder. "Not here."

"What? You have some big plans for your first time?" I raised my eyebrows.

He looked away, and I thought I'd actually embarrassed him. "No, I mean… I didn't figure I'd ever actually…" He looked back ahead, facing forward. "In a bed, though, at the very least."

I sighed. "Well, how are we going to do that? Rent a room or something?"

"I told you, I'm taking you to the water. You get on that vessel, you shove off, and I'll come find you afterwards."

"You won't," I said. "You're stalling. You agreed to it to get me to shut up about it, but you have no intention of actually mating me, do you?"

He let out an affected breath at the phrase "mating me" and that made my stomach turn over. "Uh, I shouldn't do it. Maybe with some distance, yeah, I can talk myself out of it," he said quietly.

I groaned. "Look, losing your virginity in a speeder has to be better than not losing it at all, right? Pull *over*."

He didn't say anything.

"I know," I said, tugging the shirt I was wearing up over my head. I didn't have a supporter on because I hadn't really had time to get dressed, and so I was entirely bare from the waist up.

He turned to look at me, his gaze honing in on my bare breasts. He didn't say anything. He breathed noisily, looking at me.

I leaned over, coming closer to him.

"You, uh, you do seem *really* mature," he said in a tattered voice.

I giggled, reaching for him. I put his hand on me.

His eyes widened. "Spirits!" His hand moved from my breast to my forehead. "Temperature check, occupants of speeder."

The speeder chirped. "Male wvorn, temperature thirty-two noxecs, normal temp, female human, temperature forty-four noxecs, abnormally high, suggest immediate medical attention."

I slumped backwards into the seat. "I'm in heat. Your presence is triggering the heat."

"No wonder our scents are going crazy," he said. "You have suppressants back in your dorm. Should we go back?"

"Well… what about the watervessel?"

"I'm not putting you on a watervessel in heat," he muttered.

"Afraid I'd fuck my way through the entire crew?" I said in a lilting voice. "Because I'd do that even if I wasn't in heat."

He let out a snort. "Put your shirt back on."

"Not going to pull over?"

"Speeder, access networks," he said.

"Nets accessed," replied the speeder's electronic voice.

"Likelihood of heat suppressants stopping heat once peak temperatures have been reached?"

"What species?"

He considered. "Wvorn," he said.

"Fifteen percent," said the speeder.

"Spirits in the sacred groves," he muttered. "No point in going back for the suppressants, is there?"

I shrugged into my shirt. I was starting to feel a little bit apprehensive. "I haven't, um, gone into a full-fledged heat since, uh, since…"

"When you were eleven?" he said.

I nodded. "And the doctor that I saw said that it wasn't a full heat, that I hadn't actually really broken over into one. So, if I do this, it's going to be intense."

"Yes, it's totally perfect," he said. "We're on the run from a maddened gladiator with a grudge who wants to kill you, and we have about two hihors until you're in full-on whining, ass-in-the-air mode, I figure."

"What's that mean?" I said. "Whining?"

"You've never watched much girls-in-heat porn, huh?"

"That's not real," I said. "Those alien girls are pretending. That Toth stuff, there's no way—" I broke off. "I'm going to be like *that?*"

He was on the holodisplay, scrolling through results.

"You're going to… you're going to have sex with me, right? If I'm whining like that? You're going to take care of me, aren't you, Sevren?" My body lurched in apprehension, and I felt a strange wave go through me, something I hadn't felt before. I *was* hot, wasn't I? I rubbed at my heated forehead.

"Yeah," he breathed. "Don't worry, baby girl. I'll take care of you." He punched something on the holodisplay. "There."

"A fuel station?"

"We need credits," he said. "Otherwise, we can't pay for a nice room somewhere to hole up and ride this heat out."

"You're a gladiator with an agent. You get paid for fights."

"Yeah, but I can't take any credits out of my account without leaving a very traceable trail," he said.

"How are we getting credits from a fuel station?"

"Uh, you can stay in the speeder. I'll go in and hold the place up." He reached back and touched his blaster.

"Armed robbery is your plan?" I said.

"What? You got a better one?"

* * *

sevren

She didn't explain her plan real well until we were inside the fuel station and she was up on the counter with her shirt off and rubbing her tits in the guy's face.

I don't know why I cared.

She was not really my mate. I had no claim on her. It was gross and sick for me to demand any ownership of any part of her body, even if this heat thing was forcing me into her bed and I wasn't exactly going there unwillingly.

She'd indicated that she had no real difficulty handing out her body to random men like it was candy.

So.

Yeah, the blaster in the guy's face and me growling, "Touch her and you die," that was over the top.

She looked at me with huge eyes, annoyed, her expression all, I-was-handling-this-fine. But when she went back to the scared attendant, she was cool as a trickling dark stream. "Open up your drawer and give us your credits," she said with a smile.

He gave us the credits.

"Put your shirt back on," I said to her for the second time.

She shrugged at me, tugging her shirt down and crawling down off the counter.

I addressed the attendant. "I'm putting this on stun, okay? You're going to sleep."

"No, wait, come on," said the attendant. "If you—"

I stunned him.

She glared down at his slumped and unconscious form. "So, when I said, 'I'll distract him and you get in there and take the credits from his drawer,' you interpreted that as, 'Let's do armed robbery anyway?'"

I stuffed credit chips in my pockets. "Uh, you neglected to explain this distraction business was going to involve showing him your tits."

"Well, what did you think I was going to do?"

"I don't know," I said, taking her by the arm and guiding her toward the door. "There are lots of other ways to distract someone."

"None that work nearly as well in my experience. I mean, case in point, my boobs distract you. You stared at them for—"

"Stop," I said.

"You know, you can't just tell me what to do."

"Baby girl, get back in the speeder."

"You think they're yours just because we're mated? I don't see why, because if you wanted them, you could have touched them, like, *ever*."

Then I did something crazy and reckless that was fueled entirely by the fact that all the blood in my body had rushed very much the wrong way. I pressed into her, slid my hand under her shirt, and palmed one of her breasts.

She let out a cry.

I huffed. She was soft and springy as I gave her a squeeze. Her nipple stiffened right away.

I let go of her. "I want them." Then I went over to the speeder.

She stood there, lips parted, staring at me, not moving.

"Baby girl?"

She drew in a breath and threw herself into the speeder.

* * *

I'd had my breasts squeezed before.

Obviously.

Truth was, guys never did enough of that kind of stuff. I always had to beg for it or move their hands or touch myself. Not that it even mattered, because it wasn't leading anywhere, of course.

I could rub my own clitoris for as long as I wanted, and if I did, it would feel good, a nicer feeling than touching my kneecap or the tip of my nose or something, but it would never feel orgasmic, whatever that feeling even was.

The way it had felt when Sevren had just squeezed my breast and my nipple had gotten hard and rubbed against him?

That was… *wow*.

Good, *really* good, so good that I felt stupid for ever having bothered with those other guys. If I'd known it could be like *that*, I would have thought the other stuff was pointless.

"Sorry." He was gruff again. The speeder was moving again, and he was on the holodisplay, programming in a new course. I was leaving the navigating to him. "I shouldn't have done that."

"Done what?"

"Really, it was a weird thing for you to say," he said. "When should I have been fondling your breasts, exactly? When you were a little kid, that night you were in heat and came and rubbed them all over me? Then? Is that when I should have been staking my claim on your body parts? Or just in the past however long it's been since I walked in on your gang bang?"

"Oh, right," I said. "I was just… I don't know why I…" Actually, this shirt was starting to feel…

stimulating. It was touching me everywhere. I wriggled inside it, letting out a little sigh.

This was my heat coming on, actually. That was why it had felt so good when he'd touched me. That was why my nipple had decided to stand up like a good little soldier right away.

Oh, look. Both of my nipples were all erect now, just from this freaking shirt rubbing them. I sighed again.

He looked up from the holodisplay. "What do you want me to say to you, baby girl, that I thought about it? That I wanted you back then? You know I did or I wouldn't have left."

I swallowed. "Uh… that wasn't your fault. It was just, uh, biology." I wriggled again. "This, um, this shirt is kind of… I think my heat is starting to come on a bit more. I guess that's just biology too." Was I going to start whining now? Rubbing myself on the floor or the speeder seats, contorting my body to present my pussy to him? Begging for his cock?

He held my gaze. "You all right? Uncomfortable? I've almost figured out where we're going here. How long you think you can manage in here?"

"Manage? What do you mean?"

"You want to get yourself off?"

My lips parted.

He let out a breath. "Right, I wasn't thinking about how you never…" He gave me a little smile. "You should, baby girl. Go ahead. You can do it if I'm here, huh? Touch yourself. Maybe it'll make things a little better. Release some tension."

"It won't make it, uh, worse for you?"

He swallowed, looking away. "I don't really know. I've never smelled your…" His gaze flicked down to my crotch. "Keep those shorts on, maybe? It'll blunt it a little bit."

I nodded rapidly. "Sure, sure thing." I kept nodding.

He went back to the holodisplay.

I didn't move.

I just sat there, my whole body about to explode. I wanted to cry, actually. I hadn't ever had an orgasm, and I'd basically decided it was never going to happen. I had decided I'd probably never see Sevren again, and his presence was a necessary component for such things, and the truth was that I didn't even know how I felt about him.

When I was a little girl and I was going through my first heat, I'd had urges and wants, but I'd still thought of him like, I don't know, not a brother, not exactly, but… family somehow. And the idea of him and sex was still a little strange in a way.

But I wanted it.

I wanted him.

And I wanted an orgasm.

I had tried and tried to have one, a thousand ways, even knowing it was impossible, I kept thinking maybe there was a way around it. I'd researched and I'd experimented, injected myself with various concoctions that I put together in my own pathetic, rudimentary lab on Braven. Eventually, though, I started to turn to… other sensations. If I couldn't have pleasure, I'd have intensity, even if that intensity was painful.

And now, he was just telling me to sit back and… do it.

I didn't. Instead, I said, "The night I was in heat, I did not rub my breasts all over you."

He looked up at me, surprised.

"Or if I did, I didn't know what I was doing."

"I know that," he said, looking away. "Sorry I said

that. I kind of hate myself right now, that's all. I always hate myself, but it's particularly intense right now. You gonna touch yourself?"

I squared my shoulders. "Why do you hate yourself?"

"I'm going to fuck you," he said. "And that's really, really wrong."

I shivered, shutting my eyes and settling into the seat. "Maybe it's not wrong." I twisted my hands together, fidgeting.

"You afraid, baby girl?" he said in a soft voice.

"Of you? No, I never—"

"Of touching yourself," he said.

How could he tell? "Yes," I breathed in a half-sob. "Yes, because it's…"

"Huge," he finished. "I can do it for you, if you want."

I opened my eyes.

"But I think you should have that power yourself. It's your body. It's your orgasm. The fact you need me around to have it is already unfair to you. Touch yourself. Almost every person in the universe gives themselves their first orgasm. You should have that experience too."

I laughed a little. "The power of jacking off."

He laughed too. "Look, give me a hisec here, and I'll get this set up, and we can do it together. I'm about ready to burst, and I haven't… it's been a long time."

Twenty gecycles, right?

"You get started first, though," he said softly. "It won't take me very long to come. You'll need to figure yourself out a little, do some exploring."

"O-okay," I said. I took a deep breath and then slid my hand under the drawstring of the pants I was wearing. I let my hand slide down over my belly, down, down, down until I was sliding over my mound.

I gasped. That felt... wow. I was really sensitive there, and I usually wasn't this sensitive. I wasn't sure if it was heat, or Sevren, or both, but it was nice.

I stopped there, exploring a little, just rubbing over my mound, and then down to the creases on either side of my labia. I was stunned at how sensitive I was. I hadn't expected it to feel so good all over down here. I ran my fingers all over and then I pushed in a little — just some pressure —

Oh, *stars*.

I groaned.

That was almost too much. I was crazy, crazy sensitive. I couldn't believe it. If it had felt like this to touch my pussy all this time, I would never have left my room. If other women felt like this, how did they do anything else?

I thought it had to be more sensitive because of my heat.

No way did it feel this good normally. No way.

I slid one finger between my labia, and I was ridiculously wet, I realized. Sopping. I slid over my clitoris for the first time, and my body pulled tight, as if there was string that was inside me and it had been tugged on. The sensation was bright, sweet, and overwhelming.

I let out a whimper.

My core clenched.

What was *that*?

I writhed back into the seat, dragging my finger over my slippery clitoral hood, letting out noises I couldn't contain, because this was... this was...

Another little clench, like my body was trying to

warm up for something.

I liked those clenches.

I liked how this felt.

This was *astonishing*.

I found a soft and slippery rhythm, gently rubbing myself up and down, and I was almost immediately yanked on again from that same tight string of pleasure inside me. It pulled me out into space, and suddenly I was on a journey, past supernovas and bright stars and black holes, speeding up with every hisec, rushing deep into a bright, lovely center of gushing goodness.

I kept making noises, but they were tiny and wondering, disbelieving little small sounds as my journey grew deeper, darker, and better with every stroke of my finger.

Then, I accidentally slid my finger lower, and that was better there. More sensitive. It felt so good. I wanted to rub it all, and I found myself starting to make circles, surrounding my clit, all around, then touching the tip and then starting the circuit all over.

And the string inside me pulled me around and around and I felt dizzy and whirling and gasping and —

A noise from Sevren.

My eyes snapped open. I half expected to find him with his pants open and to get my first sight of that cock of his, which I was eager to see. I wanted to look at it pretty badly.

But he was totally clothed. He was just... watching me. The expression on his face was awed, as if whatever I was doing was something inspired.

I locked my gaze with his, my lips parting.

"You're beautiful," he murmured.

I smiled at him. "It feels... like an adventure in

space, like a journey, like… it feels *good*."

"Touch your breasts," he said, nodding at them, his voice barely audible.

"Oh," I said. "Good idea." I was only using one hand, and I had a whole other hand, and I pushed that up inside my shirt, which was all bothersome and rubbing me anyway, and I found one of my nipples and squeezed.

My eyes snapped shut and I bowed up in the chair.

Now, I was some glowing, spinning thing in space. With my hands on these two separate pleasure centers, I'd been ignited. Somehow, they were connected, even though they were on opposite sides of my anatomy, and they worked together in the very best of ways.

I rubbed my nipple, biting my lip, concentrating on whatever it was that was building between my thighs.

I gasped, and dipped back into my sweet, wonderful journey, swirling back into my pleasure.

And then, suddenly, there was a rush of Sevren's scent. It burrowed into me, all over, tendrils of tree sap and the smoky notes of coffee, and I went boneless, and my pleasure kicked itself stratospheric.

I opened my eyes in slits, and he'd unzipped his pants, and his cock was thick and red at the tip and weeping a little bit of pre-come, and I knew that was the source of the smell, and I wanted to *lick* it.

I licked my own lips instead. I bit down on them, and I watched his hand dragging itself over his cock, and I was suddenly sucked out to the farthest reaches of space, dipping down into the darkest, deepest vacuum and then deeper still.

My body released, pleasure booming out like an exploding star, and I was having an orgasm!

It was good, waves of it still rippling through me in

sweet little bursts, and I hadn't realized it would feel that good. I hadn't realized it would be like this.

It was…

Tears were coming to my eyes.

My breath hitched.

I convulsed against the chair, and my pelvis shook and my shoulders shook, and Sevren's scent was heavy on the air, and every breath I drew in came out as a sob.

He made a couple answering sobs, his head bowed. He gasped and then he looked up out the front of the speeder. It was fine, we were on autodrive, but… He sorted through the center console for something to clean himself up with.

I stared at him, my hand still inside my pants.

He wiped himself clean, tucked himself away, and the scent went duller. He put the soiled rag in the trash slot, and then looked up and saw me staring at him.

"Oh," he rasped. "Did you…?"

I nodded wordlessly.

He raised his eyebrows appraisingly. "Good?"

I let out a helpless laugh, covering my mouth with one hand, and then the laugh broke into more sobs and I shut my eyes.

"Are you all right?"

"Are you?" I said.

"Not my first, baby girl." He sounded gently amused.

"But the first in twenty gecycles," I said.

"Uh… no," he said.

I sat up straighter. "But—"

"I mean, there were times when I was in your radius back then and I…" He coughed. "I was working on a theory that I could get off before I went around you and maybe I wouldn't get hard, like if I drained my balls."

I blinked at him.

"It didn't work." He shrugged.

"So, you were skulking outside of my window while I was eleven, rubbing one out?"

"It's not like it was in front of you."

I huffed, shaking my head.

"It's still been a while," he said in a low voice.

"Yeah, but..."

"Best one of my life," he said.

I turned back to him.

"Your scent, your expression, your... everything about you." His voice wasn't strong. "It's never been anything like..."

I gave him a small smile. "Well, it was, um, I mean I really liked... Good for me, too."

He grinned back. "Did it help with the heat coming on at all?"

I wriggled around in my shirt, which didn't seem quite as stimulating. "I think so." And then I realized he still had a hard-on, because he was still sticking up in his pants, even though he'd zipped up. "Didn't it do anything for you?"

He looked down. "Oh, I got a knot."

"A...?" I furrowed my brow. "You mean like a coital tie. Wovrn have those and no one told me? Didn't anyone think I needed to know that?"

"It shouldn't happen unless my cock is getting squeezed, like they're not supposed to form unless I'm already inside you—er, a woman." He made a face. "But my pants are tight because of... it's... a hard-on with a knot doesn't go down so easy, that's all."

"Why didn't you tell me?"

"Me?" He touched his chest. "When did we discuss my penis?"

"That time when I was in heat, when you told me it would not touch me, while it was, you know, touching me."

He turned away, embarrassed. "That's not exactly how I remember it, baby girl. And, yeah, that was a perfect time to bring up knotting, just right then."

"So, when we do it, you're going to... you'll have a..." I bit my lip again, harder. "I'm going to be taking a knot."

"I can probably keep it down," he said. "I mean... I'm kind of out of practice, but I can probably control it."

"Seriously? It's a thing you can control?"

"Kind of?" He shrugged. "If you're afraid —"

"Oh, no, this is not fear," I said. "I want it."

"Oh," he said in a different, deeper voice. "Oh." Then he gave me a look I could only term hungry. He pulled up the holodisplay. "Forty hidosecs until we get to our destination, looks like." He let out a breath.

I let out a breath too, and a wave of hot warmth went through my body. I suddenly got a wave of shakes, my teeth chattering.

"Spirits," he said. "I guess that didn't do anything for your heat at all, huh?"

I rode it out, body tensing.

It passed.

I panted.

"I'm so sorry, baby girl," he whispered. "I don't have a blanket to give you. I'd give you my shirt, but..." It was half burned off.

"It's fine," I said. "I'm fine."

I shut my eyes.

It was not fine.

The intensity that was building in me was like nothing I'd ever felt before.

FIVE

I gave her my shirt anyway.

The teeth chattering jags only came three more times on our way to the cabins I'd looked up, which was where we were heading, where I'd set our course for.

On Bravren, when a couple mated and the woman went into her first heat, they'd leave the village and go off to what was called a dewin. In my village, almost all of the dewins were in a set of nearby caves which also housed hot springs. Women in heat tended to like dark, small, warm places.

It didn't entirely make sense, what with being in heat. You'd think they'd want to cool down, but no. Warm and humid. The hot springs and the caverns were perfect.

In some other villages nearby, they didn't have handy caves, and they built underground tunnels or they made other small cavernous-type dwellings for their women.

Obviously, I could not take her to a cave, but I had another idea.

I had been fighting on Kalion off and on over the past nine gecycles. There was a huge arena on an orbiting space station around this planet, and I fought there often. Because of that, I'd occasionally been taken out to places on the planet Kalion for drinking and boozing and women—not that I could really indulge much in the latter. At first, this was done by the Toth handler who owned my contract, and then—when I'd earned it out—I'd be wooed by sponsors who wanted me to wear their logos emblazoned on my shorts when I fought or to endorse their products, that kind of thing.

Anyway, I'd been out to these cabins before, because some bigwig who owned a shoe company had bought them all out and brought four or five of us gladiators out here for a days-long party.

The cabins were built into a cliff. They overlooked a huge river that was flowing out into one of Kalion's many oceans. Kalion was covered in a lot of water with only a few land masses which were habitable.

The rooms were cozy and dark and warm, and the rooms in the back of the cabins were deeper in the cliff and didn't have any windows. Anyway, I thought they might work, that she might be the most comfortable there, and I knew that the best way to get her heat to break was to make sure that she was comfortable.

Well, that and fuck her a lot.

The prospect of that made me feel both eager and revolted. Not because of her. Nothing about her was revolting. But…

I'd fought this for so long.

I was giving in now only because the heat was impossible. I couldn't abandon her while she was in heat. She'd be too needy, and I wouldn't do that to her, wouldn't leave her alone in that way. If I'd had someone else who I could trust to take care of her, that would have been one thing. Then I could have packed her off on the watervessel as I'd planned.

But we had to do this.

We *did* have to, right?

I hadn't caved to this idea too easily, had I?

I still didn't even have a plan for Izar Fjass. It would be easiest to kill him. I didn't take killing lightly, of course, but he was a grizzled, violent, psychotic gladiator with no one who cared about him. It was the path that caused the least amount of suffering. For him, too. He'd been driven out of his head by the pain of the loss of his brother. He'd get relief if I put him to rest.

But.

If I killed him, the guild was a problem.

So, that left the options of running from him forever or until he got tired of it.

Or trying to talk him out of it somehow. Which, yeah, he was not known for being reasonable. Maybe I could convince him to allow me to make amends for the death of his brother in some other way?

Maybe there was a third option. Kill him and somehow find enough credits to pay back the guild for what they thought he was worth.

Yeah, that was definitely going to happen. I was sure I'd just find a fat pile of credits lying around somewhere.

Spirits, I was probably on a security vid from that fuel station I'd held up, and I was probably on the hook for that. Maybe for shooting a cop-bot too. Of course, the guild could clean all that up easy.

All of these things were problems I was going to have to address in three to five days, when I got Eventh's heat to break, however. She was all I was going to be able to think about until then.

When we pulled up to the cabins, she was shivering into my shirt, and I left her in the speeder while I went to secure the room.

The woman at the front desk looked me over, sans shirt, still healing my burn wounds, all shaved up for the ring, and I could tell she wanted to ask me a lot of questions.

But I gave her a look that I'd learned from being a gladiator, a look that said not to talk to me because I broke people's bones when I got a little annoyed, and she got quiet and worried and stuttered a lot as she handed me the key.

The cabin I got was the smallest, and it had the least amount of windows. It was also the cheapest, but I thought it was going to be best for our purposes.

And I was rewarded with Eventh's sigh of relief when we walked inside. "It's better in here," she said. "It's just *better*."

"Let's get the plasstoves going," I said, turning them until they glowed dully and heat began to come off them in waves. I settled her on one of the couches and then swathed her in blankets and told her not to open the door to anyone.

I headed down to the corner, where there was a tiny shop next to the cabins. There was food there, basic kind of stuff. I got some ration bars and fruit. She wouldn't be hungry per se, but I'd need to get her to eat, because it would take a lot out of her.

Huh.

I knew all about this.

How'd I know all about this? I'd never truly prepared to be a newly mated man taking my own mate through her first heat, not really. I'd not given it a lot of thought when I was in my early twenties and all the men I'd grown up with in the village were going through it. But I guess I'd paid a lot of attention to them when they talked about it around the bonfires in the village, swilling the nexberry wine we brewed and giving each other advice.

I guess I must have absorbed it somehow.

I hurried back with the food, and I was wary.

Izar shouldn't have been able to trace us, not without our bracelets, and he shouldn't have been able to follow us, not with having been stunned. But I didn't like leaving her alone either.

I was relieved when I burst back into our warm little space and found her curled up in a ball on the couch, going through another set of teeth-chattering shivers, entirely alone.

To be sure, I checked the cabin. There was this outer area, which had a couch and small area for preparing food—with a sink and countertop but no cooking implements or anything. And there was a bedroom with a hii grax sized bed and an adjoining bathroom.

When I got back to the couch area, she was rubbing her cheek against one of the pillows, gritting her teeth, making a tiny noise in the back of her throat.

"Hey," I said. "We got here just in time, I think. How are you doing?"

"I'm hanging in there." Her voice was breathy. She was freaked out, and I could hear it in her tone.

I sat down next to her and pulled her into my lap.

She curled into my chest immediately, humming her approval, and she started using my chest like she'd been using the pillow. And, uh, my chest? Still bare. It felt…

Okay, well, this was happening anyway, so, fine.

It's going to feel good, Sevren. You're going to put your dick in her.

I forced myself to take a deep breath. "Shh," I said in my most soothing voice, wrapping my arms around her. "You're fine. You're just fine. It's all going to be okay."

"Is it? How soon until I'm whining and begging like the pathetic, crying girls on the porn?"

"Baby girl, you're not going to be begging. I wouldn't do that to you. I'm not going to torture you, come on. I won't let you get anywhere near that bad."

She shivered against me, letting out a whine. "Okay. Okay, good."

I hugged her closer. "You want to do anything now?"

"Did your knot go down?"

"Uh…" I gently moved her to examine myself inside my pants. I was hard—but I'd been hard since I got close to her earlier that night. I didn't know if this was the same hard-on or if it had gone down and I'd gotten hard again. I'd been a little preoccupied as of late. "Yeah, knot's gone."

"But you're, um, you're ready to go. I can feel that."

"Uh huh," I said. "Don't worry about me. Anything you need from me, I can do. You hungry? You want to get a little food in before this gets crazy?"

"No, I'm not hungry at all. I couldn't eat," she said.

"Okay, well, then let's go to the bed," I said.

"Oh," she said in a different voice. "Bed now?"

"We don't have to," I said.

"Is it happening now? Already?"

"It doesn't have to," I said, stroking her hair.

She pushed up to look into my eyes. "Can you smell… them… the other guys I was with? On me?"

"No, baby girl," I breathed, but I didn't find the mention of that made me feel good. The jealousy rose in me like a dark wave. "No, you're all I can smell. Your scent's potent right now."

"They're dead," she said with a little noise. "I don't think I've processed that yet." She put her face back against my chest.

I rubbed her back. "Shh, don't think about that."

Her teeth started chattering again. She rubbed her face against me, letting out a low noise in the back of her throat, her hips starting to jut out a little.

I rubbed her back, my hand going down to feel the place where her spine ended but not down to cup her buttocks. "Shh," I said again.

"Ugh," she said.

"It probably feel better to just give in to it, baby girl. But on the bed, okay? I'll carry you, if you want."

She rubbed her face. "Give in?"

"Yeah, to get in the position," I breathed. My cock twitched. Spirits, what was she going to look like that way? Was that how I was going to fuck her, with her ass in the air and her face flush against the bed?

No, not like that.

Not our first time.

I didn't want to end up ranskking her.

Control yourself, Sevren, I thought, and then I picked her up, hands under her knees, cradling her against me, and swept her off for the bedroom.

There, I tossed her on the bed, and she went for it immediately, hands down, face down, up on her knees, legs spread.

She was dressed, but her scent filled the room like a powerful drug.

I panted, gaping at the sight of her.

She whined. "Sevren, it's good like this. You were right."

"Yeah," I whispered, coming closer, running my hands over her hips.

She moaned.

I trailed my hands lower, to clutch her thighs. I climbed up, knees on the bed, and pressed my pelvis against her.

She moaned. "*Sevren.*"

"Shh, okay, we're, uh, we're..." I swallowed. "Okay, sweet one, just breathe."

"Knot me," she said in a low, scraping voice. "Right now. Please."

"Shh," I said, giving her thigh a squeeze. That was normal, too. The begging. Except I promised her she wasn't going to have to beg. Except I also was determined not to take her from behind like this the first time either. "Here," I said, reaching around and undoing the drawstring of the shorts she was wearing.

She let out a low, long approving moan. "Yes, Sevren, yes."

I climbed back down off the bed and put my feet on the floor and then scooted her closer to me. I peeled her shorts over her hips, revealing her wet, red slit to me for the first time. It was all right here, on display for me, just offered up. And the *scent* of her. She was invading my senses, all nexberries and springtime. I put my nose against her wetness, just breathing her in.

She twitched.

I licked her. One long, sweet lap, clit to her opening, tasting her.

She tasted better than she smelled. So sweet.

A groan from her, her hips jerking.

I held her still, concentrating my tongue on her clit, licking her there slow and soft and deliberate.

She groaned again. "Oh, stars, that's good."

"Yeah?" I rumbled into her sex. "You taste like dessert, baby girl."

She giggled. "Fuck, were you always going to be like this? Say things like that? You're so perfect, Sevren."

My heart squeezed. She shouldn't say things like that, because I was going to want to say things too.

Whatever you do, do not tell her you love her, I ordered myself.

Right, that would be bad.

And it was all I wanted to say in that moment.

I made my tongue busy with other things.

SIX

Sevren's tongue was my new favorite thing.

It was only my second orgasm ever, of my entire life, but I was chasing it almost immediately, rocking my hips back against his tongue, which was thinner and wider than a human tongue, seemingly made just for dragging itself over my sensitive parts.

He put one palm up on my belly and then slid it all the way inside my shirt and started touching my breasts as he licked me.

At first, he only cupped them both, going back and forth, one after another, the inside of his palm brushing against each of my nipples and making them hard. Then he squeezed a little, and then he started rubbing his fingers over my hard nipples, teasing first one and then the other.

This drove me wilder and wilder, the sensation getting more intense as he continued, and I yelped into the bed, rubbing my face against the covers.

It was very, very nice.

With my eyes closed and the room dark and small, I felt as if I'd been pressed into a soft, safe, warm cavern, and I was being held and caressed by the very air around me, and everything was exactly right, exactly what I wanted.

Each movement of his tongue on my clit made everything seem to tighten pleasantly, closing in on me, in the most wondrous of ways, and his fingers rubbing and teasing my nipples made it better, and the way I was moving my hips was helping too.

I was nothing but a writhing, twisting, yearning creature, focused on nothing except my pleasure. It surrounded me, enveloped me, and it was everything.

Sevren made answering noises to mine—which were out-of-control animal noises, like I'd come apart. Sometimes I heard words from him, things like "taste good" or "could do this forever" and when I managed to hear them, whatever he said made it even better, pushed me farther toward my pinnacle.

Then he slid a finger inside me, and I came up off the bed with a sound that might have been a howl. It was so good to have something in there—I'd felt empty, and I hadn't realized it. "Yes!" I gasped.

"Tight little wet baby girl," he moaned, his voice all strangled.

"More," I said. "I need more."

"More fingers?" he whispered, tongue still going at my clit, and suddenly my opening was crowded full—how many fingers was that? I was stretched and filled and I clenched on them, not an orgasm, but closing in on one soon, any nsec now.

"Oh, fuck me, Sevren. Please. You said you wouldn't make me beg."

"We'll get there, baby girl," he panted, licking me, jamming his fingers inside. "You close, can you come for me?"

I let out a guttural noise. I could come. I was going to come. I writhed on his tongue, on his fingers, pushing my hips into his face.

He pinched one of my nipples.

It pushed me over. Everything suddenly constricted, like the whole room constricted, like the warmth and the darkness turned a shade I hadn't thought they could even *be*, and then I was clenching hard on his fingers, whimpering out my pleasure as it twitched and rippled its way through me.

"Good girl," he breathed. "That's good." His licks slowed, in time with the waves of my orgasm.

As it faded out, he gently lowered me to the bed, smoothing down my hips until my belly was flat against the bed.

I bucked up into his hand, and he gently but firmly pressed me down.

I gasped. That was good. The pressure was good. I liked it. It soothed me.

He slowly pulled his fingers out of me, and I looked over my shoulder to see him licking them clean like… well, like it was really dessert. It couldn't actually taste that good, could it?

Whatever, it made me clench again, and I gasped.

He collapsed next to me on the bed, breathing hard. He lay on his back, and I watched the rise and fall of his bare chest and then my gaze fell to his crotch, where he was hard and obvious and pushing at his pants.

I climbed on top of him, kicking off the shorts that were around my ankles and yanking off the shirt I was wearing too, wanting to be completely bare. I kissed him.

"Spirits, baby girl, we're all backwards," he said. "Kissing should come first, shouldn't it?"

I could taste myself on him, and I did taste… sweet. I pulled back. "Why do I taste—?"

He laughed. "Mating perk."

My eyes widened. "What do *you* taste like?"

"I don't know, what do I smell like to you?" His voice was low and rattling and I liked it.

"Coffee," I said, and moved down his body to work at the eazclasp of his pants. "Branciuth sap." I lowered my face to him, wanting to get a taste of him.

He stopped me. "Hey, hey, what are you—?"

I wouldn't be stopped. I yanked his pants open. Oh, *there* he was. He was beautiful and thick and long and I petted him, rubbing his shaft and then down to where he disappeared into his striped fur. There were a few faint stripes on his cock too, right around the base of him, and I loved them. I gave them each a kiss.

He sighed. "Spirits, Eventh."

I licked my way up to the tip of him, tongue going to his slit, and he *did* taste like coffee, like the sweet sap of the branciuth tree. The head of his cock, all down in the folds of his foreskin, he was sticky with it, and I set about licking every drop of it up. He tasted divine. I groaned, sucking the head of him into my mouth. I sucked a little more liquid out of him, and it was lovely.

"Mmm," I murmured around his cock. "I want to make you come. I want my mouth full of your taste."

"Yeah, well, I'm close," he said in a strained voice. "Wouldn't take much."

"Come for me, Sevren. Come in my mouth." I sank down on him, taking him down my throat.

He groaned. His hand came up to tangle in my hair. "Baby girl," he said—or something like that. His words were all distorted like he couldn't quite talk.

I came back up, dragging my tongue over him, and slowly descended again. Typically, if I gave a blow job, I'd keep a cock down my throat, the better to keep it all away from my taste buds and down the hatch right away, but I *wanted* to taste him, and it made me more deliberate, and I used my tongue to lick up over the tip of him again and again.

I was going way too slow for most guys. It was the speed of a three-hihor blow job, but he took about four strokes before he was gushing into my mouth. Spurt after spurt gave me more than a mouthful of his thick, smoky and sweet taste, and I was swallowing only bits of it, leaving most of it against my tongue, savoring it, enjoying it. It was leaking out of my mouth, spurting everywhere, and I just took my time.

I licked it off his shaft. Then I licked my lips. I used my fingers to get it off my chin and then I licked my fingers clean.

He was watching me with a heated look on his face, and I grinned at him.

He pulled me down and rolled me under him.

We started kissing in a fury.

I arched into him, my bare chest against his, running my hands over his back, which wasn't shaved, so I could feel his soft, lustrous striped fur.

Stars, this was good. Nothing had ever been even remotely like this with a man, and it was actually better that it was Sevren, not weird at all, because I knew him and I felt safe with him, and it wasn't even remotely like fucking my brother.

Of course, that thought seemed to go through me and make me tense.

He noticed. "Baby girl?"

I shook my head up at him, thinking of too many memories, too many times that he was there when I was small.

Was this gross for us to do this?

He touched my face, tracing the lines of my cheekbone and then my jaw, barely brushing me with his fingers. "You all right?"

"Yeah," I said, nodding ferociously. "Definitely all right."

He eyed me, furrowing his brow, striped fur bunching up over his violet eyes.

I reached up to touch his face, to brush his whiskers. His face was dear to me, never foreign or strange, even though we were different species. He always felt like home to me. "Oh, Sevren."

"What is it?"

"Just… thinking about… us being us."

He let out a resigned breath. He rolled off me, completely off, and we weren't touching at all.

I rolled onto my side. "I shouldn't have said anything. I should have known it would make you get weird."

"Am I being weird?" He was gruff again.

"You got guilty," I said. I reached out and pressed my hand reassuringly into the middle of his chest. "I'm okay. I'm not a little girl anymore."

"No, you're not," he groaned. His gaze flicked over me. "Definitely not."

"So, it's okay." I brushed my hands down over his chest. It was a little stubbly, fur growing back in. "It's not like we're related or something, not actually."

"No, I know," he said.

"We were close because of this, because we were mated, and we're supposed to…" I dragged my hand back up. "How often do they make you shave this?"

"Before a fight," he said.

"I wish you could let it grow back."

"Oh, me too. Ingrown hairs are a bitch."

I laughed. I sat up and grinned down at him, looking him over. My Sevren. My mate. He was a very attractive man, wasn't he? Wow, he was all muscled all over, and he had big, pretty shoulders and a rippling flat stomach, and he was striped and virile and mine, and he tasted good.

My heart expanded suddenly, fast and big and almost painful. I gasped.

"What?" he said.

I love you.

I flopped down on the bed and rolled onto my back. Immediately, a teeth-chattering jag gripped me and I came up off the bed, back arching, shivering wildly, groaning.

He was on top of me again, covering me with his warmth, pushing me down, soothing his hand over my shoulder, whispering calming sounds in my ear. "I've got you, I've got you," he breathed, and he kissed my ear lobe.

I wrapped my arms tightly around him, tears coming to my eyes. "I need you."

"I know," he whispered.

"But I just wasted your hard-on to taste your come. Your amazingly delicious come, of course, but why did I do that? I needed it to fuck me."

He pressed his pelvis into me. "No worries on that score. I'm your mate. You're in heat. I will be hard whenever you need it."

I gasped, feeling him growing against my leg. "Good, good, good. Perfect. Fuck me? Now?"

"Mmm." He kissed me and he eased in between my legs. He was still wearing his pants, even though they were half pulled off, and I tried to nudge them off with my feet, using my toes.

He laughed, and then sat up and shoved them off, kicking them off the bed to settle in between my thighs, both of us wearing nothing at all.

I grinned, sinking my hands into his fur, kissing his neck, and then rubbing into him, scenting him, marking him. Mine, mine, *mine*.

He let out an affected gasp and claimed my mouth.

I wriggled my pelvis against his.

He rubbed his hard cock into my clit.

I moaned. "I get your knot, right?"

He grunted. "About that, baby girl."

I pushed on his massive shoulders. "You're not going to give it to me, are you?" It was a full-on whine, and I probably sounded exactly like the little girl I had just said I wasn't. "But you have to."

"Baby girl, you know why I knot you, right?"

"Because… good." I wriggled my clit against his cock more, rocking my hips.

"The biological reason, I mean." His voice was husky.

"Oh, right, because of creating a seal so that you're, um, seed stays in there and swims up into me and…" I let out a breath. "Fuck, why am I so very, very stupid?"

"You're not stupid," he said. "You're in heat."

"I am not ready to get pregnant," I said, panic rising in me.

"I know," he said. "You're a student. You're very young. Trust me, I know."

My suppressant suppressed my ovulatory cycle, which was tied to my heat, meaning I couldn't get pregnant. But if his presence had brought on my heat, then I was fertile. I was fertile as all fuck.

"I mean, I guess I *don't* know, because it took me until now, at this moment to think of it," he said. "This moment, this stupid, stupid moment. Not earlier, when I was at the store, and I could have picked up some spermicide patches."

"Ohhh…" I squeezed my eyes shut.

"So, it's okay, though." He rubbed my shoulder. "We can fix it. I'll just go now and get them."

"Now?" I was whining again. "Now? I need you right now."

"Okay, I could, uh…" He dragged his cock through the wetness that had gathered between my labia. "I mean, I could keep the knot out of you. And not come inside you."

"Mmph." I pouted. "But I want—I *need*—"

"I would insist on going," he said. "But I just got you calmed down and lying this way for me, and if I go, you're going to be really worked up when I get back, and then *I'll* be worked up, and I'll end up ranskking you, and… and…"

"Ranskking me?" I said. "What's that?"

He groaned. He rested his forehead on my collarbone. "Spirits. I just… I want to look in your eyes while I'm pushing into you for the first time. I want to kiss you. I want it sweet, not just rough and intense, you know?"

I did. I also wanted it rough and intense, but I wanted it like this first, because of that bright expanding feeling in my chest, because of…

Love.

I stroked the fur on the back of his head. "*Can* you pull out? You have practiced that exactly never."

He let out a helpless laugh. "I gotta go get the patches, baby girl, don't I?"

"No," I said, wrapping my legs around him. "No, please. You can't go. You can't leave me like this."

He sighed.

"I trust you," I said. "You're my Sevren. You won't come in me. You'd never do anything I didn't want."

He lifted his face to look down at me, his expression intense. "Are you sure?"

"Yes," I said in a throaty voice. "Positive. *Please.*"

He surveyed me, hesitating.

"You promised me I wouldn't beg, and all I have been doing is begging, and—" My voice cut off because he thrust a hand between us, moved himself, and sank into me. He felt better than his fingers, all smooth and thick and *marvelous.* "Fuck."

"Yeah," he agreed, voice gravelly.

I undulated my hips, bringing them up to take him, and he pulled out entirely. I gasped in disappointment and anger. "Sevren!"

"It's gotta be shallow, baby girl," he said through gritted teeth. "You got to stay still until the knot expands, okay, or else it will expand inside you, and then we're screwed."

I groaned. "Fine, fine, but—"

He grabbed onto my hips, holding me down, and then he pushed back into me.

I gasped again. He felt good, but I wanted more, I wanted all of him, and I fought him, my hips trying to raise as he held me in place.

His cock was thick and good, though, as he dragged the tip of it in and out of my opening, and I liked it.

His eyes rolled back in his head and his movements stuttered.

"Good, Sevren?" I said, rubbing his arm, thinking of the fact this was his first time, that he'd never had his hard cock inside a woman before, and that it wasn't fair he had to be doing so much concentrating while he was trying to accomplish this.

"Fucking so much better than good," he grunted.

Suddenly, he jerked into me, *deep* into me.

I gasped in concern, but then I felt his knot, outside of me, and it was enormous. It was thick and wide and round, expanded all the way up to rub my clit. It felt good, so I ground myself on it, but I moaned, "Oh, Sevren, I don't know if I'll be able to take this."

"It won't get this big in you," he said in a labored voice. He was fucking me, *really* fucking me, sweet, long strokes.

I moved with him, sighing, getting my clit up on the edge of his hard knot, and it was sublime. So good. So, *so* good.

"It usually expands until it finds, uh, walls, like your pussy walls, but it was out in the open so it just keeps going until it can't anymore. If you, uh, if you really don't want it, I'll figure something out, though." He pumped at me, out of breath, caressing my hips, and then my waist, and then up to touch my breasts. "Spirits, you feel amazing."

"You too," I moaned, moving with him—against him—feeling little hints of pleasure, of yet another orgasm, starting to gather inside me.

He kissed both of my nipples, and then his mouth found mine, and I clutched at him, wrapping my legs around him, thrusting my tongue into his mouth, wanting, I didn't know what, exactly, but to have him all the way inside me, to push my way into him too, for us to just… mesh together in some way.

Yes, that was what I wanted. Definitely.

To be part of each other, interconnected, joined, *one*.

I threw my head back, breaking the kiss, letting out a cry.

He kissed my throat and then he scented me.

I moaned, liking that, feeling the pleasure in me gather up like a coming storm.

Then his mouth found my bite mark, the place he'd bitten me when I was a baby, and he raked his teeth over it.

My body when hot and tight and I suddenly went into a sputtering, moaning orgasm, so intense, so good, and I bucked and rode it against him, pushing myself nearly painfully into his knot.

"Mine," he growled at my throat.

"Yours," I whimpered. "*Yours.*"

And then the sound of a speeder alarm broke through the air, bleeding in through the walls of the cabin, all the way back to us here.

My orgasm hitched out and ended abruptly, as if the alarm had shorted it out. I groaned. "I wish someone would turn that off."

He stilled against me. "Is that our speeder?"

"I don't know. We don't know what the alarm sounds like." I was grumpy. I did not like this interruption.

He pulled out of me.

"No," I said.

He kissed me quick and hard. "Be right back."

SEVEN

I yanked my pants back up but didn't fasten them and went to the door. I slid it open just a little bit, and yeah, sure enough, that was the speeder we'd come in, blinking its lights and blaring out its alarm.

Spirits.

I fastened my pants, started out of the door, and then I halted.

Don't be an idiot, Sevren, take the blaster.

Right.

I shut the door and then found it, right next to the door where I'd left it. I powered it on and stepped out the door and went to the speeder.

I opened the door and slid inside.

The dashboard was blinking a message: *Theft location protocols engaged.*

I groaned. I was an idiot. I was an enormous idiot.

"Way to think with your dick," I muttered. How was I going to shut this thing off now? I pulled up the holodisplay and went through menu after menu, trying different things, the alarm continuing loudly. It was starting to give me a headache.

Finally, I cut the power to the entire alarm system, and the speeder went quiet.

I ducked out and shut the door.

The doors to all the occupied cabins were open and people were staring at me.

I gave them a little wave.

They saw my blaster and shut their doors real quick.

Spirits in the sacred groves, this was not good.

I stalked back to the cabin and let myself in.

Inside the door, I caught a wave of Eventh's scent, and it floored me.

Oh, I had been in the middle of *fucking her*, and it had been the most amazing thing I'd ever felt in my life. She was perfect in every way, and I adored her, worshiped her, wanted back in that slick little tight pussy of hers right at this—

I let out a breath.

"Baby girl?"

"What?" Her voice was a half-whine.

"We gotta go."

"What? No. We can't. I like it here. I need to stay here. It's good here. It's dark and warm and safe and—"

"Izar's tracing the speeder." I rubbed my face. Of course he was tracing the speeder. Why had I thought I could take his fucking speeder? Why was I incapable of intelligent thought? Was it her scent? Was it the fact she was in heat? Was it that I'd been perpetually in a state of heightened arousal for hihors now? "We have to go, but we can't take that speeder."

What were we going to do?

I guessed we could steal another speeder, but Izar would show up here, figure out who'd lost their speeder, and then get their theft location to find us.

Of course, we could have ditched that speeder and picked up another by then, maybe?

Maybe we *should* get on the water.

If we were on the water, we'd be out of his reach.

But I was not taking her through her heat in a cabin on a watervessel. That was… no.

Eventh appeared in the doorway to the bedroom, lusciously and totally naked. I took in her beautiful curves, her round and ripe breasts, and her pretty little mound. Spirits, I wanted to put my mouth all over her again.

"How are we leaving without that speeder?" she said.

I grunted, going over to her. I wrapped an arm around her waist, pulled her flush against me, and started kissing her.

She melded into me, opening her mouth, eagerly moving her tongue against mine.

We kissed for a while.

Too long.

With effort, I pulled away and deposited her back on the bed.

She went up into the position again, ass in the air, legs spread, rubbing her face furiously against the coverlet, rasping noises rattling out of her throat.

I looked at her, gritting my teeth. She was in a bad way, and I was going to try to move her?

This was insane.

"Sevren?" She managed between moans, her voice ravaged. "I can't get in a speeder."

I went over to her and sank two fingers into her, curving my thumb up over her clit. I finger-fucked her, rubbing her clit, and tried to think.

She made little grunts and whines, moving her hips against my fingers. "I need your cock again, Sevren. Please?"

"Shh, no, baby girl, I can't." I shoved another finger

in, moving quicker on her clit.

"I *need* it." She was practically sobbing.

Spirits, this was exactly how I promised her that I wouldn't let her get. It was the stress of the situation, feeding her heat in not-so-great ways, making it unpleasant for her.

It was very hard to think when I was touching her like that, and when her scent was so powerful.

Want to taste her.

No.

Okay, what did I need?

I needed someplace safe to take her, where either Izar couldn't get, or…

What if I had muscle? What if I had someone else, or several someones who weren't focused entirely on Eventh's heat and who were not completely distracted by that?

I took my fingers out of her pussy.

She made a noise of disbelief. "Don't stop."

"Shh, I got you," I muttered, climbing up behind her on the bed, undoing my pants. My cock was still hard, and the knot—the fuck was that knot? I'd never seen anything like it. I mean, it had been a while since I was getting regular erections, but *seriously*.

I gripped her hips and pushed back into her.

She let out a sigh of relief, moving her hips, angling them, getting my knot against her clit.

Can't ranskk her, I told myself. *Get her off. Do not come inside her.*

"I know where we're going, okay, baby girl?" I muttered, fucking her.

"We can't leave," she said, her voice muffled.

I dug my fingers into her hips. "I'm going to need to go out and find a terminal so I can get in touch with someone, since we don't have bracelets. You'll need to come with me. I'm not leaving you alone."

"In public?" she moaned. "Do I have to wear clothes?"

"Yes," I said, slamming into her. She had the most perfect pussy in the history of pussies. I wanted to build a temple to it and make up a regular worship schedule. She was... *fuck.*

"I don't know," she said. "I don't know if I can."

"Yeah, you can," I said. "We'll do that, and then we'll take the speeder to a meet-up point, and he'll pick us up. We can mess around on the way there, but he, uh, I don't think he's going to want to watch us..."

"Who is he?"

"He's a friend," I said. Oh, fuck, I was getting close. I wrapped my hand around the base of my dick, behind the knot. *Let her get off. Wait.*

"I can't. I *can't.* There's no way. Can't we stay here?"

"No," I said. I mean, maybe I could kill Izar, right, but then... what would I do with the body? I was not going to break her heat while some dead gladiator was moldering out in the other room, and I didn't see myself burying him— "No. We have to go."

She let out a moan of disappointment, but then it turned into something else, and she moved her hips and let out another sound, a *different* sound, and two hisecs later, I felt her flutter-clenching on my cock, and I almost came inside her.

I yanked out, slapping my dick against her back, and I spurted rope after rope of wet semen over her skin.

Fuck.

She collapsed on the bed.

I went with her, pressing into her, thrusting my hips into the soft swell of her ass, my balls emptying themselves with two more jerks.

She groaned.

I grunted.

That was *not* how I wanted that to go. "Don't move," I said.

She writhed. "Feed it to me."

Spirits.

She looked over her shoulder. "Please. I can't reach."

"No, baby girl, no. We don't have time to…" My mouth was dry. I was imagining it, dragging my fingers through my jizz, transferring it to between her lips, feeling her lick me clean with her tongue… "Later, okay, I promise, when we get settled, you can… but for now, I'm just going to clean you up."

"We're settled here."

"I know, and if I wasn't such a fuck-up, it wouldn't be like this." Of course, if I'd never come to her at all, she wouldn't be in heat, and this wouldn't even be *happening.* I went into the bathroom and got a wet cloth. I came back and used it on her back.

She liked that. She writhed against my touch, sighing and leaning into it, scenting my hand when I couldn't help but caress her cheek.

I was hard again by the time it was done.

I helped her get dressed, and I put on my pants, and then we left the cabin.

She clung to me, letting out little gasps as we walked toward the speeder. Spirits of the sacred groves, she was very obviously in heat. This was so bad.

We made our way to the front desk where I'd rented the cabin.

The woman there eyed Eventh with something like horror. "No, uh, we don't have a communication terminal here."

"You're joking," I said. "How can you not—"

"Everyone has a bracelet!" she protested. "And you're not borrowing mine, so don't ask. Did you drug her?"

"I'm in heat," Eventh growled at her. She was holding onto me, melded against my body, clinging to me for dear life.

"Oh," said the woman, blinking, looking even more horrified. "Uh, they, um, down the street at the tavern, there's a terminal there."

"Fine," I said, and Eventh and I left the front desk and made our way down to the tavern.

At the tavern, there was a guy with a huuq instrument, strumming it and crooning mournfully in Cobran, which was a trade language from the Lanisson sector. I knew enough of it to get by, so I could tell that the song was about some girl who'd cheated on him and broken his heart.

The tavern was mostly empty except for about ten different men sitting at the bar, all nursing drinks, all of whom eyed Eventh in a way I did not like at all.

She was rubbing her face into my chest and thrusting her hips out, though, so it was probably hard for them not to stare.

We found the terminal. I put in a credit chip and it drained the balance a bit and then spit it back out at me.

I rubbed Eventh's back and held her against me as the connection was made.

She let out noisy breaths. "I'm sorry. I can't help it. I'm trying not to—"

"You're fine," I told her. "You're just fine. Whatever you need. We'll be out of here soon."

She groaned, sagging into me, able to stop moving

for a few hidosecs.

Right, I'd forgotten about the way our emotions moved through the bond during heat. We could influence each other that way, and my job as her mate was to be projecting soothing feelings through the bond to her. I needed to take better care of her. She'd been feeling all my stress instead, and I'd been making it harder for her.

I forced myself to take deep, slow breaths and release the rest of my own tension.

Eventh visibly relaxed even more, sighing against me.

The terminal popped up a holoprojection of Conlach Mattres, an old gladiator friend of mine. He was a scarencs from the planet Jenthe, scaled all over, triangular ridges on the top of his head and all the way down his back.

"Whoever it is who has this number—" He broke off as he recognized me. "Well, sands, if it isn't Sevren. Long time, buddy."

"Long time," I said. "Very long time. You doing all right?"

"Oh, you know, can't complain, but still do *constantly*." He chuckled.

I tried to laugh too, but I wasn't quite up for it. "You still running that resort down on the shore?"

"I am," he said. "You still working for the guild?"

"I am," I said.

"Who's that? Do you have your arm around a *girl*?"

"This is, uh…" I grimaced. I lowered my voice. "I told you about Eventh."

"Oh," he said in a different voice. "Well, but, she's, uh, how old is she now?"

"Twenty," I said tightly.

"Oh," he said, relieved. "Well, that's… that's *fine*, then. Isn't that fine?"

I sighed heavily. "I need a really big favor."

EIGHT

Back in the speeder, Sevren stroked his hands up and down my arms and down my torso, talking to me in a low, even voice. He buckled me in, telling me I was fine, that everything was okay, and that I could relax. He tightened the buckle, and I tested my hips against it, pushing into it, but he secured it, so that I couldn't really move my hips, and that was a relief, that pressure.

"Thanks," I breathed.

"Yeah," he said. "I'm, uh, I know I'm terrible at this, baby girl. I'm so sorry. Worst heat ever. I'm going to make it up to you."

"It's not terrible," I said. "It's so much better near you. You're the best thing. You're my favorite thing."

He kissed me, a soft, long, thorough kiss, and smoothed his hands all over me again, strategically avoiding my breasts and pelvis. Then he got into the other side of the speeder, programmed a new course into it, and we took off.

"So, this guy is going to help us?" I said.

"He's got a bunch of ex-gladiators working for him," he said. "If Izar shows up, they'll keep him from getting to us, and they'll contain him. I can concentrate on you, and if we can focus, we can get through it, and maybe even get your heat to break early."

"Mmm," I sighed. "Is that possible?"

"Back on Bravren, guys talked about it, yeah, about how to draw it out, how to get it over with, things like that."

"People want to draw it out?" I said, thinking I could maybe see why, because it was unpleasant and also *wonderful* all at the same time.

"Uh… in the beginning of a relationship, yeah. It's pretty typical that the first heat will result in pregnancy after a couple is mated, and then there's no heat at all during the pregnancy or for a couple gecyles after, while she's nursing, and so, there's a sense of it being a last hurrah for the younger couples. But then, after a couple kids, it becomes an annoyance, and if you're actively trying to not get pregnant, even more of one."

"Because wovrn heats are frequent," I said. If I went off my suppressants, I'd have a heat once every gemoon, so basically a fourth of my stars-shined life would be spent in heat. If Sevren interfered with my suppressants, that would mean that I'd be forced to be like that if we were…

But what was I thinking?

How could I fit Sevren into my current life? How could I fit into his?

I definitely couldn't fit heats into it. I could not do this every fourth fogemoon, no way. That was really the entire reason I was at school, after all, though. I'd gotten my scholarship because of my promising research that I'd done basically on my own, with a dinky lab I'd attempted to assemble back on Bravren and mostly experimenting on myself.

"Very frequent, yeah," he said. "But, uh, if a woman gets pregnant every time, she might only go into heat

once every few gecycles. And the knots, the heat, it's…
pretty effective at, uh, at pregnancy."

"Yeah," I breathed.

He'd stopped at the store on the way back to the
speeder and bought the spermicide patches. We had
them now, so we were safe. It would be fine. We were
not going to be effective at pregnancy, no way.

"You want kids, Sevren?" I said.

He looked up at me, surprised. "What?"

"Did you not hear me?"

"I guess that's something I never thought about." He
settled himself back into the speeder's seat, facing
forward, shaking his head. "Basically, it's impossible."

"Obviously, it's not, and that bag of spermicide
patches proves just how possible—"

"Why are we doing this?" He gave me a look. "Let's
not do this."

"What are we doing?"

He sighed, shutting his eyes. "What if I said yes?
How would that make you feel?"

"Yes? Yes about what?"

"Yes, I want kids," he said, opening his eyes.

"You do?" I couldn't help but smile at this, though I
didn't know why.

"It's a hypothetical, Eventh. If I say that, how's that
going to make you feel? Your emotions are volatile
right now, and we're not in a great position, and any
extra stress or negative emotions—"

"I think it makes me feel good." I shrugged. "Which,
uh, which is stupid, because the only way you can have
kids is with me. I might be able to conceive with
someone else, but it would be really difficult, so—for
the sake of argument—if there are children in our
future, we'd have to make them together—"

"Enough." His voice was firm.

"Well, we can't do that," I said. "I mean, I can't be pregnant right now, because I'm really busy with school."

"You know, I don't know anything about you being at school," he said, turning to me with a look on his face—the look he used to give me when I would do something he thought was particularly amazing when I was a kid, like when I learned the Common alphabet or could recite math figures. It made me feel good but weird. He had that older-person-proud thing going on, which… "How'd you get that scholarship?"

"I applied," I said, shrugging, hunching down in the seat, reacting as if I were some embarrassed teenaged kid instead of the person who'd been jammed gloriously full of his cock and grinding my clit on his knot a very short time ago.

"Don't be like that," he said. "After everything you went through, it's amazing. Your parents were captives in a Toth lab, and then you had to suffer through being mated with me, and—"

"Don't be like *you're* being," I said, annoyed.

"How am I being?" He scoffed. "I'm proud of you."

"Yeah, like you're my uncle or something. Stop it."

He let out a breath, and then he grimaced and rolled his shoulders, uncomfortable. It was quiet.

The silence swallowed us, and my heat surged. I started to work my hips against the seatbelt, letting out little half-whines.

"I'm *not* your uncle," he growled.

I started to shiver, a wave of heat working through me.

He turned on me, baring his teeth. "Settle."

I did. My hips stopped and the shivers went away. I

gaped at him. "What'd you do?"

He rubbed his face. "Fuck, fuck, *fuck*."

"How can you do that to me?" I said. "That some weird wovrn thing? Your species lets men just control women when they're mated? That's horrible. I want to find some way to suppress—"

"It goes both ways, baby girl," he said tersely. "I get your emotions through the bond too. It's only during heat, and it gets strengthened the more we…"

"Fuck?"

"Are close."

"That's why I got the scholarship," I said. "Because of our bond. Because of being in heat as a little girl. Because of not having orgasms. I started studying human hormones, trying to figure out how it is we're so compatible with so many species, why things like altering me with a wovrn mating bond are even possible, looking for the links in human DNA."

He drew back. "Really?" He was stunned. "*That's* why you're in school? You're like a science genius?" He didn't sound proud in that uncle way now. It wasn't patronizing. It was genuine.

I preened, awash in his praise, and it was good, like when he made me come. I might have groaned a little. "I'm not… a genius," I breathed.

"It sounds really complicated."

"Well, I still haven't succeeded," I said. "At first, I started it because I wanted to see if I could unlock my orgasm, you know, with hormones or something. But whatever the bond does, it's locked down tight, and I never made any progress with that. However, I started to see some side effects that made me think I might be able to make a different sort of suppressant, and that's what I presented in my scholarship application."

"Wow," he said, grinning at me. "That's amazing. I can hardly believe it."

I beamed at him. "I'm *not* a little girl anymore."

"No," he said, shaking his head. "You're not at all." He bowed his head. "Spirits, I've done nothing with myself."

"For me, though," I said, my voice breaking. "You became a gladiator for me. You stayed a gladiator for me."

He looked up at me.

"But you could stop now?" I twisted my hands together. "You could do something else, anything else. You could go back to being the chieftain."

He snorted. "Oh, yeah, I was a great chieftain."

"Were you not?" I didn't know about this.

"Knocked off every day to play hide and seek or dolls or shit with you, and, uh, then I ran off and left the planet. I'm sure Millicen is doing a much better job than me. My sister was meant to be chieftess."

"So, you don't want to be chieftain? What do you want?"

He shrugged, spreading his hands. "Right now, baby girl, I want to get you through your heat and do something about Izar Fjass. And then... yeah, I don't know. It's been a long time since I thought that way, a long time."

"Twenty gecycles?" I whispered. "Did I take your ambition from you, Sevren? Mating me?"

"No, baby girl. No, it didn't feel like that. Before you, I wanted stupid, silly things. I wanted to be an adventurer from a story, a hero from some holovid. Not a real thing. And then, after you, I felt... focused. Like, I always knew what to do, and it was whatever was best for you."

My lips parted and my stomach twisted. "I can't be that to you, Sevren. That's too much. I release you from that. You don't need to *do* that."

He met my gaze and gave me a little smile, one that told me that there was no releasing him. But what he said was, "Okay, baby girl. Whatever you want."

Stars.

No, I couldn't let him be that way. If he was going to be so stupidly devoted, I could at least use my influence for good. "Well, I want you to quit being a gladiator. It's too dangerous."

"Yeah, I'm not real attached to it either." He shrugged.

"And… and I want you to think about something to do for yourself," I said. "Because that's what I want, that's what would be best for me, if you were happy."

"You happy, baby girl?" he said, looking away from me. "That why you're doing 'blood play'?"

I grimaced. "You want to bring this up, huh?"

He stared out the window.

"It's just… if there's no orgasm, I need… something."

"I get that," he said.

I huffed.

He glanced back at me, swallowing hard, the knob in his throat bobbing. "No, I really do. I understand why. But does it make you happy?"

"Well…" My shoulders sagged, and all the fight went out of me. "No, I guess not. But that's just that part of my life. The sex part of my life is admittedly frustrating. Maybe demeaning. Maybe embarrassing. Maybe a little bit, uh, disturbed." I studied my knuckles. "But the rest of it, my research, my time in the lab, my classes, the work I'm doing with the professors and the other students, it's really, really good. It makes me very happy. It excites me. It's my reason for getting up in the morning."

"Yeah, that's a good thing. That's a real good thing."

"You think I should stop the sex stuff."

"You're the one who said it was disturbing."

"Maybe you and me…" I bit my lip. "Is there any way we could…"

He let out a breath. "I don't know."

It was quiet.

He cleared his throat. "Uh, I don't see how I could fit into your life, exactly. What? I'll be the thirty-five-gecycles-old guy hanging out, waiting to be let into your dorm room and throw you into your heat? You rearrange your schedule for us to have four days of full-on fucking? That doesn't sound workable, baby girl, I gotta say."

"No," I said, feeling defeated. "It really doesn't." I sighed. "And even if we could work that out, we couldn't really socialize."

"Mmm." He nodded. "Yeah, I'll come to your university parties. This is my ex-gladiator boyfriend. He's older."

I snorted. "Oh, fuck. That's…"

"And it's not necessarily easier on my side," he said. "You heard Conlach, didn't you, how weird he got, wanting to know how old you were? And he's my friend. So, let's assume I find some other kind of job, *not* being a gladiator, and then I manage to make some friends. If I bring you out for dinner or something, will they all look at me like I'm some kind of creep, because, I mean, look at you?" He gestured.

I grimaced. I could definitely see where he was coming from.

"Maybe I *am* a creep."

"No," I said immediately. "You're good to me. You care about me. No one cares about me like you."

He nodded firmly. "No one does." He sighed. "But that doesn't mean that I'm good for you, or that *any* of this is good for you. That doesn't mean all of this mating bond stuff hasn't really messed with your head, baby girl."

"Well, yours too," I said. "The mating bond took things from you too."

He nodded, sighing.

"And still continues to take things from both of us," I said. "Because we're... we can't..."

He reached across the speeder and took one of my hands in his. "Maybe something kind of, uh, occasional?"

I nodded. "Maybe. Maybe that could work. Like once every four gemoons or something, I might be able to handle getting thrown into a heat. And we could just meet up somewhere, in a hotel or something and..."

"Yeah," he nodded, squeezing my hand. "Yeah."

I smiled. "I think I might end up needing that."

"Whatever you need."

I wrapped my hand around both of ours. "I don't want to not see you at all, Sevren. I miss you when you're gone. You don't know how much I miss you."

"I think I might know, actually, baby girl."

I pulled him closer and kissed him.

He kissed me carefully but with increasing pressure, and when he broke away, it was only to scent me. He whispered darkly in my ear, "You need to get off again? We'll have to be hands off after we ditch this speeder and Conlach picks us up."

"Mmm... yes, please," I said in a throaty voice.

"Can I use my mouth on you?"

I grinned. "Ask nicely."

"Please, please, baby girl, I need to taste you."

"Well, if you need it," I sighed, "then how can I deny you?"

NINE

I was beginning to wish I'd bought myself another shirt when I was buying food or when I was buying spermicide patches. I didn't seem to be thinking big picture in this situation. I was hyper-focused on solving various problems, but I couldn't think to anticipate other problems.

Eventh and I ditched speeder in the dark and trekked through a path in some marshland to the agreed-upon rendezvous point with Conlach. It was cold, and I was shivering as we walked. Eventh was shivering too, but I didn't know if it was because of waves of heat going through her or because she was actually cold.

"So," she said, huddling into me, "we couldn't have brought the speeder to meet him?"

"No, because Conlach is paranoid and doesn't want Izar coming there."

"But he's not going to be at the rendezvous point. It's literally a spot where we're getting in his speeder and driving off, yeah? A random spot?"

"I begged him for the favor. We're doing it his way," I said.

She groaned. "Well, for the record, not my favorite part of the evening."

I laughed, tightening my grip on her. "Yeah, mine either."

She looked up at me. "What was your favorite part? Was it when you lost your virginity?"

"You're going to keep teasing me about that, aren't you?"

"Oh, only until the end of time," she said, giggling, snuggling in against me more.

"I could point out how unfair that is," I said. "I could also point out how it's just rubbing my nose in you and however many men it is that you've slept with, all of whom I want to strangle, behead, and rip the spines out of." I was matter-of-fact about this.

"Wow, stars, overreact much?"

"Losing my virginity has made me a little possessive."

"Only a little," she said, nodding. She snuggled against me, sighing. "You know that there's no comparison between you and any other sexual experience ever, right?"

"I mean..." I tightened my grip on her shoulders. "I'm not being serious. You're your own person. I've always told myself that something age appropriate was better for—"

"And besides, you told me you did unspecified sexual acts with a bunch of other women, and what do you think I want to do to *them*?"

I laughed. "Okay, yeah, you have nothing to be jealous about with whatever pathetic experiences I've had, trust me." I cleared my throat. "Besides, we're not... we weren't together before, and we're not together now, and there's no... reason to be jealous."

"We've always been together," she countered.

"Yeah," I breathed, not trying to deny it. "But we're

also not."

"I know," she sighed, snuggling again despite her words. "It's going to be okay, though, it will."

And somehow, she soothed me. I was right about the bond going both ways.

We walked on in silence, pressed close, until we came to the end of the path.

Conlach's speeder was waiting for us. The doors to the back seat were open, and he was leaning against it, arms folded over his chest, grinning at us both. "Any messes you two make in my speeder, you are cleaning up, Sevren."

"Spirits," I said. "We're not going to—"

"I'd shake your hand or give you a hug or whatever, but I don't think so," he said. "Not with whatever you two have been doing. Get in there."

I nudged Event into the back seat and climbed in after her.

Conlach walked around to the driver's side and climbed in. He got the speeder going, set a course, and then we were off.

Event leaned in against me, and I put my arm around her.

I watched Conlach. He looked the same. Maybe a little older, maybe his eyes were a little lined. He still had that tattoo of a thorny jelxa plant climbing up on his neck, peeking out from beneath his clothes. He still wore one dangling earring on one side—he'd always had to take that out for the arena.

He turned around, the autodrive engaged, and looked us over. "You lost your clothes, I see?"

"Uh, there was a speeder accident," I said. "My shirt got burned, and the tatters of it weren't worth wearing."

"And I was in the middle of a gang bang," said Eventh, rubbing her face against my chest.

I shut my eyes. So, she was going to be like that. Great. Perfect. I opened my eyes again, rueful.

Conlach caught my gaze, raising his eyebrows. "Uh… okay?"

"Don't judge him," said Eventh. "He can't help what he's mated to."

"Baby girl," I muttered, sighing. "Come on."

Conlach laughed.

"It was not a gang bang," I said archly, deciding to go with it. I didn't care anymore. *I fucked her.* "It was a threesome, am I right?"

She looked up at me.

"And they both ended up dead," I said, and now I was grinning. "Very, very dead."

She rolled her eyes. "You would be like that about it. I mean, here I am traumatized by your arch nemesis or whatever trying to kill me—"

"Hey, don't give Izar more significance than he has to me. He's just some crazed gladiator."

"Yeah, let's talk about Izar," said Conlach, letting out a snicker. "Definitely a safer topic, I think. What happened with him? I heard about Griz's untimely demise, but that was an accident, right? He fell over the side of the ring?"

"Definitely an accident. I certainly didn't mean for it to happen," I said. "Izar must have figured out at some point that the reason I was never on the deathmatch circuit was because of my limp dick, so he put it all together and tracked her down. He's much better at tracking things that it seems like he should be, I think."

"Yeah, I always figured him for a musclehead," said Conlach. "But, you know, tracking her down probably wasn't too hard. Not like she was hiding or anything?"

"No," she said, with a little sigh, her back arching, hips jutting out.

I smoothed a firm hand over her spine, cupping her backside, holding her still.

She let out a relieved huff of air.

Conlach laughed again. "Maybe I should drive."

"No, I'm good," said Eventh. She shut her eyes. "I, um, I might be tired."

"Really?" I said, reaching up to stroke her hair.

She yawned. "Maybe."

"Sleep, then, baby girl," I rumbled, kissing her on top of the head.

She sighed again, snuggling close.

Conlach looked from her to me and then back again, shaking his head slowly.

I gave him a look, telling him to just let it go. "Anyway, Izar taunted me with it, and I tracked her down, which, yeah, didn't take long. She wasn't hiding. So, I got there in time, and then we've just been on the run since. I can't go to the authorities, because they'll turn us over to the guild, and the guild is likely to let him kill her in front of me just to make Izar happy."

"He's that big of a deal these days, huh?"

"He's out of control," I said, sighing.

Eventh's breath had gone even and deep. She was asleep. I could tell. I continued to stroke her hair.

"She asleep?"

"I think so," I said.

"Threesome? Gang bang?" He spread his hands wide. "What the sands, buddy?"

"It's none of your business," I said.

"Maybe you were worried about nothing. You didn't want to corrupt her, but she's been busy corrupting herself, huh?"

"It's not like that," I said. "You know what mating bonds are like. She, uh, can't have an orgasm without me. I think it… she's not okay, that's all. But I don't know what to do. All I do is destroy this girl's life, you know? Everything I do makes things worse for her. And now… this…" I shook my head.

He shrugged. "I don't know, Sevren, she sounds a little crazy. Is she crazy?"

"Stop."

"Nothing like a crazy woman," he said. "Lots of it is fun, and then, you know, twenty percent of it is like being eaten alive by a sandsnake."

I snorted. "It's not like that."

"Well, it actually *is* none of my business," he said. "And I personally have sworn all that off."

"Oh?" I said, lifting my chin. "I thought, uh, there was that greeicx girl you were knocking boots with? That didn't work out?"

"No," he said, shaking his head. "Nah, the arena nightmares… I scared her off. I'm too screwed up for a woman, not to mention too set in my ways to make room for one. I have an arrangement with a lady who lives on the other side of the bay, and she and I just meet up probably about once a season and spend a little time, and then she goes her way, I go mine. I like it, and she does too. It's a very nice arrangement."

"Is it?" I said thoughtfully, thinking of my conversation earlier with Eventh. "So, that's working for you?"

"Like a charm," he said. "Now, here's what I didn't tell you when you got in touch. You sounded desperate, so I didn't think you'd care, but I should probably make you aware before we get back to the resort."

"This sounds serious," I said.

"It is a little. I'm, uh, a double agent these days. I mean, that's overstating it, really, but I am in the middle of setting something up, something with a lot of moving pieces, and I'm working with the resistance."

I let go of Eventh, sitting up a little. "What?"

She moaned, stirring against me.

I sat back, stroking her hair again. "The resistance? Really?"

"You want out? If you don't want to be there—"

"I didn't say that." I swallowed. "Wow. That *is* serious."

"I'm not going to tell you details," he said. "But I will say to stay clear of all of it, okay? There's a ccael, if you see him, don't engage. And there are going to be Toth, rich Toth, around the place, and they are the marks, so don't engage with them either."

"I'm not… we're going to be…" I stroked her hair.

"Right, I figured. You're holing up with your girl and fucking her brains out and you won't even be leaving the bungalow, yeah? That's how it'll go."

"It should," I said, nodding. "Hey, bringing Izar down on you, that's not going to be a problem?"

"He'll never find us." Conlach waved that away. "Don't worry about him. And what could he really do anyway? Like he's getting past my security. No, it's fine. It'll be fine. Just stay clear, yeah?"

"Not a problem," I said. "Hey, I appreciate this, and you know that it goes without saying that you can name your price for anything in the future. I owe you. Any favor you need."

"No worries. We're friends, Sevren. Friends help each other out." He shrugged. "Besides, I wanted to meet your child bride."

I glowered at him. "She's not my child bride."

"Right, your tot-mate."

I gave him a withering look.

"I mean, she *does* seem very mature now."

"Yeah, none of that," I snapped. "Eyes up here." I gestured to my own eyes.

He laughed. "You ain't got to worry about me, like I said. I've sworn off all of it, crazy girls included. The twenty percent that's like getting eaten alive, it's worse the more your bones ache. I leave the crazy ones to the younger—" He cringed. "What am I saying?"

"What *are* you saying?" I said pointedly.

"Gang bangs," he muttered, turning around to fiddle with the holodisplay.

"Shut up." I settled closer to Eventh. "She's just… mouthing off. She's pushing, testing me."

"Why would she do that?" He looked over his shoulder at me.

Because I left her, and she hates me for it.

She was just trying to hurt me, because I'd hurt her. She didn't know that it had nearly killed me to be away from her.

I shrugged, not willing to get into this with Conlach.

Besides, she was wrong. I *had* to leave her. She thought she wanted me, but I knew better. I was older, and I loved her, and I would protect her from anything that would hurt her. Including myself.

Conlach spoke again. "I'm just saying, if that's what she's into, you sure you're enough for her?"

"*I'm* what she's been looking for," I said in a low voice. "I'm her mate. Obviously nothing else is going to satisfy her."

He nodded. "Gotcha." He shook his head. "Weird."

I rolled my eyes. I felt tired, too. I shut my eyes and sank into the seat.

It felt as if no time at all passed.

"...Sevren? You asleep?"

"No," I grunted, opening my eyes.

"You're going to make me repeat all that," he said, chuckling.

"Repeat what?" I yawned.

"I probably couldn't," he said. "I was just yammering about mating bonds."

"What about them?" I shut my eyes again. I was probably going to fall asleep again, wasn't I?

"They seem kind of horrible. Great way to be tied down and stuck in something that you might very easily grow out of."

"Well, usually, amongst my people, you wait and don't choose someone until you're really sure. It's a big commitment. People know that and they're careful."

"That's not what you did."

"No."

"Yeah, and I've always thought it was a horror show for you, and you were being so noble all for that little girl you left at home, but now... it was a horror show for her too? Nothing you did mattered?"

"Maybe not," I muttered.

"If you could go back in time would you bite her again?"

"What? Let her die?"

"Nah, just pick some four-gecycles-old kid and have him bite her or something."

No way in all the sacred groves. Mine.

"That might have been better for everyone involved, I guess," I sighed.

"Sands, yes, it would have been." He laughed.

“Nothing you can do now, though.”
	“No,” I breathed.

TEN

eventh

I wasn't asleep, but I pretended to be.

So, I heard, and it hurt.

But of course he'd rather not be mated to me, and I shouldn't take it personally, because I would rather not be mated to him, also. So much of what had passed between us had been pain, and I'd wished for something different many times.

Stars, I'd cursed his name sometimes, called him every insult I knew, railed at him for leaving me, for abandoning me, for mating me, all of it.

But that was before.

We'd made love.

It had been interrupted and it hadn't been the way I thought either of us wanted it to be, but we'd been joined. He'd been inside me. I'd felt him moving with me, and I'd felt us all entwined and…

Better for everyone involved?

How could he say that?

I was awake when the speeder stopped, but I pretended to be asleep, and he picked me up like I was nothing, cradling me against his chest, and carried me. I opened my eyes to see that the sun was coming up and that we were at the shore. There were a lot of shores on Kalion, because there were a lot of oceans.

This looked like the shore to a bay, though, judging by how calm the water looked, a deep blue tranquil pool of water that rippled gently.

Hadn't Conlach said something about a bay?

I bet, judging from where we were and how far we'd traveled, that it was the Achis Bay, because this was a tourist location, and I'd heard the word resort thrown about a few times.

I lifted my head, and I could see that there were rows of thruster bridges out over the water of the bay, with walkways that jutted out to meet them from the land. That was where we were, an a cliff of sorts. Built on each thruster bridge was a building. Some were small, some were large. They all seemed to have decks surrounding them and furniture scattered around for people to sit out and stare down at the bay and the cliff and the sky above. "Are we…?"

"You're awake, baby girl." Sevren's voice rumbled in his chest.

"Are we going out in one of those?"

"You don't have a problem with heights I don't know about?" said Sevren, amused.

"No," I said, struggling against him just the same.

He set me down on my feet.

Conlach was coming for us from the opposite direction, carrying a pile of bedding—sheets, pillows, blankets. "This way," he called. "These two are empty, and Sevren said the smaller one."

Sevren gave my shoulder a squeeze. "Sorry they're so airy. I know you'd rather something closer to the ground, darker, that kind of thing."

I looked up at him. Would I? I thought I would. Was that a heat thing? Odd. He honestly seemed to know more about my own heat than I did, and I was grateful he'd paid attention to gossip in the village back home.

"But we'll be safe here. There's all kinds of security and there's no way up this cliff except the way we came, and Conlach's guys will stop Izar before he can get near us."

"Not that he'll find you," said Conlach. "He'll never trace you here." He stepped out onto a bridge and headed toward a small building with a two-story porch that wrapped all around and several rocking chairs perfectly set up to watch the sunrise over the bay.

Sevren guided me to follow Conlach.

We stepped onto the walkway, and I felt a little dizzy. I wasn't afraid of heights, but we were high up. I clutched the railing and Sevren laughed gently at me, urging me along.

Conlach already had the door open. "Welcome to Bungalow Number Three," he said in an announcer voice. "Well equipped with a full-stocked replicator, two bathrooms, upstairs and down, and a master suite with a glass ceiling so you can look at the stars."

Sevren winced as we came inside behind him. "Glass ceiling? Really? Is there another bedroom?"

I looked around at the kitchen and dining area, which was all open. There were tall windows lining the place, and the sun was beaming in as it rose in the sky. I squinted at it, and it didn't feel good. I hunched up my shoulders.

Conlach turned to him. "There is, actually, a tiny little thing down here." He pushed open a door beneath the wide set of steps that led up to the bedroom that Conlach was talking about. "Only double bed in there, not a nice hii grax size."

Sevren went to peer over his shoulder and nodded. "It's better." He beckoned to me.

I came and looked in. There was only one wall of windows in this room, so yeah, I guessed it was better. It did seem cozier because it was small and the bed took up most of the room.

Sevren went over and pulled the curtains shut tight over the wall of windows. The light dimmed.

I sighed.

"Yeah?" he said.

"We'll make it work," I said, nodding. I smiled at Conlach. "Thank you so much for this. We, um, we're sorry to impose."

"When you strip the bed, toss the sheets in here," said Conlach, leaving the room and opening a closet where there was a bin. "And you can ring for new sheets whenever you need them, as *often* as you need them—"

"You're enjoying this," said Sevren, folding his arms over his chest.

"Maybe a little," said Conlach.

"You remember that time that you fell head over heels for that girl on that planet out in the Garn System?" said Sevren. "And I had to run resistance with your handler while you were making time with her, and the whole time you teased me about how I was like one of those von-monks from Nilk?"

Conlach cringed. "I teased you? That was cruel of me, wasn't it?"

"Just go away," said Sevren.

"Sure," said Conlach. "Have fun, kids." He slapped Sevren on the shoulder. "Enjoy the crazy while you can."

I glared at him. Conlach did not understand me, but he was helping us out, and he had come all the way out to pick us up and this was a very nice bungalow, all things considered. If someone wanted to rent it, and he couldn't because he'd given it to us, it would cost him. I'd let it slide, but really.

I wasn't crazy.

Okay, maybe sort of crazy. But no one else got to say it, only me.

Once Conlach was gone, it was just me and Sevren, and it was suddenly awkward.

Was it because it was light out? I couldn't figure anything else that would make a difference.

I wasn't sure what to do with myself. I felt shaky from the heat, but somehow the sun had forced it down to curl up inside me, and it was resting at the back of my spine like a sleeping animal. I didn't feel like moaning or getting into position or rubbing myself all over everything.

Well.

I mean, maybe I did wish I could do those things, because they'd give me some relief, but I didn't feel comfortable doing them. I hugged myself, and I wanted to find someplace to curl up in a ball. Could I crawl into the closet?

"Baby girl?" said Sevren.

"Yeah," I said softly.

"You seem like you're a little less affected," he said. "I don't know if that's because you're getting through the heat or because it's retreated and is hiding because we're in this big, bright space."

It was the second thing. I didn't say anything, though. I shrugged.

"Conlach said he'd work on getting us some clothes sent up. You hungry? You want me to see what's programmed into the replicator?"

I shrugged again.

"Shower," he said finally, firmly, as if this was decided.

I found that oddly calming, that he was making decisions for me. Heat was very fucked up, and I hated it. "Okay, I'll take a shower."

"Good," he said. "By yourself, get scrubbed and clean, and when you get out, you can eat while I shower, and then we'll..."

I bit down on my lip. *Then you knot me?* The thing curled up against my spine jerked at this thought.

"Maybe nap or something," he said. "Just get comfy, yeah?"

"Okay," I said.

"Okay," he said, and he came over, wound an arm around me, and kissed my forehead.

I put my face into his chest and breathed in the scent of him. It was better when we were touching.

So, maybe I should have told him to come into the shower with me, but I didn't. I showered alone, and I couldn't seem to get the water hot enough. I ended up on the floor, hugging my knees to my chest, teeth chattering as waves and waves of heat racked my body.

Finally, the worst of it left me and I managed to turn off the water, drag myself out, and wrap up in a thick, fluffy towel that was there.

I told Sevren I didn't want any food. Instead, I dove naked, hair still wet, under the covers of the bed in the small, dim room, and I huddled there with extra pillows.

For a while, I felt warm, but then my teeth started chattering again.

That was how Sevren found me when he got out of the shower.

"Baby girl, you should have called for me." He

climbed into the bed and pulled me into his arms, and when my body touched his, everything was better. I scrabbled up, pressing into him everywhere I could, wrapping my arms tight around him, moaning.

He clutched me tight, smoothing his hands down me like he had when he buckled me into the speeder. "We should have showered together. I'm an idiot. I thought… I thought you'd want space, but I should have known better. What was I thinking?"

"Sorry," I murmured into his skin. "Sorry, I should have called for you."

"No, baby girl, you didn't do anything wrong." He kissed my forehead and then my nose, and then I captured his lips with my own.

In moments, I was pressed back into the bed, his body warm and firm and heavy on me, warming me everywhere, and we were both very naked, and our bare skin was fresh and clean from the shower, and I suddenly really liked the turn of events.

I started to writhe against him, rocking my hips against his hips and I felt him getting hard against me.

"Mmm," he sighed. "Hold that thought." He suddenly vaulted off me.

"No," I cried. "No, don't leave me." I was piteous.

"Back in a hisec, baby girl," he assured me, and he was, with a spermicide patch, which he applied to me and I felt it dissolve into my skin and then he was back, pressing against me, and kissing me again.

I wound my arms around his neck, and I moved my tongue against his. I liked the way our bodies felt against each other. I hummed in appreciation as we kissed and kissed and kissed.

When he pulled away, it was to scent me, first on one side of my neck and then the other.

I sighed, tipping back my head, offering him my throat.

He kissed me there, using his tongue.

"Now," I breathed, "I get your knot, right?"

He panted against my skin.

"Right?" A note of panic crept into my voice. "You're not coming up with another excuse."

"No more excuses, baby girl," he breathed, kissing lower, over my shoulders, raining kisses against my skin until one collided with his mark.

I gasped.

"Mmm," he rumbled and kissed it again, more deliberately.

I sighed, wriggling my hips up into him, wrapping my thighs around his body.

He licked me there.

I groaned, feeling it in my clit, like a warm burst of a sudden blossom. His scent was heavy on the air, all around me, pleasant and sweet and dark and complex, coffee and the sweet scent of tree sap. I arched my back, pushing my shoulder up into his mouth, and he began to lick me there in long, sloppy strokes, driving his very hard cock against my thigh as he did and making low, affected noises.

So, he liked licking me there, too, huh?

What was that about?

I didn't know, but I felt him all around me, as if his mouth there triggered our bond, and I felt turned on and aroused but also safe and cherished the way he always made me feel.

My breasts tingled. My body felt ripe and loose. I bucked against him, twisting my hips around as he thrust, and he suddenly wasn't thrusting against my thigh anymore, but sliding against my pussy, where I was wet.

So, *so* wet.

When had I gotten that wet? Was it just from his mouth on the bite mark on me? Oh, man, that was so weird. It was kind of messed up, but it was also hot and kind of nice in some other way, and all of those strange, warring sensations twisted around in me as I rubbed into him.

His hard cock was slippery against my clit, driving up against me, his underside against my slick center, and I enthusiastically pumped my hips, liking the sensation of him there—long and sleek and hard, perfect to grind on.

He moved his mouth from my bite mark, but his hand covered it and he fingered it, and each stroke of his finger made my clit clench.

He closed his mouth on one of my nipples.

I moaned. Good, good, good.

All the while, our hips were moving in tandem against each other in that very nice way, his cock between my labia, rubbing against my clit, getting dripping wet from how slick I seemed to have gotten down there.

He sucked hard on one nipple, and then the other.

And then he pulled his hips back further, and his cock pulled out between us, the tip pointing straight at me, and when he pressed his hips back down, his cock didn't go over my clit again, it went down, down, down and buried itself in my pussy.

I gasped, stunned, because that had never happened to me in my life. Honestly, I could count on one hand the men who'd correctly put themselves inside me. Usually, I had to reach down there and do some guiding.

But this…

No handling on either of our parts, and he was just *in* there.

He made a tattered sound, lifting his head from my breast. "Oops."

I giggled. "We were heading there anyway."

"Yeah," he breathed. He moved up, face over mine. He kissed me. "You sure?"

"I mean, you're already in there—"

"About the knot," he said. "Even if I don't end up ranskking you, it's going to be in there a while. We're going to be, uh, stuck together."

I grinned, touching his face. "You want me to beg, don't you?"

"Hey, no, I said you wouldn't have to."

"But I've *been* begging," I said, pumping my hips a little, pulling him in deep and letting him back out. "So, what's a little more?"

He kissed me again. "You really don't have to—"

"Knot, Sevren," I said in a rasping voice. "Please, give it to me. Knot *now*."

He kissed me harder, groaning, sinking into me, deep into me, deeper than he'd been before.

I bowed back, gasping, crying out at how deep he was. It was the edge of pain, but I liked that edge. Stars, I usually blew past that edge into higher sensations of intensity, so this… pleasure mixed with a little bit more? It was just fine with me. "Knot me," I panted. "Knot me, knot me, *please*, knot me."

He cut me off with more kissing, and pierced me deep again and then pulled out and then in and then—

My eyes opened because I felt it. The resistance, the way that when he stroked down, he wasn't coming out, he was taking my body with him, tugging on the inside of my pussy, stretching my skin.

Oohhh, that stretched my *clit*.

I gasped again. "Stars, Sevren, stars."

He gritted his teeth, grabbing my hips, repositioning us, easing his way into a rhythm. His breath was coming in labored gasps. "You okay?"

"Definitely, okay, it's perfect, pull out a little more when you thrust?"

"Are you...?" He furrowed his brow. "That doesn't hurt you? I'm stretching your—"

"Clit," I said.

"Ah," he said with a grin and then he did exactly what I asked.

I let out a deeply satisfied groan and then we fell into his rhythm together.

As he got comfortable, I could swear his cock swelled even bigger. His knot was pretty huge, and with the stretching and the extra way it filled me up my clit was getting all kinds of happy, just rubbed from a bunch of different angles, and I felt again like there were blossoms opening as he stroked into me, like I was in a garden full of bright flowers and they were nudging fuller and wider the longer and longer it went.

When my orgasm came, it was a burst of petals, one after the other, all scattering into the air and fluttering down in sweet, wonderful clenches as I came off it.

ELEVEN

eventh

Sevren must have come at the same time, or within hisecs of me, because I felt him twitching within me, and I could also feel how much more slippery I was in there, his knot sliding around a little more against my opening.

But it wasn't coming out. It was in there good and we were, like he said, stuck.

In the wake of our climaxes, we rested, catching our breath, his face buried in the crook of my shoulder, my fingers moving idly through the fur on his back.

He pushed up on his arms and looked down at me. "So, if it did hurt, would you tell me?"

"It doesn't hurt." I ran my hands over his shoulders. "It doesn't hurt at all."

"But would you like it if it did?"

"I..." I squinted up at him. "Is this really the conversation you want to have while you're stuck inside my body?"

He grinned. "I take it, from that answer, that yes, you would like it, and you think I wouldn't like you liking it."

"What? My head hurts now. I like that you like that I like that you like?"

He chuckled, lowering his face back to my breasts.

He nuzzled me there, sighing.

I sighed too. "That's nice."

"Yeah?" He suckled me.

I writhed.

He thrust.

I met his thrust. "Is… if you get worked up and come again, does that just double the amount of time we're locked together?"

"Yup," he said.

"Oh, wow," I said.

"And, I mean, there's a one hundred and seven percent chance that I'm going to get worked up again." He sucked my other nipple into his mouth.

I moaned.

He pulled off, tonguing my hard nipple. "You wanted it. You were begging me for it. You were like, 'Knot, please.'"

"Are you making fun of me while my pussy has swallowed your cock?" I said. "Is that wise?"

He snickered. "Ooh. Swallowed? This is your imagery?" He thrust again. "Regrets?"

I shook my head. "Um, no, none. Not even a tiny regret. Get worked up and fuck me again, please."

"Harder?" He raised an eyebrow.

I felt a rush of excitement and I nodded wordlessly.

He turned his attention back to my breast, his hips started to move in me. He scraped his teeth over my nipple.

I let out a yip.

"Want that, baby girl?" he said hoarsely.

"Yes," I whispered.

"Mmm, me too." He bit my nipple, but gently, not too much pressure.

I writhed, crying out.

He soothed his tongue over it, and then bit again, starting to move his cock in me as he did. This bite was a little harder, but the soothing was more. He continued, fucking me in a steady rhythm and using his teeth in increasing intensity on my nipple.

When he had me panting and practically sobbing, he went to the other nipple and did the same thing, and then I was scrabbling at his back, crying out his name, jerking my hips against his as he sent me tumbling into a world of red, scalding pleasure, each sensation more intense than the last.

Finally, I came, gasping, my body tender, my nipples throbbing and sore and huge, but he kept going, fucking me through my spasms and he kissed his way up my body to my shoulder.

He applied his teeth to my mark.

I went wild. "Oh, yes, yes," I said, clutching handfuls of his fur and yanking.

He grunted. "Yes?"

"Bite it, bite it, now." I groaned.

He did.

I came again, a hot gush, more intense than anything I'd ever felt, too much—pleasure that felt like it wrenched me in two.

He grunted, sinking his teeth into me there again, and he came, and he fucked me through both our orgasms, his teeth in my neck, his pelvis jerking into mine.

Finally, he was still and we both lay there, still connected, splayed out and spent.

My whole body felt like a worn-out, sparking plastorch. I was *done*.

He lifted his head to kiss me and to soothingly kiss my mark, licking it, whispering that he hadn't broken the skin, and then pulling us over, me on top of him, "so I don't smother you," he said. Then he fell asleep.

He was still hard.

The knot was still holding us together.

I wriggled on it, liking it, and curled up against his chest.

I slept too.

* * *

eventh

I woke up when Sevren's cock softened enough to slip out of me.

He didn't stir as I rolled off of him. The light was coming around the window shades, and I must not have slept for very long, not by the position of it. I didn't like the light. It was too bright.

I made myself comfortable by curling up around his body and pulling the covers over my head.

But I could still see the light, and I couldn't sleep.

I thought… my heat hadn't entirely broken, I didn't think, but I thought that knotting session had done it some good. I didn't feel as feverish, and I was a little hungry. I decided I'd go out to the kitchen area and make something light in the replicator. If I got chills or my teeth started chattering, I'd run back to Sevren.

Decided, I climbed out of bed and fished up the robe I'd worn from the shower off the floor.

Except, ugh, it was wet.

I took it off, and ventured out to find that Conlach was as good as his word and had brought us clothes! I pulled on a pair of loose pants and a flowing shirt, both made of very comfortable material. They might have also doubled as bathing suit coverups, but I didn't care. They weren't see-through, and I figured that was the kind of clothing that might be on hand at a resort.

I made my way into the kitchen, which was all windows, so many windows, and I cringed in the light, hunching up, feeling that same sensation of my heat curling up down near my spine. My head ached a little too. There were shades on the front and side windows, but none on the back, I guessed because it looked out over the bay and the horizon and whoever built these bungalows figured that the only reason you'd close the blinds was to keep people from seeing in, not to keep the light out.

Gritting my teeth, I went around yanking curtains shut and pushing buttons to pull down blinds.

And as I was doing that, I came face to face with another person on the other side of the window.

She was human, with deep brown skin and short dark hair and she looked shocked and chagrined. "Sorry!" she called through the window, her voice muffled by the clear material between us. "We were told no one was in these bungalows."

I hit a button on the side of the wall and the window slid up so that there was nothing between us. "Just got here a few hihors ago," I said. "It's no problem."

She eyed me with concern. "You're, um, here on a little vacation? For fun?"

I hesitated. Why was she asking me this? Something in her tone didn't indicate casual curiosity. Then I got it. I remembered the conversation I'd overheard while I was pretending to be asleep about the resistance and whatever it was that Conlach was up to and how we were supposed to stay clear.

She was talking again. "It's only that we thought that there wasn't anyone here, especially not on this side of the resort—"

"It's not like that," I said. "Conlach told us to stay

out of your way. Don't worry. His exact words were, 'Don't engage.'"

She went still, her expression changing. "Oh. So, you're, um, not here for a little trip away?"

"We're hiding out from a crazed gladiator who's trying to get revenge on my, um, well, it's a long story, but anyway, we're busy. We're staying in this bungalow, and we probably won't even come outside."

"I'm going to Conlach," she said. "Really, he should have told me you were here. He apparently told you things, and I don't know how I feel about that. Crazed gladiator, huh?" She bit down on her lip. "Sorry, I'll let you, um, get back to… whatever it is you're doing." She tried a smile and turned away. "I was just taking a walk out here on the deck, looking out at the bay." She turned back. "I'm Sienne, by the way."

"Eventh," I said.

She pointed at the bungalow next to us. "This one? Is it still empty?"

"As far as I know," I said.

"Great, I'll just go walk over there, then," she said, giving me a little wave. "Nice to meet you."

"Yeah," I said, although I really didn't know what to make of that exchange. I pressed the button to make the window close and then I closed the curtain and blinds and went on to finish my task.

I felt better when I had the room semi-dark, but my heat also decided it was a great time to wake up.

So, I ended up trying to program the replicator while my hips were jutting out and I was bent over the counter, rubbing my face on it. My whines must have woken up Sevren.

He was just there, behind me, soothing his big hands over my hips, pulling me up from the counter and banding one arm around me to keep my back flush against his chest. "What are you doing, baby girl?"

"Failing miserably at feeding myself," I said, sagging into him.

"You gotta let me do this kind of stuff," he said, kissing my temple.

I groaned, laying my head backwards on his shoulder. "So, I'm just an invalid now, incapable of anything because my body is trying so hard to get knocked up?"

"Yeah, that's about the way it is," he said.

"Not fair. Biology is stupid," I said. "Your species' biology is stupid. I'm going to change it. I'm going to figure out how to turn it off with hormones and take back control."

"Okay," he said. "But right now, what do you need? You want food or cock?"

I gasped, turning his arms, pressing into his firm chest. "Knot! Knot me again."

"No."

"What?" I looked up at him disbelief. "You already did it, and you can't just—"

"Because you're hungry, and we'll be stuck together," he said. "I will shallowly fuck you right here against the counter if you want, though? Or I can bundle you up in blankets on that couch and get you something from the replicator. Food or cock?"

"Cock," I said immediately, turning back around and putting my cheek back against the counter. "Cock please, now, Sevren." I whined again.

He chuckled, pressing back into me, and then he peeled down my pants to expose me, leaving them around my thighs, keeping my legs trapped close together. He reached around to rub my clit as he pressed inside me, and he did fuck me shallowly but very thoroughly, and I came twice, each time squeezing hard on his cock and letting out soft sighs of deep satisfaction.

When we were done, he picked me up and took me over to the couch and bundled me in blankets and went back to the replicator.

I snuggled in the blankets, hugging a pillow, groaning. "Mmph, I *am* hungry, but I don't want anything heavy, you know?"

"Soup?" he said.

I sighed. "Perfect." I sank into the blankets and pillows and waited.

He came over with a cup of soup and a cup of hot tea.

I grinned up at him. "Perfect," I said again.

He smiled down at me. "Eat, baby girl, you need your strength."

"So much more fucking, right?"

"A couple more days probably," he said.

I sagged into the couch. "I don't know if that sounds really, really great or just exhausting."

He sat down opposite me. "Probably both?"

"Are you eating?" I glared at him sternly over my cup of soup. "Feed yourself, Sevren, you need your strength too."

"Yeah, I'm on it." He kissed me on the forehead and went back into the kitchen.

TWELVE

I lost count of how many times I fucked her.

With my knot, without my knot, in the bed, in the kitchen, in the shower, on the balcony outside once — when it was dark and the sky was a blanket of glittering stars overhead.

I tried not to think about what it meant or what I was doing or whether I should be doing it.

She was in heat, and she needed me, and that was that.

And the other stuff I found myself doing, the stuff that got a little more forceful now and again, that was for her, too. She liked it, and I wanted to please her. Same thing with the mark on her shoulder, the one I spent too much time fondling and licking and worrying at with my teeth. It made her hot, so I did it.

It didn't have to mean anything, and I didn't have to think about it.

I especially didn't have to think about making that mark on her in the first place, which had been the antithesis of anything sexy at all, a moment of utter panic and desperation.

I shouldn't have even been there.

Dannor hadn't been pleased that I was there. He never liked me around, and especially not then, not while Belini was giving birth. But I had to be there.

Back then, if you'd asked me, I would have said I was in love with Belini, and maybe I was, maybe it was real. Maybe whatever I felt for Eventh was a thing tainted by biological urges, something that couldn't be love because it was forced by my body and by my animal instincts.

It was only that it felt so much more intense than whatever silly adolescent thing I'd felt for Belini.

The difference was, wanting Belini was about me. I wanted her because I wanted her to want me and to make me matter. If a woman like that thought I was worth something, then I would be, that was the way it was in my head. It wasn't about her. Sure, I wanted her, and sure, I was willing to do things to make her happy, but I didn't know what it was to be devoted to a person, to love her more than I loved myself, to put her first, above everything, to be willing to die or kill or lie or suffer for her.

So, Eventh, what I felt for her, it felt more real.

However, maybe it was forced. Maybe a thing like that, if it's not a choice…

Did I choose to love her?

I don't know, I thought I did. The bond could connect us and it could make her important to me, but I was the one responsible for the choices I'd made. I thought I chose her again and again, and the first time I did was that moment when I bit her.

Of course I didn't bite Eventh for herself, not then, I did it for Belini, and I did that because I wanted Belini to want me, even then.

I don't know how I thought it could even still be possible. Belini had never returned my affections and she'd always been obsessed with Dannor.

When I first found that lab where they were being held captive, it was because I was off exploring, neglecting my chieftain duties, which I seemed to always find any and every excuse to do. I'd made excuses for my wanderings, saying that I was exploring to look for things for the village and for my clan, but the truth was that I just wanted to see what was out there.

I'd found the lab, which was tunneled into the side of a mountain, and I'd crawled through the air ducts that crisscrossed the place, and that was how I'd found Belini's cell.

Immediately, I wanted to rescue her. It was a story I'd heard so many times, about the hero who rescues the girl and then they live happily ever after together. She was human and pretty and—even to a kid like me, in the middle of nowhere—the allure of a human girl, the species most desired by the Toth, it was like some fantasy come to life.

But Belini wouldn't leave without Dannor, and I went to find him for her sake.

I got them both out. We crawled through the air ducts together, and the Toth never knew what had become of them, not even when I went back to the lab after Eventh went into heat that first time and bargained for suppressants.

Belini was pregnant with another man's child, which you'd think would have clued me in to the fact that she was taken, but I was relentless in my pursuit of her. No wonder Dannor never liked me. I was such a gratts back then, really.

So, when Belini went into labor, I was there. Not with her, but outside the hut, pacing and worrying and waiting. And when the baby was born and she was convulsing in seizures and turning purple, and Belini was screaming at Dannor about those injections they'd gotten, I didn't really think, I just… bit.

I remember wresting the baby out of Belini's arms.

She screamed at me, "What are you doing?"

I put my mouth on the baby's shoulder and bit down, and there was blood, and Belini let out this horrible sound, and Dannor tore Eventh out of my arms and handed her off and tackled me to the ground and probably would have strangled me.

But Belini was holding the baby and saying, "She's breathing, she's breathing."

And the sound of Eventh's healthy wails rent the air. They made my heart feel painfully razed. I couldn't handle her screaming. Never could bear it when Eventh was in any kind of distress.

I couldn't even talk about it or explain myself until Belini had the baby tucked to her breast and was feeding her and Eventh had been quiet, content.

And then I told them what I'd done. "I was thinking about Conna in the village over the ridge," I panted. "The human whose ship crashed? She could live inside the ship, but she got sick when she came outside, until she mated with the chieftain there. So, I thought… I thought maybe it's the bite, somehow, just alters humans. And she's a baby, so I mean, I can't mate to her."

"Mate?" Dannor had glared at me. "What are you talking about?"

Her blood was still on my tongue. It tasted like nexberries.

I'd explained and Dannor's solution to it all had been, "You stay away from my daughter."

But no matter how I tried, I could never stay away.

Now, she was lying in my arms, and I was buried in her body, my knot still expanded, holding us together, and she felt the way she always did, like the other part of me, like the most important aspect of the universe, like a precious gift I'd been entrusted with to protect and care for.

I ran my nose over her mark and she sighed happily.

It had been days.

Her heat wasn't breaking.

There wasn't any cause for concern. It was normal for a heat to last as long as six or seven days in some circumstances, and I remembered a couple back on Bravren who'd once extended it for nine. He'd sprawled at the bonfire afterwards, sipping his nexberry wine, talking about how chafed his cock was and it had been one of those times when a person is bragging even while he says he's suffering. He was proud and satisfied to have done it.

But I didn't want to drag this out, and I'd been doing everything in my power to make it break earlier.

Admittedly, there was one thing I hadn't done, and that was ranskked her.

But I couldn't see what difference that would make. The ranskk was me, not her. It was me losing control, going out of my head and fucking her in a blind fury. I didn't want to do it. Thinking of doing it made me feel sheer terror, so intense that I didn't want to examine it, and so I shied away from it all and *didn't* think about it.

"Mmm," she said, "are you gearing up for round two?"

"That what you want, baby girl?" My voice was dark and deep and I nosed her mark again.

She hissed. "I… I'm tired, Sevren."

"Yeah." I moved to kiss her mouth soft and quick.

"Well, let me turn you and we'll spoon, huh?" It was the best position for sleep when we were still joined with the knot, and I'd gotten adept at moving her around on it.

"I mean… just… you said we were going to try to make the heat break early, and…" She brushed her hand over my shoulder. My fur was growing back where it had been shaved, and I'd given her little abrasions from rubbing it against her accidentally. Spending time tending the little burns had turned to sex several times. Of course, she was in heat, so everything turned to sex. "Did you change your mind because you like licking my mark so much?"

I went stiff. "I don't… I do it because you like it," I muttered.

She snorted. "Um, nonsense, you like it *too*."

"I'm not trying to drag the heat out." I kissed her again. "Let's turn you."

"Wait." She stopped me. "Can we talk about that ranskking thing?"

I settled back on my knees, lifting her legs up, putting them together. "Nothing to talk about."

"Sevren," she sighed.

Carefully, I scooted around, arranging her legs as I did, moving behind her, moving her onto her side, all while still inside her. It was a little complicated, but we'd figured it out.

"I don't even know what it is," she said.

I pushed an arm under her neck and wrapped my body around hers. "It's just a thing that can happen to me when you're in heat, but I feel like it could be, uh, dangerous."

"Dangerous?" She lifted her head and twisted to look at me. "Seriously?"

"I'm not ranskking you," I said, sounding sullen. "Go to sleep."

"I guess I don't get it," she said. "Because I'd think you'd want the heat over, already."

"You just said *you* want it over," I said.

"I mean, I'm tired," she said. "And I know you wish… you think it would be better for everyone if we weren't mated."

I let out a little sigh. "You weren't asleep."

She sighed too.

"How much of it did you hear?"

"All of it." Her voice was small. "And I think I met one of the people with the resistance."

I had seen them a few times. I'd had short conversations with Conlach a few times when he'd come by to check on us. I usually went out on the porch to talk to him, usually fresh from Eventh's pussy, while she was still naked somewhere, and it was usually awkward.

I had seen the ccael a few times from far off. He was pretty distinctive, what with all the tentacles and everything. The human woman seemed to be with him. He'd had his arm draped over her shoulder once, I thought. I didn't know what it was all about, and I wasn't asking any questions, as per Conlach's instructions.

I hadn't seen any Toth, even though Conlach had indicated I would. That was fine with me. I'd rather not see any Toth, if it came down to it.

"Are you worried about whatever Conlach's doing?" I said. "Is that why you want the heat broken, so we can get out of here and away from all of that?"

"No," she said.

"I guess you just want to get back to your life," I

said. "But even if your heat breaks, baby girl, we still have Izar to deal with."

"I know," she said.

I hadn't even been thinking about that, spending too much time actively not thinking about how I felt guilty for all the indecent things I was doing with Eventh's pussy. I needed to solve that problem, and I was no closer to that.

She entwined her fingers with mine, settling her cheek against the bicep I had under her neck. "But how are you going to deal with him? You said you can't go to the police or anything? And the guild won't do anything?"

"The guild cares about their bottom line. If I was filthy rich, I'd just kill Izar and compensate the guild for their monetary loss."

"Oh," she said.

"Sorry," I said. "I don't like killing people. You shouldn't think that because of that accident in the ring with Izar's brother that I'm some kind of bloodthirsty—"

"I would never think that about you," she said. She pressed her hips back into me, something that her body did instinctively in heat. "Maybe that's why you don't want to break the heat, so that you don't have to deal with that."

I sighed, settling a little of my weight against her hips, pressing into her, giving her the pressure she needed. "It would be better, actually, to have that taken care of. It makes me crazy, you being in danger from him. And I'm so sorry that I put you in danger. This is another reason why it would be better if we weren't mated."

"Yeah," she said softly, in that same tiny voice.

"You'll break my heat and find some way to get rid of him and then you'll go off on your way and leave me again."

I settled a hand on her hip. I nuzzled her bite mark again. "I thought we said we'd try something occasional. Every few gemoons or so."

She arched into me, when I made contact with the mark. "You want that, though?"

"Uh, yeah," I said in a low, growly voice, and my cock twitched in her. I thrust a little.

She moaned. "You're not just agreeing to it for my own good or something, because you think I'm having sick and twisted sex that's bad for me?"

"I think whatever it is with *us* is sick and twisted," I rasped, and I thrust into her again.

She pushed back with her hips. "Is it?"

I nuzzled her mark. "Me being preoccupied with your scar is probably the most twisted of all."

"Mmm," she groaned, and now she was rocking into me.

I rocked back. Round two it was. "I mean, baby girl, I don't want you fucking other men. I want you all to myself."

She gasped.

"I shouldn't," I said. "Wanting you like this, having you like this… I don't even know how to accept that it's happening. I hate myself."

"No, you don't," she disagreed.

I let out a breath. "No, I don't," I agreed. "But we both know I'm bad for you."

"Do we know that?"

I licked her mark. "We do."

"Mmm, you don't *feel* bad right now," she sighed.

I rolled into her, pressing her belly-first into the bed,

rolling my hips against her. My knot stretched her pussy this way, and it made her whine. I fucked into her and she whined more, rubbing her face against the sheets.

"It would be better if we weren't mated," I said. "But if you're asking if I ever want to let go of you, the answer is never." I licked her mark, grazed my teeth over it. "You're mine," I growled.

"I like being yours," she said in a strained voice. "I like it when you knot me and possess me and stay inside me all stars-shined day, because it's *your* pussy and everything's *better* when your cock is filling it up."

I grunted, fucking her harder. "Well, that's fucked up, baby girl."

"I like it fucked up," she gasped.

"I know you do," I managed. I brought my teeth up around her scar, not really biting her, just using my teeth to play with it.

She loved that, and she bucked her hips into me, moaning, and she got wetter—so fucking wet.

"So, if the ranskking is dangerous…" she said in a scoured voice.

I grunted, biting down hard on her mark and then soothing it with my tongue while she let out a pleased cry and got even wetter. "I should do it for you, then, baby girl, huh, because you like it fucked up?"

"Yes, yes," she breathed.

I groaned.

"You're fifteen gecycles older than me," she gasped. "You took care of me when I was a baby."

"Eventh," I growled.

"You're my mate and my family and my everything, and it makes me hot to think of how problematic all this is, Sevren, so *ranskk me.*"

I was fucking her in an erratic rhythm now, probably pulling out a little hard on her pussy because my knot was stretching her, and she was probably getting a little bit hurt, but I couldn't stop. The ranskk was coming now.

Spirits, she'd forced it out of me, hadn't she?

"Should I beg you?" she said in a throaty voice.

"Yes," I said darkly.

"You like it when I beg?" Her voice was dark too, knowing, mature.

I convulsed, the rhythm of my fucking going even more erratic. I slammed into her. "Yes," I gasped. "Beg me, baby girl. Beg me *now*."

"Please," she moaned immediately. "Please, Sevren, ranskk me. Ranskk your baby girl. Ranskk your baby girl nice and *hard*."

The world went red.

THIRTEEN

I came aware of myself lying on my side in the bed.

I was alone.

I sat up, and the first thing I saw was a smear of red on the sheets. It was a long, thick line, and it went all the way up to the pillow. I put my nose to it.

Nexberries.

Eventh's blood.

Where was she?

It wasn't… it wasn't a serious amount of blood.

Oh, trying to make yourself feel better about that, huh, are you? What did you do to her?

I was already out of the bed, calling her name as I left the dim, small bedroom where we'd spent the bulk of the last few days.

I was naked, and I looked down at my body. Oh, look, more blood on me. It was smeared over my collarbone, and then I felt something dried at my chin.

So, you bit her.

"Eventh?" I called.

I moved out into the front room, and the window shades were open, and Eventh was out on the porch. She wasn't alone. She was dressed and talking to to the ccael and the human woman.

I ducked back into the bedroom before they sighted

me. I tugged on a pair of pants.

Hidosecs later, I was out on the porch and Eventh turned to me, smiling a sunny smile. I noticed the difference in her scent immediately. It was much more blunted. Her heat had broken.

Well.

That was what we wanted, wasn't it?

"Morning, sleepyhead," said Eventh. "I thought you were going to sleep for a thousand gecycles."

I wiped at my face, trying to wipe off the dried blood, embarrassed. What was I doing out here? I should excuse myself, go back inside, do something.

"This is Caspe and Sienne," said Eventh, gesturing to the ccael and the human. "This is my, um, my Sevren."

I raised a hand in greeting. "Nice to meet you both. I'm going to go…" I pointed at the door.

"No, stay," said Eventh. "I've been talking to them about what they're doing here, and I think I have an idea. It might solve all of our problems, too, yours and mine."

Solve our problems? What the spirits was she talking about?

"Don't ambush the guy right after he's woken up," said the ccael, giving me a smile.

I eyed his tentacles. He had a lot of tentacles, and they were moving while he was standing there. They weren't moving frantically around, but they drifted and undulated in the air. It was unsettling.

"I'll…" I looked down. "Put on a shirt." I disappeared back into the bungalow.

When I got back, having cleaned the blood out of my fur and wearing a shirt, the three of them were sitting on rockers on the porch, looking out over the bay.

"There he is," said the ccael. Caspe was his name, I

remembered. "More awake now?"

I sat down in one of the rockers too. "Conlach said we should stay clear of whatever it is they're planning."

"No, I know," said Eventh. "But I was curious. I was up with the sunrise this morning. I just felt…" She stretched, grinning. "Reborn."

I felt like I'd been crushed by a Plembian tirecraft, but fine. If it was energizing for her, great.

"Anyway," Eventh continued, "I made this huge breakfast—there's some still in there, if you're hungry, actually—and then I was out in the sun, eating, and I saw them walking, and we struck up a conversation and one thing led to another, and…" She shrugged.

"You're a gladiator?" said Caspe. "Eventh says they bullied you into an unfair contract and now you're past your prime with no other skills and feel trapped?"

"Trapped?" I said. Past my *prime?* I was thirty-fucking-five. "I don't think—"

"So, you enjoy fighting other men for an audience?" spoke up Sienne.

I sighed, bowing my head. "No one likes their jobs, right?"

"My point is just that you have no reason to love the Toth," said Caspe. "Look at what they've done to this entire galaxy, look at the injustices they've inflicted. The way they treat other species, as though we're not equal to them, as though the Toth are somehow superior—"

"No one likes the Toth," I said, but I was feeling irritated. "Is this some resistance recruitment spiel? Because if so, Eventh, your main objection to my continuing to be a gladiator was that it was dangerous, and the resistance sounds about ten times more dangerous."

"No, it's me they recruited," said Eventh, laughing.

"We didn't," said Sienne. "You volunteered. And it's not settled yet."

"Well, I don't need his permission," said Eventh, eyeing me.

"I thought he was your mate," said Caspe. "Conlach said you two were working through your heat out here."

"Conlach isn't good with keeping people's business to himself, is he?" said Eventh.

"He can keep quiet when he needs to," said Sienne.

"Maybe permission isn't the way I'd put it," said Caspe, shrugging. "I mean, Sienne is her own person and I would never limit her in any way, but I also, yeah, would appreciate the chance to weigh in on conversations about what happens to her body."

"What?" I spoke up.

"It's not suppose to be like *that*," said Sienne, "or *I* wouldn't be doing it."

"I'm very confused," I said, and I was glaring at Eventh, practically growling.

"Well, we can set up perimeters, and I'm happy to strangle the life out of him with my tentacles if it goes too far, which I think I said before," said Caspe. "I'm going to be there, because I'm going to be dealing." He nodded at me. "If you have specific perimeters, you let me know."

"Perimeters for what? Dealing what?"

"It's a grasic game," said Eventh. "High stakes, underground, a lure for some rich Toth noblemen."

Grasic was a game that was played with a special holoboard and a set of a certain kind of holochips. There were lots of permutations of it, and all of them involved various levels of betting. High stakes grasic games could get into huge amounts of credits, the kind of thing that could buy and sell planets.

"Why is the resistance hosting grasic?" I said.

"We're trying to get a certain Toth here," said Caspe. "A Toth with secret knowledge about a certain hidden weapons cache. We're going to fix the game towards a certain outcome, get him nice and liquored up, and hope that he'll be happy to brag to a pretty girl."

"Me," said Eventh, grinning at me.

"We had another girl lined up," said Sienne. "But she fell through. She wasn't human anyway. I'm going to be there, and he might talk to me, but we have it on good authority that Eventh here is more his type."

"It's no big deal," said Eventh. "I just sit on his lap and flirt with him. Maybe let him grope me a little, kiss me, that kind of thing—"

"Okay, so here is where we'd set perimeters," broke in Caspe, gesturing with two tentacles.

"And I'd get paid," said Eventh. "I said that you really needed the credits, and they agreed to give me all of the entry fees that they're charging the players to enter the game. Then I'll give it to you, and you can use it to pay off the guild, like you were talking about."

My lips parted.

"It's good, don't you think?" she said. "I mean, unless you don't actually want to kill Izar, which I would understand. I mean, you really aren't bloodthirsty, and I know that you don't want to be—"

"I don't have any problem killing him," I said in a low voice. "He deserves it, and it's probably better for him anyway. He's lost it. He's in need of putting down."

"This is the gladiator that you two are hiding out

from?" said Sienne. "The one trying to kill Eventh?"

"Conlach told you this?" I said. "He really isn't good at keeping his mouth shut, is he?"

Caspe laughed. "Well, maybe he's a little chatty, sure."

"But, baby girl, I don't need you to get me credits," I said, shaking my head. "And definitely not like this."

"Well," said Eventh, "if it's some matter of pride or something—"

"That's not what it is," I interrupted.

"Maybe we should let you two talk it over in private," said Sienne.

"Sure," said Caspe.

"There's nothing to talk over," said Eventh. "He has no say over what I do."

"He's not your mate?" said Caspe.

"Not really," said Eventh.

I let out a huff of air.

"Isn't that right, Sevren?" said Eventh.

"Yeah," I said, nodding. "It's right. I have no say over what you do." My voice was dull. "And I guess you do want to get back to your life at some point, and this will be the easiest way to take care of Izar."

"Exactly," said Eventh.

"I don't think I really need to be part of this conversation, then." I stood up.

"Um, Caspe, let's let them talk alone," said Sienne, getting up as well.

"No, no," I said. "You guys have at it." I nodded. "Sit down, really." I pointed. "This breakfast you were talking about, Eventh? It's in the kitchen?"

"Yeah," she said brightly. "But you don't have to go."

I shrugged. "You want me to stay? You think I want

to hear all the details about you getting groped by some Toth? No thanks." I went inside.

I found the food.

It was cold. I didn't care. I ate it anyway, barely tasting it. I didn't know what to think or feel at the moment. I hated this plan of hers. I hated it.

And had no right to hate it.

Besides, it was for a good cause, right? Get some weapons away from the Toth and into the hands of the resistance? I couldn't get in the way of that.

What the spirits had happened during the ranskk?

Had that... was that any part of why she was acting like this, why she was so insistent that I had no say over what she did? Even if I wasn't her mate, and she wasn't mine, I still cared about her, and I could have some input if she did things like this, right?

But it was just like her, actually.

I'd found her being fucked by two different guys and she didn't care about what anyone did with her body.

Including you.

I felt ill.

She was back inside in twenty hidosecs, and she found me in the kitchen, still eating.

I wanted to touch her. I was used to touching her. She'd needed me touching her all this time, needed me to put pressure on her body and soothe her and to... to fuck her.

Now, she wasn't in heat, and I shouldn't.

I looked at her and then looked away, setting down the fork I was using to eat the breakfast casserole she'd made in the replicator. "Where did I bite you?"

"You don't remember?"

"I don't remember anything about being in a ranskk."

"Oh," she said, surprised. She came over and sat down next to me. I was at a stool at a raised breakfast bar that served as the only table in the bungalow. "Well, I guess I maybe should have realized since you went all grunty and nonverbal." She laughed a little. She pulled aside her shirt to show me her mark. It was freshly bitten into, teeth marks over the marks I'd made before. They were scabbed over, not even bandaged.

I got the urge to take her into my arms and use my tongue on it, lick it to soothe it and to encourage healing there. I did actually have coagulants in my saliva. It was a thing with my species. But she looked scabbed up already.

Maybe I'd licked it a lot during the ranskk, after the bite?

"I'm sorry," I said, looking away.

"No need. When you did it, it made me have a crazy orgasm and then you licked it and I just came and came and came, and that was when my heat broke."

I nodded. "Right. Well, I'm glad it worked."

"You don't seem glad at all."

"I am." I nodded. "This… all of this… it's better if it's over with."

"We don't have to stop fucking just because I'm not in heat anymore," she said. "I mean, I am menstruating now which does put a little crimp in things, but I'm game for shower sex or sucking you off or —"

"No." I shook my head. "No, that's…"

She raised her eyebrows. "You grossed out because I'm bleeding?"

My jaw twitched. "That's definitely it, baby girl. You see right through me." Oh, when had I gotten this sarcastic, and why was I taking it out on her, anyway? Why not keep fucking her, really? What did it matter?

She folded her arms over her chest and surveyed me. "I don't understand you at all."

I sighed. "Well, I guess you don't really need to, do you? I'm not your mate. I have no say over what you do. There's nothing here, Eventh. So, don't worry about it."

Her mouth tightened and she looked hurt.

I went back to my plate and started eating again. "This is good. You programmed this into the replicator yourself? I didn't see it on the menu."

"I, um..." Her voice was tight, but she took a deep breath, recovering. "Yeah, I guess it's one of my hobbies. I try to find ways to use certain spices and keep that plastic replicator-y taste out of it."

"It's amazing. Delicious, really. Sorry you've been eating the shit I've been making it spit out."

"No, you've been—" She broke off.

I looked up at her.

She wiped at her eye. "You were very good at taking care of me." Her lower lip was trembling.

You made her cry. I felt it like the bolt of a blaster beam to my gut. I hated it when she cried. I didn't know if I'd ever been the source of her crying before. What the hell was wrong with me? My lower lip started trembling too. I got up too fast, knocking over the stool.

"Oh," she said. "Let me help you—"

"I got it." I set it upright. "It's fine. Uh, I'm going to take a shower."

"Yeah," she said softly. "That's, yeah, you're probably sick of having my smell all over you."

I choked. *Did* I want to take a shower? Her potent scent *would* be gone then.

She looked up at me, wiping at her eye again.

"What?"

I shook my head. My chest was tight.

"Would you go away, please, before I just fall apart in front of you?" she said, furious, on the verge of tears.

"I'll give you some privacy," I whispered. "Spirits know, you haven't had any in days."

FOURTEEN

eventh

I wished I hadn't pushed for the ranskk.

I wished my heat hadn't broken.

I missed him.

He let me have the big bedroom, the loft, up the stairs, with all the windows, and I wished I was back in the small bed we'd shared, which would maybe smell like him, smell like *us*, and where I could relive every hisec of our bodies being joined.

But it was all stupid, because…

Because there was another part of me who was deeply relieved it was over, and who relished the sweet relief of being able to stand in the sun and whose body was glad enough not to be twisting into contortions, waves of heat running through me, shivering, being needy and desperate and so, so horny.

It was over. I was glad.

I didn't understand why it had to mean that everything was different with us, though. Maybe it was my fault. I'd been so mouthy with him that night before he ranskked me, saying all kinds of things that had felt really hot and good at the time but which I looked back on now with a bit of discomfort.

Like, it *was* weird that he'd been my childhood playmate and best friend and that I'd grown up being toted around on his shoulders and that now I was begging him, *Ranskk your baby girl?*

That was…

I mean, what *was* that?

Maybe I'd just pushed him too far, and he didn't know how to live with himself.

I didn't even know what I wanted from him.

We'd already had the discussion about how he didn't fit into my life and I didn't fit into his. We'd already both determined there were tons of reasons we couldn't be together.

So, I shouldn't want *anything* from him.

Except I did want something.

I simply didn't know what it was.

And the way he was treating me now, mostly ignoring me, spending his time tracking down Izar and making his plan for how he was going to go after him? It hurt.

I would have thrown myself into preparing for the grasic game, but there wasn't really much to do in order to prepare. I didn't even really need to know much about the rules of grasic, because I wasn't playing, I was just flirting with the Toth. I did study up, though, even though I already knew the basics, because it was something to do.

I made food in the replicator, and we both ate, but he shoveled food in his mouth while staring at the holodisplay of a borrowed bracelet and we didn't talk. We slept separately and we only exchanged words here and there about things that didn't matter.

Finally, one night, I couldn't handle it, and I slammed my hand down on top of his bracelet, pushing down his holodisplay, and I said, "You said you never wanted to let go of me."

His gaze flicked up to mine, surprised, confused. "What?"

"When we were... when we were having sex, you said—"

"People say all kinds of things during sex, baby girl," he said. "I'm not holding you to the things you said."

I drew back, because hadn't I been thinking about how I'd said stuff that made me uncomfortable?

He looked away, and then started to pull his bracelet back up.

"Don't," I said. "We need to talk."

He blew out a long, low breath. "Women always want to talk," he muttered.

"We *need* to," I said.

He shrugged. He fiddled with his fork. "What about?"

"Just... us, I guess."

"Is there an 'us'?"

I licked my lips. Why had I started this conversation? "I mean, yes, there is. We're, you and me, we've been through something together, and we..."

He glanced at me again and then away.

"Sevren, there will always be an 'us.'"

He nodded slowly. "Yeah, sure, I guess so. It's just, uh, it's awkward now is all. When I look at you, I think about all the things I did and said, and I feel..."

"What do you feel?"

He shrugged again.

"Well, do you want me?"

His head snapped up. "What? What kind of question is that?"

"I don't know. Answer it."

"No." He glared at me.

"No, you don't want me, or no, you're not going to

answer the question?"

He scoffed. "Let's drop this."

"If you don't want me, just say it. You don't have to worry about hurting my feelings. I know that I'm not the sort of woman you'd probably want for yourself. I'm sure you'd want someone who was older and less… less slutty, I guess. I mean, it must kill you to think that you've only ever had sex with me, and I can't even count the number of people—"

"Eventh."

"Which is why you don't want me. So, just say it."

"We are *mated*," he snapped. "Obviously, I want you."

"That's not the same thing."

"Fine." He raised his gaze to mine, looked deep into my eyes, and said it, in a very even, matter-of-fact voice. "I do not want you, Eventh Johns."

I pulled back, letting out a little gasp. "Fuck you."

"You just asked me to—"

"I want the truth."

"Okay, well, I don't know what that is."

"You either want me or you don't."

"Do *you* want *me*?"

My jaw worked. "Yes. I'm in love with you."

He let out a harsh, noisy breath. "No, you're not."

I was going to start crying. "M-m-maybe I'm not. I don't know. I never felt anything like this, and now you won't even look at me, and it's killing me, and—"

"Shh," he said, his voice going soothing, like when I'd been in heat. He reached over and pulled me into his lap.

I sobbed in relief, curling up there, grabbing a fistful of his shirt, pressing my face into his chest. He still smelled like coffee and branciuth sap, but it wasn't nearly as pronounced as it had been when I was in heat.

He wrapped his arms around me and settled his chin on the top of my head.

I struggled to swallow my sobs.

"I love you, baby girl," he breathed in my ear.

I let out a gasp.

"I've always loved you. I will always love you," he said.

I lifted my face. "I love you, too. I love you, Sevren, I—" I put my mouth on his.

He kissed me, a soft, sweet kiss, our tongues dancing. And then he pulled away. "Spirits. I wasn't supposed to say that to you."

"But—"

"No, baby girl, because I know I love you, and I know I want you, and I know when my cock is inside you, it's the best thing I've ever felt, but I..." He shook his head.

"But you want someone who doesn't do gang bangs?"

"Baby girl, you don't need to keep doing that."

"You don't like it when I bring it up. Just admit that I'm too much of a slut for you—"

"There is nothing you could ever do or say or be that would make me stop loving you," he said evenly.

I drew back, letting out a little noise.

"You don't need to push like that. I know you think that you did something, but this distance with us, it's not your fault. You don't need to test the limits to see what's going to push me away. That's not why I left. It's not why we can't..."

A long silence.

"Can't what?" I whispered finally.

"Be, uh, together, I guess."

"So, then why?"

He rubbed the fur on his face the wrong way, shaking his head. "I don't think all the pieces of us fit together into anything." He rubbed it back down.

I let out another noise. My lower lip was starting to tremble.

"We're not really mates. We're not in love. There's nowhere to go from here. We already talked about it. So, don't you think it'll be easier if we just make it about heat? When you're not in heat, I'm just your… older family friend."

"Fuck that," I said. "You have never been that. No one in my family really even likes you, for one thing. My mom, I think she feels sorry for you, and my dad hates you, and I—"

"Okay, well, whatever I am, when you're not in heat, it's not sexual. Doesn't that make it easier?"

"No."

"It makes it easier for me, then." His voice was hard.

I swallowed.

"How do you want it to be different?"

"I don't know," I said. "I just thought…" I leaned in and kissed him again, and he kissed back. I rested my forehead against his. "Couldn't we just pretend I was still in heat now? Couldn't we sleep close or do this? Kiss and touch each other?"

He sighed. "That's what you want?"

I eyed him. If I said yes, would he do it?

He touched my face, gazing into my eyes, and I knew the answer to that question.

I climbed out of his lap. "You'd do it for me."

He looked up at me.

"You'd be close to me because I wanted it. That's

what you do. You always have. But what about what *you* want?"

He looked away.

"Do you even have things you want, Sevren? Things that are just for you, that aren't about me?"

He didn't answer.

I shook my head.

"When I want you, it's for me," he said softly. "I can't make myself believe that sticking my dick in you is, uh, is doing you any favors."

"But—"

"When you were in heat, I guess…"

When I was in heat, then he could justify it, because I was so needy. "So, that's why it's easier for you not to touch me now."

"I'm not good for you," he said.

"Maybe you could be."

"No, we talked about how being close to me will fuck with your suppressants and throw you into full heats once a gemoon, and how you can't possibly have that kind of interruption in your schooling and your research. And you told me the research was the reason you get up in the morning."

I found I had nothing to say to that.

"Would I like to take you back to Bravren and ranskk you till you were pregnant? Would I like to keep you pregnant or nursing for eight or ten gecycles, and for us to have five kids? For you to be at my side while I'm the chieftain of the clan? Would I like to wake up with you in my arms every morning? Would I like you to be really mine? *Really* my mate? Are you asking if that's what I want for myself?"

I took a step backwards.

"It's not," he said. "I'd never do that to you. I'd

never make you give up your life or drop out of school or any of that. I couldn't want it, because I never want things you don't want. I… is that because I love you, or because the bond makes me… I don't even know."

"I meant… a thing you want for yourself that has nothing to do with me," I said. "Do you have things like that?"

It was his turn to be quiet.

And the silence stretched on and on.

"You know, baby girl, I'm very glad we talked," he muttered sarcastically.

"You gratts," I said, glaring at him.

"The grasic game is two nights from now. I don't see any reason to wait to go after Izar, though. You'll be safe here. There's so much security. I'm going to leave in the morning. I'll kill him, and then when I come back, you'll have the credits, and that'll be that. This will all be done. You get in touch when you want to go into heat again, I guess, and we'll meet up, like we talked about."

"Oh. So, that's just it?

He nodded. "Isn't it?"

* * *

sevren

"How'd you decide to buy this resort?" I was standing in the doorway to Conlach's office, which was at the bottom of the hill below the cliff where the bungalows were located. The shore, a little beach where the deep blue water of the bay lapped gently against the land, was visible from the window. It was morning. I'd left without waking Eventh.

I didn't know what to say to her.

Conlach was bent over a replicator which was spitting out coffee. "Had the credits, seemed like a nice

156

place. I didn't overthink it, to be honest."

"You didn't want to go back to Jenthe?"

"You ever been to Jenthe?"

"It's a desert planet, right?" I said. "Uh, except the Colony, which is an oasis. Is it… awful?"

"Awful is stating it nicely," he said, laughing. "Eh… I volunteered to take the gladiator post for the sake of the child king of my tribe out there. He was too young, and I said I'd do it in his place. Turned out, six or seven gecycles later, the bastards got him anyway. He was in the arena for gecycles. It was pointless, the sacrifice I made. Did nothing."

"That's rough," I said.

Conlach shrugged. "And, uh, if I'd gone back to Jenthe, it would have been like that again. It would have been about the good of the tribe and being a martyr and more sacrifice, and I guess I was just done with that. Time to take care of myself."

"By buying a resort and working with the resistance." I bowed my head, thinking this over.

He brought his coffee over and leaned against his desk. He surveyed me. "You don't approve?"

"Maybe you can't stop sacrificing for causes, Conlach."

He snorted. "Eh, maybe not."

"But the resort? You wanted to own something like this?"

"Yeah," he said. "I like it here. It's peaceful. And I figured this was a way to live on the water in all this beauty and tranquility and still make some credits on the side. Of course, I didn't take into consideration how much work it would be. I thought, after fighting in the arena for over ten gecycles, this would be like an easy retirement."

Retirement.

I shook my head. Thirty-fucking-*five*.

Conlach had some gecycles on me, of course. I couldn't say how old he was, but we were not peers. He'd been out of the game for a while now.

"Why you asking me this?"

"I'm going to quit the arena once I get this all taken care of. I have no idea what I'm going to do with myself."

"Oh, I thought you and crazy human girl would be settling down and raising cubs. You call them cubs on your planet?"

"No," I said, shaking my head at him.

He sipped his coffee, grinning. "Not cubs."

"Not cubs. Children."

He snickered.

"And, no, it's, uh, it's not like that."

"Because she's too crazy to be a mother."

"Because of a thousand things."

"You were always out there taking care of people, you know, Sevren. You were like the surrogate gladiator mom to all the little newbies."

"I was *not*."

"I'm only saying, I always figured you for a dad someday."

"Am I a dad or a mom, then?"

"Is there really a difference? You know what I'm saying. You're, uh, nurture-y." He made a careless gesture with the hand not holding his coffee. "Like, when what's-his-face, that chamliss? You remember, started with a—" He snapped his fingers. "Gralins. You remember him? When he lost that necklace that he was all sentimental about because it was his good luck charm and you stayed up all night with him looking for it and got everyone else in on it?"

"Anyone would have done that."

"No." Conlach shook his head. "No, it's just you, Sevren."

I squared my shoulders. "I don't know what I think of that. I think I might feel a little disturbed, actually, you know, given my history with Eventh."

He flinched. "I didn't mean it like that. It's not connected, anyway. Some other man, he would have been mated to her and he wouldn't have been that way with her, like you were? You have that nurture-y thing, and so it kicked in. You would have been that way with her regardless, right? You were close to her family. Didn't you say that you spent half your time babysitting all the kids in your clan?"

"Well… but that was because she was there."

He raised his eyebrows. "Was it?"

I furrowed my brow, thinking that over. Huh. *Did* I want kids? Why was this something I'd never really thought about?

Eventh wasn't wrong when she pointed out how weird it was that I didn't have hopes and dreams for myself.

"All right, so maybe I like taking care of people, helping people," I said. "But how's that supposed to help me figure out what to do once I'm not a gladiator anymore? I will need to make credits somehow. What will I even do?"

"You know, it's not as if there aren't lots of jobs that you can do in which you help people, and then people pay you for your help."

I gave him a withering look.

"No, I mean it. People appreciate being able to compensate someone for a service, also. It's better than being beholden. Help people. Charge them. It's not that hard."

I let out a laugh.

"I do not, however, recommend buying a resort like this, because it's a headache and a half."

"Or working with the resistance?"

He shrugged. "Well, what can I say? That's been kind of fun."

"The ccael doesn't weird you out?" I said.

He shrugged. "We all look weird to someone."

"You think he… those tentacles, does he…?" I decided not to finish that question. "Uh, anyway, I basically came by to ask you to look after her."

"Protect her from the ccael?"

"No, he seems pretty… he and that other human… just, you know about the game and everything and what she's going to be doing."

"We're talking about Eventh, right?"

I nodded. "I know she's…" I used my toe to draw a circle on the floor. "I know it's no big thing for her to sit on some Toth's lap and be, uh…" I looked up at Conlach. "Like you keep saying, she's a crazy girl. But still, *I* worry."

"Caspe won't let anything happen," said Conlach. "It's his girl on the line, too, and he's incredibly protective of her."

I nodded. "I'd stay and watch over her, but…"

"But if you did, you'd stop it? Wouldn't be able to handle some man with his hands all over her?"

"Basically."

"This is what I mean about crazy women, Sevren."

"Right, well, it's a biological mating bond, so I'm kind of screwed here."

He laughed. "That's a good excuse, I guess."

"You'll keep an eye on her, then?"

"Of course," said Conlach. "And you be careful with Izar. Don't underestimate him."

"Of course not," I said. And I hadn't underestimated him. I'd checked to see if he'd tracked me—if he'd found evidence of that fuel station Eventh and I robbed or anything like that, and he hadn't. I'd covered that up myself. Of course, doing some of that, there had been a tiny chance that my movements had been tracked, and that someone could have figured out where we were, but only a tiny chance.

And besides, Conlach had security here. That was the entire reason we were here. It was safe here.

"Thanks for everything, buddy," I said to him. "The bungalow and everything, it was just what we needed."

"Glad to be of service," he said, grinning.

We shook hands and I took off.

The sun was still working its way into the sky, reflecting bright on the bay. I sped off in a a speeder I borrowed from Conlach, off after Izar.

FIFTEEN

I woke up and Sevren was nowhere to be found.

I went looking for him and found Conlach instead, who herded me back up the cliff. "You can't be down here. You need to stay up and away, tucked into the bungalow. We can control who can get in up there, and you are safer, and Sevren would not be pleased if I let something happened to you. I promised him I'd keep an eye on you. Where the sands are you going anyway? I thought you were staying here and helping with the grasic game."

"Where *is* Sevren?" I said. "I'm looking for Sevren."

"Oh." Conlach sighed. "Well, he could have told me he ran off and left you without so much as a goodbye. Maybe you got reason to be crazy, girl."

"Look, I'm not crazy," I said. "You don't get to judge me. You don't know what I've been through or how difficult it's been to be mated to someone since the day I was born."

Conlach looked me over. "The world's a bed of jelxa spikes, girl. Everyone's got some sob story or other. Crazy is as crazy does."

I decided this was not the salient point of this conversation. "So, he left."

"He left," said Conlach.

"He say if he's coming back?" I said.

"He didn't talk with you at all about it."

"I mean..." Maybe he did. In a general, roundabout way. "Was he going after Izar?"

"That was the plan, I thought, yeah," said Conlach.

I sighed heavily. "Well... I guess I'll go back up to the bungalow and be alone, then." It honestly wasn't that much different than it had been when he'd been there recently, anyway, since we hadn't been doing a lot of talking and everything had gotten odd after my heat broke. Truthfully, it was odd before my heat broke also, just in a different way.

"Hey," he said, "uh, I don't mean to pry, and you can tell me it's none of my business, but I gotta say, I've always been curious about whatever happened. What'd he do to you?"

"What?" I said.

"When he ran off and joined the guild to get away from you? Is that why you're screwed up? Because he did something inappropriate when you were a little girl? Like what did he do to you? Did he, uh..."

"*No.*" I drew myself up. "Of course he didn't do that. He never touched me in any way that was even remotely gross when I was a kid."

"Oh," said Conlach, furrowing his brow. "No?"

"Did he tell you he did?"

"I just figured there's some reason why he hates himself so much," said Conlach, sighing. "Never mind."

"No, why *does* he hate himself?" I said. "Why can't he...?" I clenched my hands into fists. "You know, I *do* have a reason to be crazy."

Conlach smirked. "Don't we all, though?"

I went back up to the bungalow and made myself

something on the replicator. I was so used to having Sevren around that I made two portions. This depressed me, and so I ate both portions.

I didn't know what was wrong with me, really.

That conversation I'd had with him where he'd talked about keeping me barefoot and pregnant, his little woman in the village, it…

I knew that was the life of a lot of the girls I'd grown up with, and I didn't even think it was a bad life, necessarily. It depended on how you were built, I guessed. There was this girl named Missa who'd I'd grown up with who had fallen in capital L love with this other guy in the clan, and they ended up mating way earlier than their parents or anyone else thought was wise, when they were both eighteen gecycles, and she had her first baby by the time she was nineteen.

They were really happy, though.

I've heard people say that sort of happiness is being content with a simple life, but it didn't seem to me that there was anything simple about having children and living in the village. Though we weren't entirely primitive out on Bravren, we still relied on hunting, gathering, and a certain amount of farming to feed ourselves. We didn't have replicators or food stores or restaurants. It wasn't like the city. Just surviving on Bravren was a job in and of itself. It wasn't simple. It was hard work, consuming work, and raising children at the same time only made it harder.

So, I didn't buy that simple business.

I just wasn't built to find it satisfying, I guess. The thing about the life on Bravren was that it was demanding but that it wasn't innovative. There wasn't much room for discovery. You did what your parents had done and their parents before them. It was all about tradition and belonging to the clan.

I could see how that *could* be satisfying, being part of something bigger than yourself, assuming the clan as your identity, being absorbed into the warm arms of togetherness and acceptance.

It was just…

Well, maybe it was because I was human, except I didn't think so, because my parents seemed to love being part of the clan, and I had met Conna, from the wovrn clan over the ridge, and she was the mate of their chieftain, and she loved it too.

I needed to have my own identity. I needed to distinguish myself in some way. And I never felt as alive as I did when I was working on solving some problem or trying to figure out something that no one else had figured out yet.

I wasn't going to be happy doing what women had done for generations and generations before me — having a husband and having babies and… existing until I withered away.

I needed something else.

It was only that, with Sevren, all my life, really, but especially when I was in heat and he was taking care of me, I felt a different thing. I felt distinguished and important and singular, but not for anything I did, just because I was *his*.

It felt so good.

It broke me that it was gone.

Why couldn't I somehow have both things? Why couldn't I have Sevren *and* my research? That should be possible, right? Women did that. This wasn't the dark times, a few generations ago, when all the women were dead and the Toth were locking us up and turning us into baby-making machines.

I was contemplating this and also feeling sick because I'd eaten way too much replicator food (and somehow also considering that I might have room for some kind of dessert if I wanted to program that into the replicator) when Sienne showed up at the door to the bungalow.

"Is everything okay?" I said. "Has something gone wrong with the plans for the game?"

"No, everything's fine," said Sienne, laughing. "Don't jinx us, Eventh, stars."

"Sorry." I laughed a little. "You want to come in?" I stepped out of the doorway.

She followed me in. "I actually was just, um, wondering if you had any extra spermicide patches."

"Oh," I said. "Yeah, definitely. Hold on, I'll go and grab some for you."

"One's fine," she said. "The resort store is out, and I like to have one for emergencies is all."

Only one? I blinked at her.

She shifted on her feet, embarrassed. "I mean, because—"

"It's fine," I said. "I'm sure you guys are just too stressed to get it on or whatever, and that's why you only want one. You'll have to forgive me. I was just in heat, and it was nonstop, and... I've never been in an actual relationship, so I don't even know what it's like." I flushed. "Never mind." I hurried out of the room and went to find the spermicide patches.

When I got back, I held out two of them. "In case there's two emergencies?"

She chuckled, shaking her head. "There won't be." She took them. "But, uh, I feel compelled to say that it's not because we're too stressed. I don't know why, but I guess it's a point of pride. Everything is very, uh, steady and healthy and vigorous in, um, that department of our lives."

"Okay," I said, eyeing her. "Well, then I think I'm going to be compelled to ask why only one? If you have an implant, you should know that they're extremely effective—"

"No, I don't have an implant. Those things make me feel like I have a big clear dome over my head or something."

"Huh," I said, shrugging. "I'm curious about that. What kind of implant did you have?"

"Uh, I tried a couple. They were all that way."

"Maybe it's estrogen suppression," I said. "Sometimes people can be sensitive to that. I've been toying with an implant that's primed to only release hormones a day or so before ovulation, instead of a constant stream. That way, you're only getting an influx of progesterone for a few extra days besides during the luteal phase, which is when you're progesterone dominant anyway."

She blinked at me. "Are you like a science genius?"

"I'm a student," I said. "But, yeah, I got my scholarship because I'm working on experimental birth control and heat suppressants."

"Right, because… why do you have a heat anyway?"

"Well, you still never explained to me why you only need one patch."

She cringed. "Oh, because it's a big thing for Caspe to, you know, ejaculate."

"But you just said that you were very steady and vigorous," I said, raising my eyebrows.

She lowered her voice. "Okay, when ccael ejaculate, their penises fall off."

I stiffened. "What?"

"It's hotter than it sounds?" She cleared her throat. "So, like, he doesn't do that often. Usually, he just uses one of his other, um, appendages for, you know…"

"Oh," I said in a different voice, thinking of the tentacles, *all* of the tentacles, and the way they moved around and the suction cups and… "You're a lucky woman, aren't you?"

She shrugged. "I mean, can't complain." Then she gave me a very big grin and let out a giggle.

I might have giggled too. "Well, take two spermicide patches anyway. For the future."

"Thanks," she said, tucking them both away. "So, your heat?"

"Yeah, my body got mutated by a mating bond when I was a baby. It was an accident. Sevren saved my life. He didn't mean for us to be all…" I intertwined all of my fingers and wriggled them.

"So, how often do you go into heat? Usually, it's like every four gemoons or so, right?"

"Once a gemoon," I said. "Like a human menstrual cycle."

She made a face. "Sounds horrible." She considered. "Or not? Is it actually great?"

I giggled again. "I don't even know. This was my first real heat. I've been on suppressants my whole life, but this one broke through, and we didn't have any choice."

"Yeah, he's your not-mate that has no say over what you do," said Sienne. "I don't mean to pry or anything. We don't have to talk about it."

"Nothing to talk about," I said.

"So, you're both happy with that arrangement?" she said. "Because, none of my business, but he didn't sound that happy about it, if you want to know the truth."

"Oh, fuck him," I muttered. "He left me this morning without even saying goodbye."

She flinched. "Ouch. Sorry."

"It's impossible, anyway," I said. "We can't ever be together."

"Sometimes, impossible things can work out," said Sienne. "Caspe and me, we were archenemies."

"Archenemies?"

"Well, we hated each other and tried to ruin each other's lives for a long time before we started fucking, and then, it was only hate sex, nothing besides that, and then… well, long story, but *now*, sometimes, when I'm putting on these patches, I get a pang."

"What kind of pang?"

"An I-want-babies-with-this-man-sooner-than-is-intelligent pang?"

"What's the problem?" I said. "He doesn't want kids?"

"I think he does," she said. "And I do too, but not yet. I want to keep doing our work for the resistance. I guess I could keep fighting the Toth and be a mom at the same time, but…"

It made me think of having my research and being with Sevren at the same time. "But that would be hard," I said.

"Really hard," she said. "And dangerous. It's one thing to put myself in danger, but to put my child in danger? How can I do that?"

"Sure," I said. "Sure, I get that."

"I know I'm making the right decision," she said. "But still, I get that pang, and it hurts worse every time I feel it. I won't hold out forever."

"But then you and Caspe will have kids and quit the

resistance, and you'll live happily ever after," I said. "You know that's going to happen."

"I hope that's going to happen," she corrected. "But you feel like you don't have a happily ever on your horizon, is that it? You're bitter?"

"It's impossible," I said again.

"But you want it? Because I think he wants you, too, so what's in the way with you guys, huh? Maybe you just need to talk—"

"No, we tried to talk," I said. "It didn't matter. There are problems. If I'm near him, my suppressants don't work, and I can't live like that, and he's kind of way too old for me, and I grew up like he was my, I don't know, *not* my brother, but my family, and whatever it is with us, he's convinced it's *wrong* or something, but it doesn't *feel* wrong."

Sienne furrowed her brow. She started to speak.

"I guess it's just complicated," I cut her off. "I don't really want to talk about it."

She eyed me. "Are you sure? Because I'm here to listen."

"I'm sure."

"And I'm kind of dying of curiosity. How much older than you is he?"

"Fifteen gecycles."

She considered. "That's... yeah... I mean..." She shrugged. "But whatever, that doesn't make it impossible. And he's *not* your family, is he?"

"No, but I guess to him, it feels... he was fifteen when I was born. He took care of me when I was a baby. He gets guilty. And then he gets so guilty that he abandons me. Over and over again."

"I get that," said Sienne.

"You do?"

"Well, being guilty. I get *that*. I had a brother who was killed, and I blamed myself for it," said Sienne.

"Oh, wow, I'm so sorry," I said.

"I did stupid things because of it," she said. "I felt guilty and I kept trying to punish myself. I put myself in danger, and Caspe saved me. More than once. But I saved him too. We saved each other. Maybe your wvorn's going to realize he's being stupid and come back to you."

"Maybe," I said quietly.

"In the meantime, you will have revolutionized birth control and heat suppressants for the entire galaxy." She grinned at me.

"I'm not even close to a revolution," I said.

"Well, I think you'll get there," she said. "And I think it's important what you're doing. I, for one, appreciate having the choice. Otherwise, it's like biology is destiny or something, and it's good to be empowered in that way."

"What do you mean?"

"Just that if we didn't have contraception, I'd be forced to have babies, and it's cool to rise above that and have agency over my body and my life and all that. You're doing good work. I think you're doing things that can make the galaxy a better place."

I smiled. "Thanks." I wanted to keep doing that. Why did I also want Sevren so badly?

"Choices are good, Eventh," she said. "I hope your wvorn makes the right choice and comes back to you." She grinned. "Thanks for the spermicide patches."

* * *

sevren

Izar wasn't there.

I'd come all this way, and he was nowhere to be

found.

The gratts had tricked me.

There was his bracelet, sitting right out on the bed. I'd tracked that here, all right, assuming it would be attached to him, but he wasn't here.

It hadn't been a terrible assumption to assume he'd be here—which was my own quarters in the gladiator barracks. When I'd tracked him down and discovered his bracelet here, I figured he would be here.

From his perspective, it made sense. He couldn't track me anymore, so he'd figured I had to come home eventually. Of course he'd go there and wait for me.

I had made an elaborate plan of how I was going to draw him out, because I didn't want to get into an altercation on the guild's property. It was better for us to go elsewhere.

Drawing him out wasn't ideal, because honestly, the best way to deal with him would have been to sneak up on him and put a plasknife in the back of his skull while he was sleeping or something.

But if I'd done that, then there would have been a conspicuous body, and the guild wouldn't have been pleased.

So, instead, I made my elaborate plan.

I traveled straight to the barracks that day, and I skipped check in and went in through a back way, so that the guild wouldn't know I'd come back. It hadn't been easy finding the codes to get through those doors and override the locks and permissions. That, in and of itself, had taken me the better part of two days.

Once inside, I crept through the corridors, ducking out of sight the hidosec I heard voices, hiding in alcoves and bathrooms while other gladiators ambled along to head for training or to get food or to prepare for a fight.

It took me considerably longer to get to my room than it should have taken.

When I got there, it was empty.

Empty except for his bracelet, of course.

On the wall, scrawled with a shaky hand, was a message that said, *I will take the thing that means most to you, just as you took it from me.*

Fuck.

I immediately got out the bracelet I was using.

But no.

I didn't want to use the bracelet here, because the guild would have a registry of the transmission if I used it on their network.

So, instead, I made my laborious way out of the barracks, again hiding whenever I saw someone, not wanting to indicate I was there at all.

And then, when I got out, I tried to contact Eventh and Conlach.

Jammed.

Not on my end, though, on theirs.

I couldn't get through to the comm in our bungalow. I couldn't get through on Conlach's bracelet either.

This horrified me.

Izar was there. He was interfering with communications there.

Desperate, I tried the main line for Conlach's resort, but an answering service picked up with a recorded message to leave a message, that regular business hours were over.

I had to go *now*.

It had taken me two Kalion sun-cycles to get here in the first place, though admittedly, a lot of that time had been taken up in getting to the space station where the barracks were located, and the extra time had been because of wanting not to leave a trail, so I'd had to get a ticket under an assumed name, and I'd had to acquire the credentials to pull all that off.

So, now, with my assumed name and credentials, that would shave a good amount off the time it would take to get back to the resort.

But it was still going to take me too long.

I tried again to contact Conlach again, and then Eventh, and then the main resort line.

Still jammed.

Main resort line still went to a machine.

How had Izar found us?

Was it because I'd covered our tracks with the robbery and the cop-bot? It had been a tiny risk, but maybe he'd been able to exploit it.

After everything, I *had* underestimated him.

There was a decent amount of security at the resort, because Conlach hired ex-gladiators for that precise reason. And with the Toth there, he would be keeping security tight and alert.

Izar was out of his mind and taking stupid risks.

I had to hope that he'd be stopped before he could get anywhere near Eventh.

But I sure would feel better if I could warn someone or if could be there.

Because if anything happened to Eventh—

Well, nothing could happen to her.

SIXTEEN

eventh

I shook my head at the ensemble I was wearing. "This is too obvious."

Sienne was lounging on the bed in the upper bedroom in my bungalow and Caspe was in the doorway.

"Obvious is good," said Caspe. "Speaking as the only person in this room attracted to women's assets, wear that."

"Trying to make me jealous?" said Sienne, shooting him a grin.

"I didn't mean that I was specifically attracted—should I leave the room?"

"I'm going to take this off, so yes," I said.

He ducked out, closing the door behind him.

The thing I was wearing was basically two triangles that covered my breasts with some strings and then a slinky, sparkly pair of pants that clung to me like they were painted on. "We're trying to hook this guy, Sienne," I said. "Obvious is not good. We want a hint, but we want him to feel like there's something to discover."

She shrugged. "Sounds good to me." She raised her voice. "Caspe, what do you think?"

"I think when you go to watch women take off their

clothes on stage, they don't start out with much on," he called back.

"Trust me, men don't know what they want," I said, shaking my head at the door.

"Uh… I think women just make men more complicated than they are," replied Caspe, through the door. "Women overthink everything."

"Oh, you never overthink stuff," said Sienne.

He snorted, but he didn't respond otherwise.

"This thing," I said, pulling a red cape-like top over my head. "Is a tease." It was cut low in the front, and it had slits up the sides. The bottom half of the garment was all fringes, which revealed tantalizing bits of skin here and there. I was covered almost entirely but it didn't seem like I was covered. It seemed like any hisec I could turn in some way and some naughty part of me would be revealed.

"I see what you're saying," said Sienne.

"You can come back in, Caspe," I said.

He opened the door and looked me over.

"See?" I said. "The other outfit says, 'I'm a sure thing.' This outfit says, 'I have things to show you, but you can't see them yet, and you want to see them just because I've refused to show them to you.'"

He cleared his throat and turned to Sienne. "She's like a genius?"

Sienne laughed. "This is what I've been saying. Also, she does science stuff in labs and things. She's intimidating."

"I will not be intimidating," I said. "Trust me, I know how to not be intimidating. You want to be a challenge, but attainable. You want to be the promise of an adventure, something that can be conquered and enjoyed."

"You've given this a lot of thought," said Caspe.

I shrugged, going back to the mirror and fiddling with the fringes. "For a while, I guess I thought of it like my own challenge, like if I could seduce anyone, if no one was impervious to my charms, it would mean…" That I mattered? That I was worth something? That—

Stars, I was pathetic.

I glowered at myself in them mirror. "Never mind. I need to do makeup."

"Not too much," said Caspe.

"Trust me," I said, shooting him a look. "I know what I'm doing. I'm a genius, remember?"

"And humble too," he said with a grin.

I ducked my face down, embarrassed. "Sorry."

"Just teasing you," he said. "Meet us at the end of the walkway at the top of the cliff in…" He checked his bracelet. "A hihor? That good? Enough time for your makeup?"

"Absolutely. I won't need that much time."

"Then we'll leave you to it," he said.

Sienne got up off the bed and gave me a grin. "You look great. This is going to be great. Everything will be fine."

"Thanks, I needed that," I said with a sigh. I was nervous, no matter how much I was blustering and pretending to be in control of everything.

Sienne and Caspe left me, and I went into the bathroom to do makeup.

It was makeup that Sienne had gotten for me, nothing that I'd brought on my own, since I obviously had come with nothing. I didn't put too much on. I mostly concentrated on my eyes and lips. It was about accentuating and otherwise only about concealing flaws.

Done, I surveyed myself in the mirror, looking at the finished product. I looked good. I took a deep breath, still feeling nervous.

From below, there was a crash.

SEVENTEEN

eventh

I started down the steps immediately, but then I stopped myself. Stars knew what that noise was, and I wasn't going to be an idiot. Going down to investigate a strange noise and calling out, "Who's there?" was not intelligent.

Instead, I retreated in my room and looked around for something that could be considered a weapon.

There wasn't a lot here, but I ended up brandishing a metal nail file from the makeup kit and descending the stairs.

As I did, I noticed that the front door was open and the breeze was coming inside, fluttering the curtains.

My heart started to pick up speed and my grip on the nail file felt a little slippery.

Maybe I should go back upstairs and shut myself in that room in there, just barricade myself in.

Right.

Barricade myself with what?

Then I'd be trapped.

No, I was *not* an idiot.

So, I hurried down the rest of the steps and rushed out the front door. I ran down the walkway, heading for the rendezvous point with Caspe and Sienne.

Except it was early, and they weren't there yet.

I didn't have a bracelet, though there was a communicator in the bungalow. Of course, to use it to contact anyone, I'd have to go back inside.

Nope. Not doing that.

I kept moving. I went all the way downstairs to Conlach's office, but it was closed up and no one was in there. There was a security guy at the main entrance, though, a big scaly looking guy—not a scarencs like Conlach, but some other lizardy-type species. I ran over to him.

"I think someone's in my bungalow," I said.

"No way," he said. "How would they get up there? This is the only way up." He pointed to the path I'd just come down.

"Well, I heard something," I said. "And the door was open. Can you just check, please?"

"I can't leave my post," he said. "But Bifg's doing the rounds. I'll get in touch with him." He turned to his bracelet and said, "Blue Team leader, come back?"

"This is Blue Leader," came a disembodied response. "What's the word?"

"I need you to swing through Bungalow Three," said the scaly guy. He turned to me, covering his bracelet. "What'd you hear?"

"It was a crash," I said.

"Like something falling over or something breaking?"

"I don't know. It was loud. I didn't make the noise and something else did."

He held up a hand and went back to his bracelet. "Blue Leader, inspect for source of a crash, possible breaking and entering."

"Copy that. Will report back."

The scaly guy gave me a smile.

I folded my arms over my chest.

He looked me over. "That's, um, a pretty top."

I gave him a withering look. Pretty, huh?

His face turned blue-ish, which might have been his species' equivalent of a blush. He looked away, shifting on his feet.

Time passed.

I waited, tapping my foot, wondering if I should go somewhere else or stay here or… "Uh, is he checking now?"

"Should be," said the scaly guy.

"So… we just wait?"

He nodded. "Yeah, he'll get back in touch once he's looked around."

"Okay."

More time passed. I peered up at the sun in the sky and then looked out at the bay. I turned to look up to the top of the cliff, which was where I was supposed to meet with Caspe. But no one was up there yet. I didn't know what time it was. I'd left all time-keeping devices behind in the bungalow.

Finally, I said, "Hasn't it been a really long time?"

The scaly guy spread his hands. "I don't know. Maybe he got held up. I'll send a query, okay?"

"What if whatever is up there got him?" I demanded.

The scaly guy let out a noise, and it sounded worried.

Oh, stars, Blue Leader, whoever he was, was probably dead on the floor of my bungalow, and maybe he'd gotten to Caspe and Sienne while he was there, and maybe he —

"Orange Leader, this is Blue Leader," came a voice from the scaly guy's bracelet.

"Blue Team Leader report," said the scaly guy into his bracelet.

"I looked all over here. I did find a rocking chair on the back porch that looks like it might have blown over. It might have made a crash. The door is open. I don't see anything otherwise, though. I looked in every nook and cranny. All the closets and even the crawl space between the kitchen and the downstairs bathroom."

"Thanks, Blue Leader, that's very reassuring. Probably just the wind."

I blew out a noisy breath. Had it just been the wind?

"Permission to check the surrounding bungalows, Orange Leader?" said Blue Leader. "Best to be thorough."

"Permission granted. Report if you find anything."

"Will do," said Blue Leader.

The transmission ended and the scaly guy turned to me. "Well, there you have it."

I bit down on my lip.

"Hey," he said, "you did exactly the right thing, okay? Coming down here, having us check into it. You're right to be wary. But it looks like we're in the clear."

"I don't know," I said, still feeling nervous.

"Why don't you stay down here with me instead of going back up there until he's checked all the bungalows," said the scaly guy.

"Yeah," I said, nodding. "Yeah, I'd feel better if I did that."

"Great," he said.

But now, I didn't know what to do with myself. I thought about striking up a conversation with the scaly guy, just to have something to do.

Around that point, Conlach appeared, all dressed for

the evening. He approached us, looked me over and said, "That's a pretty top."

I rolled my eyes.

"Yeah, that's what I said," said the scaly guy.

"Sevren's a lucky guy," said Conlach. "But why are you down here and not in your bungalow?"

"I heard a noise," I said, and now I was starting to feel stupid. "I didn't know what it was, and so I came down here."

"We're checking into it," said the scaly guy. "We didn't find anyone in the bungalow, but Mick's looking through the empty ones up there to make sure it's all clear."

"Oh, good," said Conlach. "I'd don't see how anyone would get up there."

"That's what I said," said the scaly guy. "You're just… like you're reading my mind." He grinned at Conlach.

Conlach laughed and slapped the other man on the upper forearm. "Well, you know what they say about great minds, yeah?"

The scaly guy chuckled.

Conlach nodded at me. "I'm going to head up there and nose around myself." He got a blaster out from inside of his jacket, gave us a nod, and headed up the path.

A little while later, Blue Leader came back, said that Conlach and himself had covered every room of every bungalow and there was nothing to see. I tried to be reassured.

It was probably a rocking chair knocked over by the wind. I'd heard a crash. There was no evidence of anything else.

As for the door being open, maybe Caspe and Sienne

had done it? Maybe I'd done it?

I didn't remember closing it, and maybe they'd thought I'd left it open for some reason.

I didn't know.

"What would we do?" I said to Conlach when he came back down shortly afterward. "If Izar was here?"

"He's not here," said Conlach. "He's on the space station where the arena is, the one that orbits this planet. He's in space. Sevren tracked him out there. He's definitely not here."

"But if he faked that somehow," I said. "If he was here? We couldn't stop the game, could we? It's a big thing, right?"

"We'd contain him, shoot him if we had to, whatever," said Conlach. "No, we would not stop the game."

I took a deep breath. "Well, I guess it doesn't matter, then."

"There's no way he could be here. Even if he was, he couldn't get up to those bungalows. There's no other way up the cliff."

"What about from the other side? Isn't that possible?"

"Maybe, but it would have taken him days to get from there to here. No roads through there, and it's all wild."

I wasn't sure what to make of that. Before I could worry too much about it, however, I saw Caspe and Sienne waiting for me at the top of the cliff. But when they saw me, they made their way down, and we all went to the main lodge of the resort, which was where we'd be meeting the players.

I explained to them what had happened, and they talked with Conlach for a while about it, taking it pretty seriously. There was a discussion about redistributing security to various different points in the resort, and then we were all on our way.

The Toth who were there for the game had all been staying on the other side of the resort, in different bungalows. These were similarly constructed to the ones that I'd been staying in, in that they were built on thruster bridges and they overlooked the bay, but they were obviously newer, bigger, and fancier.

Conlach had not given us one of his nicest vacation bungalows to stay in for free, it was now clear. I eyed the gleaming row of pretty, brandy-new bungalows and wondered what they looked like inside.

I didn't get to stand around and contemplate them for too long, however, because Caspe and Sienne ushered me inside to the room where the grasic table was.

They went over everything with me again, as if we hadn't gone over it a million times already.

I know they were trying to reassure me and themselves that everything was going to go according to plan, but it had the effect of making me even more nervous. What if I messed this up? What if I'd picked out the wrong clothes? What if I was wrong about everything?

The room was relatively small, with room only for the grasic table and five chairs. There would be three players, plus Sienne and me. The room was surrounded by windows, however, which had views of the bay. The sun was sinking low on the horizon and the stars were coming out. The windows made the room seem bigger than it was, expansive and luxurious.

"Okay," said Caspe. "You two should have drinks.

Drink a little to calm your nerves, but not so much that you're not sharp."

Sienne and I went to the bar.

I found myself looking all over the room, half-expecting that Izar was going to jump out from somewhere.

I thought—for the first time in a while—about the limp body of that guy landing on top of me, his cock still inside me, and my stomach roiled.

Why had I let Sevren leave me? I should have insisted he stayed. He made me feel safe.

I sighted the security guards at each entrance, making sure to note that they were all there and everything was fine, and then I told the bartender what I wanted to drink.

I hoped a drink would settle my nerves, like Caspe had said.

It didn't. It made me have to pee.

I thought about asking Sienne to come with me. She had a blaster, after all. I knew that she did, and she was good with it, or so she said.

But I was probably being stupid, right? There were security guards on all the doors. I was fine.

I would prove to myself that I was fine.

The bathroom down here was all upscale, and it had fancy stalls with doors that went all the way down to the floor.

Inside, it was entirely empty, and all the doors were closed.

I glared at them.

No, not doing it, I told myself. I'm going to pee and get back in there, and I'm going to be calm.

I went into a stall, pulled the door closed, and then started to pull down my pants.

I hesitated.

Stars.

Sighing heavily, I pushed the stall door open.

Fine, fine, fine. I'd check, but just quickly. I pushed open the door of the stall next to me.

Empty.

I took a breath and went to the next.

Empty.

The next three were empty too.

And then I pushed open the next door.

EIGHTEEN

eventh

The woman in there was a Qel, and she screamed at me, curling up, trying to cover herself.

I slammed the door closed, letting out a breath. "Sorry. I'm so sorry."

"Occupied!" she snapped.

"Why didn't you lock the door?" I said, annoyed now, stomping back to my stall.

No answer from the Qel woman. I locked my door, pulled down my pants, did my business, and emerged. She was washing her hands and she shot me a dirty look.

"I'm really sorry," I said. She should have locked her door, though. Who does that?

She swung out of the bathroom, and I washed my own hands, resolving to stop freaking out now.

When I got back into the grasic room, the Toth players had already started to arrive.

Caspe thrust out a tentacle and draped it over my shoulder, which felt a little weird, but okay, whatever. He nudged me around and pushed me at a Toth, a tall man with bright fuschia skin and dark eyes—so dark they appeared nearly black. "This is Maaxx Umil," said Caspe.

He was the mark.

I grinned at him. "Oh, how nice to meet you. My name's Eventh."

"Eventh's the resort's good luck charm," said Caspe. "It just seems like whoever she latches onto for the evening wins big."

"Really," said Maaxx, smiling back at me, but it wasn't a nice smile. "What a pretty human girl." He looked me over. "I've had three different humans bear my children, you know. I adore human girls. You're quite exquisite. And what a pretty red thing you're wearing." He smirked, offering me his arm, like I was a foregone conclusion.

I had the urge to withdraw and put as much space between me and this man as possible. Not in a flirting way, playing hard to get, like I'd intended, but in a get-me-away-from-this-creep way. There was something awful about him.

But that was not my job.

However, I didn't know what it was—maybe him, maybe how scared I was, maybe that I just somehow wasn't the same person who had spent her life having meaningless hookups with men—but I couldn't do the hard-to-get thing. The best I could do was smile and put my hand on his arm and pretend like I was into him.

He settled down at the table and I sat next to him, but he wasn't having that. He pulled me onto his lap. He put his hand inside my shirt.

I flinched. I wriggled away, hopping off his lap. "I've heard of you," I said. My voice was too tight.

"Have you." He looked me over.

"Are you the Maaxx Umil who owns the weapons company?"

Caspe shot me a look, because I wasn't supposed to

bring up the weapons yet. We hadn't even started the game.

"You're interested in weapons?" He raised his eyebrows.

I swallowed, lifting my chin. "I like a man with a big gun," I said, finding some sort of footing at last.

He chuckled. "Oh, I like *you*, Eventh. And I like big guns, too. Nothing like the way a man feels with a big blaster in each hand."

"Powerful," I said. I touched his upper arm. "But you don't need a blaster to feel that way, I bet." A lot of Toth these days were half-human, because the Toth had lost their women and they'd bred with humans, since humans were so similar to Toth. But this guy, he was older—and not older like Sevren was, older like in his fifties or sixties—and he was pureblood. It wasn't always easy to tell—you had to look for telltale signs like stubble. Humans had hair. Toth didn't. Half-Toth tended to shave or wax their eyebrows, and if you were close up, you could see that. This guy, though, he was naturally hairless and touching him, pretending to be impressed with him, it was unsettling.

I wished I hadn't volunteered for this now.

I didn't think I liked this.

He pulled me back onto his lap. He put his hand back in my shirt. "Well, Eventh," he whispered in my ear, "after you help me win, if you really want to see some big guns, I could take you on a trip. Would you like that?"

Well, this was going well. I tried not to seem overeager. "A trip to see your weapons cache? Your big, secret stash? Is that real?"

"Oh, it's real, Eventh." He squeezed my breast.

I gasped, but in pain. "Where is it?"

He chuckled. "If you really are a good luck charm, I'll take you there."

"Hands where I can see them, Maaxx," came Caspe's voice, which sounded light and amused, but I could hear a hint of threat beneath it and I was grateful he was there. "How do I know you're not keeping extra holochips up her shirt."

Maaxx laughed, but he moved his hand. "You're the one who introduced her to me." He set me down on the chair next to him. "You don't help men cheat, do you Eventh?"

"Of course not," I said.

"I like a fair win," said Maaxx. "It's the sweetest that way, you see. No risk, no reward."

Behind me, the sound of shattering plasglass.

I turned to see a bright beam of blaster fire and a hulking figure crashing in through the window.

Beside me, Caspe slumped over the grasic table.

Sienne screamed, and there was answering blaster fire.

Maaxx had a blaster too, and he was shoving me behind him, opening fire.

From outside the room, came screams and the sound of even more blaster fire.

The door burst open.

Izar walked in.

NINETEEN

eventh

What the stars was going on?

The guy who'd come in the window was down, hit by Sienne's blaster fire, but who *was* he?

Izar wasn't firing, but someone was. I could hear blasters and screams and yells from outside in the main room of the lodge.

Maaxx wedged his body between mine and Izar's, pointing his blaster at the gladiator. "What's going on here?"

Sienne yanked Caspe upright. There was blood all over the grasic table.

Was Caspe…?

My heart beat a wild, hot rhythm at my temples.

"All I want is that one," said Izar, pointing at me.

"No," I said, shaking my head. "Because Maaxx here is going to take me to his weapons cache on Taichh, isn't that right?" Okay, was I seriously still trying to get the location of the weapons cache out of this guy? I wasn't even that dedicated to the resistance cause.

"Not Taichh," said Maaxx, glancing back at me. "You're very interested in that, aren't you, Eventh?"

"Not me, him." I pointed at Izar. "He made me do it. Shoot him."

Maaxx considered this, and then pulled the trigger.

A blaster beam shot across the room and hit right where Izar's head should have been.

Except Izar had leapt to the side and had narrowly missed getting shot. He could have opened fire on Maaxx, but he hadn't. What was that all about?

Was it because I was behind Maaxx? Did Izar have some special plan for killing me? Maybe he wanted to film it and show Sevren or something.

How could I use that?

Sienne and Caspe were on the floor now. He was all splayed out, tentacles limp and askew. She was running her hands all over his face and chest, letting out noisy breaths, muttering, "No, no, no."

"You have other people with you," I said to Izar.

"Needed to hire blasters and muscle to deal with all this security," said Izar, shrugging. He nodded at Maaxx. "Just hand over the girl and you walk away."

"Alien trash," said Maaxx. "Is that how you talk to a Toth hii kath? Respect your betters."

Izar moved fast—limbs going every which way—and suddenly, Maaxx's blaster was skidding across the floor and Izar's blaster was pressed into Maaxx's head. "Betters? I killed in the arena for your kind's amusement for gecycles of my life, but it's never enough, is it? You're parasites feeding on the galaxy's carcass."

"It's on Kailli, all right?" said Maaxx in a different voice. "The cache is in the Blain Mountains there."

Izar pulled the trigger.

Maaxx slumped to the floor, dead.

I let out a little noise.

Izar sighted me with his blaster.

I cringed.

Suddenly, Izar shifted his blaster to right next to me.

"Drop it," he growled.

Sienne was standing, ready to shoot. She tensed, gritting her teeth, and then nodded. She slowly lowered her blaster and laid it on the grasic table. "I'm sorry, Eventh."

"Caspe?" I whispered. "Is he—"

"Shut up," said Izar to me.

I swallowed. "Um… y-you don't want to shoot me here. You want t-to wait. Wait for Sevren. Do it while he's watching."

Izar snorted. "Nice try, human."

"I know," I said. "You could… fuck me. Take a holovid of us together and show it to him. That would hurt worse than just killing me. I-I'd be willing. I w-want one last chance to have sex before I die. Please? Don't kill me yet. Not yet." I didn't know what I was doing, but I figured buying time was my best bet. The more time I had, I could use it to figure something out.

Izar considered this.

Sienne dove for her blaster.

Izar shot her.

She cried out and went down.

I let out a sob, covering my mouth. Stars, stars, *stars*.

A big muscled furry man holding an enormous blaster appeared in the doorway. "Room's clear," he said to Izar.

"Thank you," said Izar, reaching over and snatching me by the arm. He pulled me against him, my back to his front, and fitted the blaster under my chin. "All right, Eventh, let's walk."

I did as he said.

We walked out of the grasic room and into the big, main room of the lodge, which was carnage city.

Everyone was dead.

People were strewn all over the floor like discarded streamers. Blood was everywhere. It pooled on the floor and spattered the walls and the ceiling. I could smell it, coppery and bright.

Movement!

Someone was alive.

Conlach was crawling across the floor, using one arm. His other arm was bloody and useless, dragging along behind him. He was going for a blaster which was lying on the floor just out of his reach.

Izar nodded at the furry guy and he shot Conlach in the head.

I watched Conlach's face jerk back and then he went still.

I started to shake. "Y-you… you can't come back from this," I said to Izar. "You think the guild is going to be able to cover all this up? This is a whole resort. You killed Toth people. *Lots* of Toth." It was maybe four Toth, but I knew I was right.

"Shut up," said Izar.

I let out a low moan of understanding. "Oh, fuck, this is a suicide mission. You kill me and then you kill yourself, right?"

"Shut *up*."

Oh, stars, it was hopeless. What was I going to do? What was I going to do?

TWENTY

"Look, whoever keeps pinging this terminal, no one's home," said the voice on the other end of my bracelet.

I'd been calling the main terminal at Conlach's resort off and on for hihors now. I had nothing better to do since I was in a speeder in the high-speed lane, going as fast as I could back for Eventh.

"Sounds like you're there," I said.

A chuckle. "Just give it a rest. No one here to book your bungalow on the bay, eh?"

"I'm actually calling to talk to Conlach."

"Conlach's not home."

"Where is he?"

"I'm hanging up."

"I'll just keep pinging. You might as well talk to me. Who is this, anyway? You work for Conlach? What do you do? Front desk? Security? Cleaning service?"

"Who are you?"

"I'm Sevren."

"Oho! This is all for you, then."

"What's all for me? Who do you work for? Did Izar hire—"

"He took your girl. Think he's having a little fun with her before he slits her throat. I'm the only one left.

Everyone else shoved off. Just keeping watch."

My stomach dropped and I felt like I was going to vomit.

"Have a nice night, *Sevren*." The transmission ended.

For hidosecs, I only sat there, not breathing, not doing anything. I could ping the terminal again, but I had my answers, didn't I?

I jerked upright and pulled up the holodisplay of the speeder, searching for an alternate route, a faster route.

I'd looked through everything, and there was no way that—

There.

What was that? What if I climbed altitude and went over the cliffs, over the water, and came around from that side? How much quicker could I make it?

Well, it was something, anyway.

I hurriedly made the adjustments in the route. The speeder swung around and climbed higher in the air.

Hang on, baby girl, I'm coming.

* * *

eventh

I was currently on my knees in front of the lodge, and Izar was standing over me with a blaster to my forehead. I waited, but the blast to my head wasn't coming.

"Mr. Fjass?" I finally said in a tiny voice. What the stars did I have to lose at this point? He was going to shoot me. I wanted to live.

"Shut up, girl," said Izar.

"No," I said.

"I will shoot you—"

"Maybe you don't want to," I said, breathless.

"I do," he said. "You see how many other people I've killed tonight? I have *no problem* killing some slip of a girl like you."

Right. Well, he was protesting too much, but I didn't want to push him, because he might shoot me just to prove to himself that he could do it.

I licked my lips. "Uh, maybe we need a different venue."

He snorted.

"How about a balcony?" I backed away from his blaster. I stood up.

"On your knees," he said.

I licked my lips. "I could… I could suck your dick. You can take a holovid of that to send to Sevren, and it'll show him just how willing I was. It'll ruin him. Y-you want to hurt him, right? Why don't you let me—"

"I don't want that from you," he said in a low voice.

"Okay," I said.

"I'm not an idiot," he said. "You think I don't realize you'd try something while I was distracted? Get back on your knees."

I didn't. I simply stared at him, my breathing erratic. "It's, um, it'd be peaceful on the balcony. There would be a view. You feel hesitant about it. I can tell you do. It might be nicer there for me. That might make it easier for you."

He shook his head. His voice had a biting lilt. "You're trying to make it *easier* for me to kill you?"

"It's not personal, right?" I breathed. "This is about Sevren, not about me. So, that's why it's difficult for you—"

"It's *not* difficult."

I pointed. "I'm going to go up onto the balcony in one of those bungalows. I'm just going to walk there. There's no one else alive, except people who work for you. If you don't like it, you can shoot me in the back.

Or, you can come with me up there."

"I'm not going to let you live, girl," he said. "The longer you and I talk, the more complicated this gets."

I bit down on my bottom lip. Then I backed away from him.

His blaster tip wavered.

My heart slammed painfully into my rib cage. I turned my back on him. I started for one of the bungalows, expecting to feel the hot pain of blaster fire cutting into me at any moment.

But I didn't.

I walked up to the door of one of the bungalows and opened it. Well, the small silver lining here was that I was going to get to see inside the fancier bungalows on this side of the resort, so that was something, right?

I hoped it was not going to be the last thing that I ever saw. I didn't really have a plan here. I didn't know what the hell I was doing. I knew I wanted to live. I knew that.

I stepped over the threshold of the door and he was suddenly behind me.

I turned to look at him.

He wasn't looking at me. He had the blaster at his side, eyeing his feet.

I let out a breath and turned away. Inside, this bungalow was a lot like our bungalow, actually. It had basically the same furniture, for instance, but there was more of it, and this bungalow was really big. It had a huge open space downstairs with a kitchen and a wide area with couches and chairs and then a game room area with some hologame equipment and a holotennis table and some other stuff.

In the center of everything, just like in our bungalow, was a big staircase leading up to the second level.

I started up it.

Izar came behind me wordlessly.

My breaths were harsh and erratic, echoing off the stairwell.

There were two bedrooms up here.

I went into the first and went past the bed and slid open the doors and then went out onto the balcony. I went over and clutched the railing and peered down at the bay. I let out gasping breaths.

Izar came up next to me, setting the blaster on top of the railing. He sighed.

I looked at him. What should I say? Should I beg? Should I offer more sexual favors? Should I try for the blaster?

He stared out into the darkness, at the rippling water of the bay, at the dark, starry sky above.

I licked my lips. "Tell me about your brother?" My voice was hoarse.

He hung his head. It was round and black, and it glinted, dimly reflecting back the starlight overhead.

"You loved him," I breathed. "He was your family. He mattered to you."

"He was the only thing that mattered, because the Toth have taken everything else. Our handler threatened our sisters, our mother, even my brother's children—and then he made good on those threats. Our handler killed them all, everyone either of us ever cared about. But still, I held on, because of my brother. He needed me. So, I kept it together. But… underneath, I'd already fallen apart. This is what I *am*, girl." He turned around, putting his back to the railing, gesturing out in the direction of the building from which we'd come, where there was nothing but carnage. "I am nothing but a killer. It is what I do. *All* I can do."

I backed up, away from the railing, letting out sharp, broken breaths. "I'm sure that's not true." My voice shook.

He let out a long, bitter chuckle. "You have no idea what I—"

And that was when I launched myself at him. I put my shoulder into his chest with all my strength.

He cried out, surprised. He flailed, his hands going up, including the one with the blaster, which went off, shooting a bright beam up above my head.

I put both of my hands in the middle of his chest and shoved.

He let out a strangled cry, tipping backwards. One of his hands—the one that didn't have a blaster—reached for me, but I danced out of the way. And he fell heels over head off the balcony.

He screamed the whole way down and landed with a splash in the bay.

I backed up, letting out a strangled, sobbing breath, backed all the way up into the bedroom. I crouched down on the floor and took more noisy breaths.

Then I got up immediately and hurried to the balcony. I gripped it and looked down.

What if he'd somehow lived?

Was that him floating?

I dashed down the stairs and out of the bungalow. I started to rush down to the dock. His body was floating fairly near the dock.

I stopped there, just gazing at his body for several moments.

After some time, I went back into the main lodge.

I didn't go into the room with all the dead people. I just knelt next to the security guard on the door—who was dead—and scooped up his blaster.

Now armed, I started out of the room when something shot out and grabbed me around the waist.

I cried out.

TWENTY-ONE

It was a tentacle.

Caspe and Sienne were leaning against each other, her dragging a blaster, both spattered in blood. They limped over to me.

I was sobbing, but I managed to explain to them what had happened, and together, we went down to the dock, and Caspe fished Izar out of the bay with one of his tentacles. Izar had hit the bottom, or hit a rock, or something. He was dead. There was blood on the back of his skull.

"What should we do with him?" said Caspe.

"It's better for everyone if he just disappears," I said. "The guild can't blame anyone if he's missing and not dead."

"Got it," said Caspe. He hurled Izar's body way out into the bay with his tentacles. It was amazing how far he could throw with those things. The current would take Izar's remains out to sea. He'd probably never be found. The sea on Kalion was vast.

Then, together, we made our laborious way to find the woefully stocked med supply area in the resort. Sienne and Caspe bandaged each other up, and I realized I didn't have a scratch on me.

"Well," she said as he used his tentacles to wrap

gauze around her wound, "I guess we got the location of the weapons cache, so it's a success in the end, huh?" Her voice was shaking.

"We did?" said Caspe. "Was I unconscious when that happened?"

"You scared the fuck out of me," she said to him.

"Sorry, babe," he said, caressing her cheek. "You scared me too, though. You were out of it when I woke up."

"I was just stunned," she said. "I hit my head when I fell," she told me. "Otherwise I would have come for you. Izar only got my arm." She nodded at where Caspe was bandaging her.

"I gotta say, sometimes I don't like how often it is I'm bandaging you up," he said to her.

She cupped his face in her hands. "This is worth it, Caspe. This is… what we're doing, it matters."

He sighed. "*You* matter, babe. More than anything. The galaxy can get sucked into a black hole. You're so much more important to me than—"

"Shh, we make a difference," she said, kissing him, stopping his words.

I felt like I shouldn't be watching this, and I looked away.

"So?" came Caspe's voice. "Where's the cache?"

"On Kailli," said Sienne. "The, um, the Paii Mountains—"

"No, he said the Blain Mountains," I interrupted.

"Oh, right," said Sienne. "That's right. You heard that in the middle of everything?"

"How'd you get him to give that up?" said Caspe.

"It was luck, really," I said.

"It was brilliant," said Sienne. "You were amazing. I couldn't believe you managed that during all of it. And then you killed him."

"I didn't... There was no real plan..." I shook my head. "And anyone would do whatever they could to save their own lives. I just got lucky." I could very easily be dead. If he'd managed to grab the railing, if he hadn't agreed to go to the balcony, if...

I wrapped my arms around myself, bereft.

"Hey," said Caspe, settling a tentacle on my shoulder. "Hey, you're all right. You're alive. And we're safe now. It's over."

Which, of course, was the hidosec we heard more blaster fire.

Sienne shook her head at him. "You *had* to say that, didn't you?"

He spread his hands. "I thought it *was*. He's dead, right? We heard all the rest of the guys he hired leaving. He settled up credits with them. What the stars?"

Sienne brandished her blaster.

I picked mine up too.

"Look, ladies, I'm going first," said Caspe witheringly.

"Um, we're the ones who are armed," said Sienne.

"I'm the one with the tentacles," said Caspe, gesturing with several of them.

"Yes, but—"

"Tentacles? That Caspe?" came a voice, and I recognized it right away.

I let out a happy cry and I rushed forward. "Sevren!"

"Baby girl," he said, his voice strangled.

I cleared the doorway and there he was. I ran for him and he caught me and pulled me into his arms. I wrapped my legs and my arms around him and buried my face in his neck.

He supported me under my rear end and stroked my back with one hand. "There was one guy at the gate, Izar's paid goon. I took care of him."

"That was the blaster fire we heard," I said. "You."

"I guess so," he said, rubbing his cheek against my cheek. "You're really okay?"

"I'm…" I tightened my grip on him, rubbing my face up against his firmly. Was I okay? I didn't think so. But I was alive. "Izar's dead."

"Thank the spirits." His voice shook.

"She killed him," said Sienne.

Sevren seemed to notice them for the first time. He set me down on my feet, but kept a burly arm wrapped around me. His arms were furrier these days, having grown in quite a bit since having shaved them. I pressed my cheek into his chest and looked at Sienne and Caspe from that vantage point. "I can't believe I let him trick me," said Sevren in a rough voice. "I've been out of my mind. I pushed the speeder *so fast* to get here."

"It was a massacre," said Caspe quietly. "Conlach, he's…"

Sevren stiffened next to me. "Spirits."

"Listen, I don't know how great an idea it is for us to stand around here chatting," said Caspe. "I don't want to be here if a bunch of local cops show up—or worse, those worthless cop-bots."

"I think those are only in the city," I said into Sevren's chest. "I don't think they work long range in rural areas."

"Whatever, the last thing we need is to be tied to this," Caspe said.

"You really think someone's coming?" said Sienne.

"That was a lot of blaster fire," said Caspe.

"Someone might have heard."

"I don't know that's going to be enough to get someone to call the police," said Sienne. "But better safe than sorry, I guess. Even if not, someone will attempt to check in at the resort tomorrow, because there are reservations, and they'll find all this. So, we can't stay."

"We have to leave the bodies, then," said Sevren. "No burying or…"

"No," said Caspe. "But we have time if you want to see him."

Sevren swallowed hard. Then he nodded.

We all went into the main lodge, gingerly picking our way around all the bodies. I kept looking at all of them—the people who worked here, the people who'd just been vacationing here, even the other Toth players… I'd never seen anything like this. I was going to have nightmares for gemoons—gecycles—eons. I stayed close to Sevren, clutching his hand, pressing into his side or into his back, and he slid his arm around my shoulders or around my waist, the movement easy and casual, as if he did it all the time, even though we'd never been like this in front of other people.

He was grim over Conlach's body, his voice raw. "Sorry, buddy," he said. "I never meant to bring this down on your head."

"It wasn't your fault," I said. "Izar went crazy."

"It was the Toth's fault," said Sienne in a hard voice. "The Toth's appetite for the arena, using people's bodies as fodder for entertainment, people's *lives* for an afternoon of fun. The Toth broke him."

No one said anything.

Sevren finally nodded. "The Toth broke him," he murmured. He looked up at me. "Did you get the information you were trying to get before all this went down?"

"She did, actually," said Caspe. "She's, uh, that's some girl you got there."

Sevren tightened his grip on me. "Yeah," he rumbled, and he kissed my forehead.

We left the main lodge and we all went out of the gate. Sevren's speeder was parked there—sort of parked. The door was open, as if he'd just dashed out of it with no thought, which I guessed he had.

Caspe gestured with his tentacles. "Our ship is this way. There's a clearing where the landing pads are."

"Are you just taking off, then?" I said.

"We could take you, too," said Sienne. "We could drop them somewhere, right, Caspe? We could hop into orbit and then touch down in any of the major cities with a spaceport."

Caspe nodded. "Sure. You guys want a ride?"

Sevren's hand trailed down my arm. He paused when our fingers touched, as if he was trying to pull away, but he couldn't quite manage it. "Uh, I could take this speeder here and you could go with them on your own."

"We can put the speeder in the cargo bay. There's room," said Caspe.

"It's not… I mean, it belongs to Conlach. Belonged. I could leave it here," said Sevren.

"There *is* only one extra bedroom," said Sienne softly.

"What? They don't have a problem sharing a bed, do they?" Caspe was amused.

Sevren's fingers tightened on mine. "Baby girl? You want me with you?"

"Of course," I said, looking up at him.

He tugged me closer. "All right then."

"Great," said Caspe. "Well, that's settled then. Follow us." He started off. Over his shoulder, "I guess we owe you credits anyway, huh?"

TWENTY-TWO

I didn't need any money to pay off the guild anymore, because no one was going to know what had happened to Izar. His body had been dragged off into the ocean, and it would probably never be found. Even if it was, it would look like an accident.

The carnage at this resort might be traceable to him, depending on how he'd paid the muscle he'd hired to help shoot the place up. I'd found out about that from the others, who filled me in everything that happened as we boarded Caspe's and Sienne's ship.

We launched into orbit, and then gathered in a lounge on the ship to have a drink before bed. At first, Eventh tried to say that she wouldn't take the credits at all, and that it should just go to the resistance. But Sienne asked Eventh if she could use the credits for her research, and Eventh said that she could, but she didn't want to take all of it.

They settled on giving half of the agreed-upon amount to Eventh for her research, and it was all decided.

Caspe and Sienne were cozy. She was practically on his lap, even though he kind of didn't have a lap with all those tentacles, most of which were wrapped around her in some way—encircling her shoulders or twined around her arms or ankles. They didn't stay for much longer after the credit conversation was decided.

"Well, we're tired," said Caspe. "We're going to bed."

"Yup," said Sienne patting one of his tentacles that was wrapped around her waist. Maybe more stroking it, actually. "Your room is the only other room past this one."

"On the other side of the ship from ours," said Caspe. "So, you know, hopefully we don't disturb you."

"*Caspe,*" said Sienne, obviously embarrassed.

They were gone pretty quickly after that.

I was still holding hands with Eventh. I'd been so terrified that I was going to lose her forever tonight, and having her alive and whole, it was such a relief that I couldn't stop touching her. I just needed to feel that she was solid and real.

"Bed?" she said in a coy little voice.

"Yeah," I said. "Uh, yeah, but, um..." Well, fuck, what did I think I was going to do here? How could I possibly ask what I wanted to ask of her?

She raised her eyebrows, looking confused. "Is it a problem?" Then her face fell. "Of course it's a problem. Because you hate yourself and you feel guilty. If it's that much of a thing, maybe you should just stay on the couch here." She nodded. "I can get you some blankets." She tried to get up.

I was still holding her hand. I wouldn't let her.

"Sevren?" she said.

I swallowed. "Bed," I said. "Let's go to bed. Together."

She tilted her head in surprise at this.

"Unless you don't want..."

"No, I already said I wanted you to be here with me and not in that speeder."

"Right, so, good." I got up from the couch, pulling her with me.

But then I just stood there, and she had to lead me out of the room. We went down the corridor and found the other room. The door slid open and we stepped inside.

The door slid closed, shutting us in there, and I let go of her. "You know, I didn't mean to assume anything, because after what you went through with Izar, I wouldn't ask you to, uh, to do anything for me. Not like that."

"I know," she said with a smile, putting a hand on my cheek. "Trust me, Sevren, I know that you'd never ask me to do something I didn't want to do."

"I wouldn't," I whispered.

"I guess that's why it doesn't make sense that you hate yourself or that you're guilty," she said.

"No, I know," I agreed. "I know."

And then it was quiet.

She looked away, everywhere but me. Her gaze settled on her shirt. "There's blood on this."

"Is there?" I said. "It's red, so, it's hard to tell."

"I want to take it off," she said firmly.

"Of course," I said.

"It's not my blood," she said. "I just want it *off* me."

"It's fine, baby girl."

She yanked it over her head.

I averted my eyes. I pulled off my own shirt and handed it to her. "Do you want mine?"

"Oh," she said. "I thought…"

She never finished, so I looked up at her and got an eyeful of her pretty, round breasts. I was done for. My cock stirred immediately. She was beautiful.

She gestured. "Over there. I thought maybe we could get cleaned up." She crossed the room and touched a set of sensors on the far wall. A cleaning unit opened. It was the kind with real water, like a shower, though I knew it would be short and perfunctory, the jets scrubbing and rinsing in a matter of hidosecs. Still, it was better than the forced air ones. Those never seemed to get my fur completely clean. She looked at me over her shoulder. "Get in with me?"

I hesitated. Truth was, I smelled like fear sweat, because it had been pouring out of me all night. I could wear my clothes into the unit and they'd get clean, but it was probably better to take them off and hang them up. They'd get cleaner that way and so would my body.

That was actually what Eventh seemed to be doing. She peeled off her pants and underthings and hung them up in the corner of the unit. She turned to me, showing her all of her bare, beautiful skin.

Now, I was incredibly hard.

"What if I do want something?" she said. "What if I want to get cleaned up, and then I want us to be together, but not during heat, just... you and me. Would you do that?"

I nodded wordlessly.

She held my gaze for a minute, and then she turned her back and climbed into the cleaning unit.

I came over and stripped off my clothes and handed them to her to hang up, and when I unclasped my pants and my very hard dick popped out and pointed right at her, she only looked at it. She didn't touch me.

For my part, I didn't touch her either. I wanted to. I wanted... I just... I didn't know how to *do* this.

"I, um…" She flushed, putting her hands between her legs. "I have to take out… it's like the last day of my period. I'm sure it's not much of anything. If you don't want to look—"

I was curious, actually. I'd had very little intimate interaction with women in this way. "I don't mind," I said.

And she reached in and pulled something out and then tossed it in the waste slot next to the cleaning unit. I didn't even really see what it was.

"Like I said, it's basically over." She stepped into the cleaning unit. "Close it?"

I stepped inside next to her and closed it behind us.

"It sometimes, like a horrible surprise, it comes back, but…"

I furrowed my brow. "Wait a minute, if you've been on suppressants all this time and you said you never had a full-fledged heat, isn't that tied into your, um…"

"Oh, yeah," she said. "But I've done all this experimenting on myself and I've never triggered a heat, but basically, the entire reason you bleed is just because of hormone fluctuations, so if you accidentally get that going, it just happens." She rolled her eyes. "I'm always accidentally fluctuating the wrong way, I'm afraid."

I blinked at her. "Fascinating."

"Is it?" she said. "You think women bleeding is fascinating?"

"I…" I considered. "Well, you think it's fascinating, don't you? That's why you're doing all this research on it, why it's the thing you wake up for in the morning?" I grinned at her.

She grinned back. "You only think it's fascinating because I do. You think I'm fascinating."

"Guilty," I said.

She turned to the controls of the cleaning unit and turned it on, still smiling.

We were blasted with hot water and soap—blessedly unscented—and we both had to shut our eyes and keep our mouths closed and wait it out. In a few hidosecs, it rinsed us and then kicked into the drying feature, blowing us this way and that with hot air, which made my fur stand up on my back.

"Turn around," Eventh giggled, trying to comb it down with her hands.

"It's fine," I said, laughing.

The doors opened.

Then our laughter stopped again, because we were both staring at the bed.

"Uh, baby girl?"

"Yeah?" she said.

"I thought you were dead."

"I'm not," she said.

I turned to look at her. I reached out and took both of her hands in mine. "I know. Obviously, you're not, but I thought you were. I thought there was no way you could have gotten away, and I thought he might have made your last moments horrific, and I—" A sob welled up in my throat, and I lost the ability to speak.

"Sevren." She pressed against me, her bare skin against my body. "I'm okay."

I shut my eyes, and then I wrapped my arms around her. My lips found hers. We kissed soft and slow.

We climbed into the bed, and she curled up against me, her head resting on the crook of my shoulder, and we kept kissing. She stroked my cock, and I didn't stop her.

I cupped one of her breasts with one hand and then

thumbed her nipple stiff, liking the way she sighed against me.

"I want us to move in together." I just blurted it out like that. Fuck, what was wrong with me?

She let go of my cock and sat up straight, gazing down at me in astonishment. "What did you just say?"

"I thought you were dead," I repeated, as if this was going to make her understand. It did all connect, but I didn't know how to explain how it connected.

"Well, if I *had* died, it probably would have been the best thing for you, though, don't you think? No more mating bond. You could go around casually fucking age-appropriate women. You'd be free of any all responsibilities to—"

"You're my world, baby girl, and you have been for a very long time," I interrupted. "I don't want to live without you."

"So, that's why you want to move in together?"

"It's just… it's stupid to fight it." I winced. "Or… no, I don't mean that. It's not fighting it, it's not like that. I've never really fought it, that's the thing. I've never tried to fight it. I've never wanted to fight it. I've always been in love with you, and I've always thought I should fight it and felt guilty for not fighting—"

"What are you talking about?" She shook her head at me, and it made her breasts jiggle a little, and I put my hand on one of them.

"Don't distract me," she said, pushing me away. "Explain."

I took a deep breath and tried to sort out my thoughts. "Conlach said something to me." But then I thought of Conlach's dead body, and I flinched. "Fuck, Conlach."

"It was awful," she said, eyes filling up. "I saw it

happen. I saw him die. It was so fast. Oh, stars, Sevren, all those people. All dead."

I pulled her down against me.

She clung to me.

We just held each other and shook for a few minutes.

"I'm so sorry I left you," I whispered. "That was such a stupid thing to do."

"It was." She lifted her head and glared at me. "I needed you. That's what you're always doing is leaving me, and—"

"I shouldn't have," I said. "I should never have left you. I shouldn't have left you before either. On Bravren? I should have stayed with you. We should have been together all this time."

She drew back even further. "What?" She blinked at me. "But you… I thought you couldn't control yourself, that you would have—"

"Hurt you? Do I do that to you?"

"No," she breathed. "Never. I mean, except when you… abandon me."

"Except when I assume the worst of myself for no apparent reason," I said. "Except when I think I'm going to do something horrible when there's no way I would ever have… I wouldn't have had sex with you when you were a kid! If I hadn't been so afraid, I would have realized that. I would have gotten used to your scent, and I would have stopped getting erections. I don't know about your heat, about triggering that. Maybe… But all I know is that being away from you, it kind of broke me."

Her lower lip started trembling. "It broke me too."

"No, I know that." Now, I was going to start crying. "I know that, and I'm so sorry." I sniffed really hard.

She threw herself down against me, laying her cheek

on my chest.

I ran my hand over her hair and over her back. "Conlach said something to me about how I would have been close to you even if we weren't mated, and it made me realize, like, we're more than our, uh, our bodies."

She sighed into my chest. "Biology isn't destiny."

"What?"

"Nothing," she said. "Keep going."

"So, the mating bond, it doesn't take away our choices. It makes it harder to resist things, but not impossible. You and I, we're still in control. Like, when I found out you were in heat, I chose to fuck you, and I didn't have to."

"If you hadn't, I would have been miserable."

"Maybe," I said. "But it was still a choice. We don't have control over what our bodies make us *want* to do, but we do have control over what we *choose* to do. I have control of myself. And I care about you. And I'm not bad for you, actually. I'm not... I would be better for you than whatever fucking crazy shit you're doing with your threesomes and your blood play—"

"Um, you and I did that, too, actually."

I furrowed my brow.

She shrugged, reaching up to touch her shoulder. "With the biting me and drawing blood, hence—"

"Fuck." I grimaced, letting that sink in.

"It's fine. It was consensual and we both had a really good time, so, it's fine."

I nodded. "Right, okay. I was picturing something a lot more gross, like playing with blood? I mean I was picturing—"

"Sevren, are we getting off track here?"

"Uh, I'm done." I shrugged. "I want you."

"You want us to move in together?"

"I want us to *be* together," I said. "As boyfriend and girlfriend or whatever, but I feel like this is permanent, so, yeah, I'm kind of asking for the rest of our lives."

She kissed me hard.

I kissed back, my hands migrating to her waist.

She pulled away and grinned at me. "Yes."

"Yes?"

She nodded furiously and then kissed me again. Then she climbed over me, straddling me, and started running her hands up and down my chest, continuing to kiss me, and I didn't stop myself from fondling both of her pretty breasts, and getting her nipples nice and hard.

She gasped against my lips. "I want to put the tip of your cock inside me and just rock on it until your knot gets real big and then ride you and rub my clit on your knot until I come."

I let out a noisy breath.

"Yes?" she said, kissing me.

"That sounds… um, fantastic," I grunted.

"I thought so." She reached out and positioned me against her opening.

"Oh, baby girl, you feel so fucking amazing," I sighed.

"That's just the tip of you," she said with a smile. Then she sank further onto me, taking the head of me into her wet, snug warmth.

"You *are* a genius." My voice was a rasp. "This is your most brilliant idea maybe ever."

"Mmm, well, I'm going to fuck you so good, you can't think."

I gasped. "I'm good with that."

She reached down and fondled the base of me.

"Well, that's coming along nicely."

I grunted.

She rocked against me, fixing me with a wicked glare. "You like it that I'm younger, don't you, Sevren?"

I licked my lips. "Look, I might have just said that I—"

"Admit that you like my sweet, young pussy that's wet just for your cock, that only comes for you?"

I jerked up into her, deeper.

She gasped.

"Here you go, baby girl," I said. "Here's your knot," and I drove it up against her, bucking into her, pressing into her clit. I put my mouth against her ear. "And I *worship* your pussy, baby girl. Can't get enough of it."

She bowed up, mouth open in a silent scream, lifting up over me.

I got her settled, my hands on her hips to help her balance, and she rode me, breasts bouncing, crying out at every bit of contact with my knot against her clit.

I thrust my thumb between the lips of her labia, gently rubbing her there until she sobbed and twitched out her pleasure against me, and then I flipped us, so that she was beneath me and I was over her.

She writhed. "Sevren. *My* Sevren." She ran her hands over my shoulders, and all the way down to cup my ass. She urged me into her, and I complied.

I fucked her into the bed, trapping her there and dragging my cock in and out of her sweet, slick pussy.

When I came, it was like overflowing bubbly wine shooting out of me, and it was jolt after jolt of goodness and blis—

I pushed up over her. "Spermicide patches?"

"I'm not fertile," she said, panting. "Stars, you think

I'd forget about that?"

I sagged into her, relieved, and my cock felt a little battered from that, because that wave of anxiety had kind of short-circuited the end of my orgasm. I pressed my face into the pillow next to her.

She ran her fingers through the fur on my back. "That was so nice," she said in a low, pleased voice.

"It was," I said. "It really was, except for the last moment when I had the faint heart attack, but otherwise…"

She snickered.

I lifted my face and looked down at her. I was still inside her. I was going to be hard for a while, because I had an expanded knot, even if I wasn't stuck in her. I wanted to stay just like this. It was nice inside her. It was probably my favorite place in the universe.

She giggled, stretching beneath me. "Are you going to stay inside me or are you going to fall asleep?"

During heat, our bond fed adrenaline into both of us, keeping us more alert than we might be normally, and I hadn't been quite as susceptible to the sleepy feeling that typically followed an orgasm. It had honestly been so long since I'd had regular orgasms, I'd kind of forgotten about that. "I, uh, I'm moderately sleepy."

"Moderately?"

I sighed. "I mean… I realize it was really romantic for me to say that thing about the rest of our lives, but… also, there are issues. Lots of issues, and I don't know how we're going to deal with them."

"This is what you want to talk about?"

"No." I rolled my hips against her. "No, I want to stay just like this and think non-thoughts like, 'Warm,' and 'Snug.'"

She reached up and traced her fingers over my face.

She tickled my whiskers.

I shivered a little, laughing.

"What are you going to do?" she said.

"What do you mean?"

"You're not going back in the arena, are you? Because you said you wouldn't."

"No, I'm not going back in the arena."

"Do you have to go and quit with the guild?"

"No, I just don't accept any more fights," I said. "I don't have a contract anymore, so I get offered fights and I can accept or not. I'm free from that. I do have to stop paying for a room in the barracks, but, otherwise…"

"You have stuff there? Belongings?"

"Not really."

"So, when you say we should move in together, you want to do that soonish?"

"I mean, unless you want to stay in the dorms for some period of time.

"Oh, you're not moving into my dorm room?" She giggled.

I groaned. "I really don't know how this is going to work." I rolled off of her, pulling out of her pussy.

"Mmm! You did that without any warning," she pouted. "Next time you leave my pussy all empty, give a girl a heads up."

I dragged a hand over my face. "I guess I was figuring we could get an apartment in town."

She propped herself up on an elbow and peered down at me. "No apologies, Sevren?"

"I'm sorry I'm not still in your pussy. Believe me, no one is regretting this more than me at this moment."

She smiled. "An apartment sounds good. Lots of students live with their boyfriends or girlfriends off campus. It's normal."

"Yeah, okay."

"So, whatever, no big deal thus far. We seem to be working this out. And you've already indicated to me that you don't want anything for yourself, that you simply live to make *me* happy—"

"Hey, it's not really like that," I said.

"Oh, so you do want things for yourself?"

"I..." I ran hand through the fur on my forehead, trying to sort through how to explain it. "Okay, I don't have ambition like you, baby girl. You're driven in a way that I'm not. You have your research, and I don't have anything like that. But that doesn't mean I don't want things for myself."

She grinned at me. "So, what do you want?"

"I want..." I felt embarrassed. "Simple things."

"To have me barefoot and pregnant on Braven?"

"*No.*" I sat up, looking down at her, shaking my head. "No, definitely not. Just to have you, I guess. Or... someone to, uh, to live *for*. It doesn't matter what I do, but I'll do something. I wouldn't be happy lying around doing nothing, but it's more important *why* I do it than *what* I'm doing, if that makes sense. So, I'll do something, but the *point* of everything will be... you."

"Um, this is what I was saying," she said.

"It's not." I shook my head. I wasn't explaining it right. I did need to do something, and not just because the credits I had saved up from the arena wouldn't last forever. Not just because I'd get antsy with nothing to occupy me. I needed to do meaningful things, but what gave my life meaning was doing good things for other people, especially for people I loved.

"Hey, do you want to go to school?" she said.

"No," I said. "I'm not a school kind of guy, baby girl.

I'm not like you."

"I like that we have different strengths," she said. "Yours tend toward the literal physical kind, of which I am a fan." She waggled her eyebrows.

I laughed, settling back down on the bed. "I want to do something that helps people."

"Yeah, you're good at that." She rubbed my chest.

"And I want to take care of you. I want you to take care of me. I just want us to be together. That's what I want for myself. To belong. To be part of something. We'll be a... a couple. It'll mean something."

She nodded. "No, I know what you mean. I was thinking about this. I need that, too. I need to belong to someone. But... Sevren, I *also* need my research."

"I know you do. That's why we're good together. You have your ambition, and it's enough for both of us, right? I'll help you, and helping you is what I want."

A big grin spread over her face. "Maybe we're kind of perfect together, Sevren."

"Ehh... we're avoiding all the actual issues," I said. "Like, socially, how people will draw awful conclusions about us."

"Well, I'm actually a huge nerd with no social life. I spend all my time in the lab. When I do go out, it's usually just to get fucked, and I'll have you to do that now." Her hand slid down to stroke my still-hard cock.

"Baby girl," I grunted. "We got to talk about your heat."

She sighed.

"I don't really have the right to ask you to go through that just to be with me," I said. "It's a big ask."

"No, it's worth it," she said, adamant. "I know it is. I can't live without this, without love, without you. Besides, we don't *know* that the suppressants won't work. I mean, I hadn't seen you in nine gecycles. My body maybe reacted erratically to the rush of pheromones. Even if not, maybe I can do some experimenting and adjust things so that the suppressants do work. Or maybe I can just dim it enough so that I can function. Like, if I could go to class and come home and fuck you in between, maybe it could be manageable."

"That all sounds really hopeful, and I hope it turns out like that, but—"

"It's a problem," she said, sitting up, grinning down at me. "But I actually *like* solving problems, Sevren. And this sounds like it could be a very fun problem to solve." She ran a hand up and down my chest. "At the very least, we'd both have a lot of orgasms, and, well, we have some catching up to do."

I let out a rueful laugh. "Well, you're not wrong about that, I guess."

"I'm a genius, remember? I'm usually right."

I tugged her against me and started kissing her.

She pressed in eagerly. "Admit that I'm right."

"You're right," I said against her mouth, and then we were lost to a long stretch of nothing but our tongues and lips joined together, our bodies pressed close, and all of it was perfect.

She sighed against me. "This is just what I want, Sevren."

"I don't want to go to sleep without you in my arms ever again if we can help it."

"Me too," she breathed.

"Because I love you." I put my mouth to her mark and kissed it.

She shuddered against me. "Oh, Sevren, I love you, too."

I kissed her mark again.

"You were wrong when you said we weren't in love."

"I was wrong," I agreed in a whisper. "We're in love. We're more in love than most people can ever even dream of being in love."

She pressed even closer. "Yes, yes, *yes.*"

I breathed in her scent, springtime and nexberries. I was never going to let go of her.

"We're going to make it work," she assured me. "You'll see."

AFTERLUDE: IF YOU NEED ME

eventh

I grimaced as I squeezed my blood onto a slide and nudged it into the machine in the lab.

"Anything?" came Sevren's voice. There was a holoprojection of him—head and shoulders—coming up out of my bracelet.

"Give it a hidosec," I said, chewing on my lip. "It takes a hidosec."

"Baby girl, I think I should just close the gym," he said. Sevren owned a gym now. He taught self-defense classes there, his way of using his skills and knowledge to help people. He was pretty great at it.

"I don't want you to close it," I said. "I can't keep asking you to close your business for me."

"Well, I've been thinking that I'm doing well enough lately that I might be able to hire some more help," he said. "I could have all the schedule covered here except for my self-defense classes, and I can always cancel classes."

"But then you have to refund credits, and I hate that," I said.

"We are fine," he said. "We do not have to worry about credits."

It was true that I'd gotten a grant for my research

lately and it included a stipend for living expenses. I still had the scholarship for my tuition, and I had several female-owned drug companies really interested in my suppressants and birth control implants. We were even almost to the phase of testing one of them on volunteers.

In a lot of ways, just as I'd predicted, Sevren and I were making it work.

But that didn't mean it was easy, or that everything was working.

My heat was stubborn, and Sevren brought it out of me in full force. I'd had some luck blunting it, but no luck at completely suppressing it.

The machine beeped, and I went to look at the results of my blood analysis. "Stars," I said.

"What?" he said.

"Oh, I'm just… my hormones are increasing. So, this didn't even put a dent in my incoming heat."

"So, I'm closing the gym, and I'll meet you at home," he said.

I groaned. "But… I want to stay here and try something else."

"Baby girl, you know that if you push it, you're going to have trouble driving your speeder. But I can come pick you up. I'll swing home first and get things ready, and then I'll come to your lab?"

"Okay," I said. "Give me three hihors."

"One," he said. "You know you'll be rubbing yourself on the beakers if we wait that long."

"Two then? Please?"

He sighed. "You get me on the bracelet if you need me earlier, yeah?"

"Yeah," I said.

We ended the transmission. One thing I would say

for Sevren was that he was amazing when it came to my heat. He took very good care of me. He would arrange the house in the perfect way that made me feel good, keeping out all the light, getting the temperature warm, making sure we had food, doing everything I couldn't be bothered to think about.

And, well, my heat was annoying, but it was... it was nice, too, having that time with us. I liked being close to him, and the sex was always incredible. Once, we'd gotten the heat to break in an unheard-of two days, but it had practically been a wash because we'd been so exhausted afterward that we'd both been worthless for anything else.

"Eventh?" called a voice.

I looked up to see that my sponsoring professor was coming into the lab. I sighed. Great. I had a feeling this wouldn't go well.

He crossed to me, looking over my shoulder. "What's this?"

My shoulders sagged. "I think you can see."

"Another heat?"

"I told you that I have them frequently."

"You never used to," he said.

Were we really going to do this again? "I think we've talked about this," I said.

He nodded. "We have."

"And there's legislation about discrimination for species-specific—"

"You're not being discriminated against, Eventh. You're a bright and talented scientist with good instincts. But that grant you have is going to run out, and you're out of the lab four or five days out of every month."

"Well, that's because you told me not to come in

when I was in heat." I was a little snippier than I usually would have been, and it was probably the affect of the heat coming in. It made my temper a little short, I'd noticed.

"I told you that because I came in on you and that... older man that you're—"

"My mate," I said. "And all he was doing was massaging me."

"Massaging your—"

"Hips. It's a pressure thing," I said. "I know it looks sexual, but we weren't doing anything inappropriate—"

"How old is he again?"

I sighed.

"It's only that I worry about you, Eventh," he said. "When you arrived here, you weren't so distracted. It seemed like you had a focus, and that was on your work."

"I'm still focused," I said. "But I also fell in love. Maybe you don't need a life that involves love and connection, professor, but it's a basic thing that most people *do* need, so I don't appreciate it when you act like I need to choose."

He sighed. "You're so young, Eventh. What do you even know about love?"

I sighed.

"My apologies," he said. "I don't mean to butt in where I'm not welcome. I only say this because I truly admire your work, and I don't want to see you throw it away."

"Can I come to the lab during my heat?" I said. "I would like to come back, in fact. Sometimes I get ideas, and if I can come in for an hour or two, it would really help."

"Alone or with that man?"

"Well, he helps me," I said. "And when I'm in heat, I really can't…" I was defeated. "Drive or anything. So, I need him."

"But he's the one triggering all these heats, am I wrong?"

He knew the answer to that question. I folded my arms over my chest. "You know, having the frequent heats could mean that I could be doing more tests on myself, but you deny the lab equipment, and it confounds the problem of my losing time —"

"Fine," he said. "The lab is always open to you, Eventh. But if there's going to be… massage? Take it into the break room." He pointed. "And lock the door?"

"We can do that," I said, giving him a smile. "Thank you, professor. I appreciate it. I know this isn't precisely a conventional approach."

"I'm only hoping that you can find something that will work to suppress your cycles."

"Me too," I said. "That's what I desperately want."

AFTERLUDE:
WHEREVER SHE IS

sevren

I woke up in the middle of the night, disoriented, the way I usually was after a ranskk. I climbed over the pillows in our bed to find Eventh, breathing in her scent.

Her heat had broken.

Finally.

She'd be relieved.

We'd been living together here in the city for a gecycle now, and she'd made progress with creating a suppressant that could work to stop her heat, but it was finicky. Sometimes it worked. Sometimes it didn't. She couldn't figure out why, and it was endlessly problematic for her at the lab.

I was lucky to have a very flexible schedule at the gym I owned, and I could take off work whenever I needed. I had enough help there to cover all the shifts, and I never needed to close anymore. Sometimes, I did cancel self-defense classes. And sometimes, when classes went normally, and Eventh showed up to meet me, I got disapproving looks from my students. She did look too young for me. Spirits, she *was* too young for me.

I wish I could say that I didn't care, but I did. It

bothered me to be thought of as predatory. I didn't want anyone to think I was hurting anyone, but least of all Eventh.

But every relationship had its issues, and these were ours. We managed.

This heat had been particularly intense and she'd been frustrated when her suppressant hadn't worked. We'd gone in on the second day, after a long session of knotting that had seemed to calm her enough that she thought she could work, and she'd tested four or five different permutations, one of which seemed to make a little bit of a difference, but not so much that it broke the heat.

Admittedly, once her heat started, I seemed to be the only thing that could break it entirely. Suppressants could stop it if she took them before the heat fully came on, but once it was raging, it was going to have its way with her.

The professor had cornered me while she was filling slides with blood and said some of the same things he'd said to me before, asking me pointed questions, implying that I was trying to pull Eventh away from her work.

The guy didn't listen to either of us when we spoke to him. I would have given it up entirely, but I figured I had to be polite, because Eventh worked with the guy.

Now, I got up, stretching, and I wandered out, heading for the kitchen of our apartment, yawning. I was going to get a glass of water and then probably go right back to sleep.

I heard a noise, and I stopped.

Maybe a noise had woken me?

Was someone in the apartment?

I rushed forward, thinking of danger, thinking of

getting the blaster I kept in a safe in the hallway, not thinking about, uh, pants.

So, when I came face-to-face with Dannor Johns, I was naked.

I froze.

His jaw dropped.

I put a hand over my crotch and backed up. I backed all the way up into the bedroom. "Baby girl," I snapped, finding clothes, pulling them on.

"Mmm," she muttered.

"Your father is here."

She suddenly sat straight up in bed. "Stars, what day is it?"

I told her.

"No, no, no, *no*." She got up, throwing on her own clothes and she rushed out into the hallway. "Guys, when I gave you this address, it was for emergencies, not so you could just show up here."

"Well, when no one met us at the spaceport, we got worried," said Dannor.

"We tried your bracelet," came Belini's voice.

"You're staying in a hotel. We're meeting up and going sightseeing, having dinner, that kind of thing. But you're not coming *here*." Eventh's voice was rising.

I stepped out of the bedroom, now fully clothed. "You didn't tell me your parents were coming to visit."

"No, you didn't need to know." She pointed at me. "I had it all worked out. It was going to be fine."

I gave Eventh's parents a half-wave. "Well, so good to see you both," I muttered.

Dannor pushed past his daughter and came for me. "What are you even doing here?"

"Uh... I'd think that was obvious." I spread my hands. "You want me to say it, like, out loud? Really?"

He stopped, right in front of me, both of his hands clenched in fists.

I winced. "It just happened. It's... fighting it was worse for her than giving in. I don't know if you can understand that, but—"

"How long has this been going on?" said Dannor. "How did he find you, Eventh?"

"It's... it's just..." Eventh came over and wrapped two hands around her father's upper arm. "Daddy, he's my mate. We live together."

"You *live* together?"

"You weren't going to tell us?" said Belini.

"Back away from him, Daddy," said Eventh. "I don't want him to accidentally hurt you if he has to defend himself."

Dannor snorted, shaking Eventh off. He shot me a look of pure hatred.

I felt it all rising in me—the roiling storm of shame and confusion.

Eventh put herself in between me and her father. She walked backwards until she collided with me and then she sagged against my chest. "I'm sorry I forgot you were coming. It was a pretty intense heat is all."

I put my arm around her waist, holding her there.

Dannor gritted his teeth.

"But Eventh, darling," said Belini. "I thought all you ever wanted was to figure out how to control all that. Isn't that why you're here? Why would you voluntarily let him into your life when you know that he'll trigger your cycles? You hate your cycles."

"But I love him," Eventh said, shrugging. "Would you give up Dad? Would anything make you give him up?"

Belini gave her daughter a sad smile. "I guess not."

"This is not the same thing," said Dannor.

Belini rested a hand on her husband's shoulder. "Dannor, he's always been devoted to her. He'd never hurt her. If there's anyone we could trust, it's Sevren."

"You're always defending him," said Dannor, but he only sounded tired.

"Now that we know you're safe, we'll just head to our hotel and we can all meet for lunch tomorrow," said Belini.

"Sevren too?" said Eventh.

"Yes," said Belini, giving me a smile. "Definitely Sevren too."

"Dannor," I said. "If you don't want me there—"

"Living together for how long?" interrupted Dannor.

"A gecycle," I said.

"A gecycle?" he repeated. "You didn't bring her home to Bravren? Didn't come back and install her as your mate in the chieftain hut? But you're with her? I don't understand."

"Eventh's life is here," I said. "And my life is wherever she is."

"You were always a horrible chieftain," said Belini, her smile widening.

I laughed. "I was, I really was."

"So, you… you wouldn't take her away from this," said Dannor, gesturing with one hand. His voice was a little thick.

"Never," I said.

"He's devoted to her, Dannor," said Belini again. "Come on, handsome, let's go get some sleep." She pulled on her husband's arm.

Dannor let his wife lead him away.

After they were gone, Eventh went out into the kitchen and started programming a four-course feast into the replicator. She was usually hungry after heats. "Stars, can you imagine if my heat hadn't broken? What if they'd come in, like, while you were ranskking me?"

"Do not say these things," I said, shivering in horror at the thought. "That's horrible."

"We can't go on like this, Sevren."

I raised my eyebrows. "What?" What the stars did that mean? What if she suddenly decided we should live apart, so that I didn't trigger her heat? It made sense, but I thought it might destroy me.

"I've just... I've been thinking," she said. "And I don't want to volunteer you for a thing that would be a lot of responsibility or whatever, but really, with taking care of my heat, it's practically a part-time job for you, and you're just... you know, you're so good at being, um, nurturing, I guess?"

"Uh... you're not the first person to say that to me, but what the spirits are you talking about?"

"We never really talked about kids, not seriously, but you're so good with kids. You *like* kids, right? I mean, you wouldn't say it, but you want us to have babies, don't you?"

I licked my lips. "Eventh, you are twenty-one gecycles old, and you have your research—"

"Well, okay, that's the thing. If I was pregnant, it would mean no heat for at least two gecycles, possibly three? I mean, breastfeeding could be intrusive, but, like, this heat is intrusive, and I can make it work. And you'd take care of the baby, right?"

My stomach flipped over. Fuck. Okay, so I wanted that. I was a little frightened at how badly I wanted that. I staggered over to the table. I needed to sit down.

"Sevren?"

"You sure?" My voice was scratchy.

"I think I could use the time to focus more on the implant, the one I'm trying to sell? With those credits from the sale, I could fund more research on the suppressants, and I would have two gecycles to work out the kinks on the one that I've got sort of working now. So, who knows, maybe when I started cycling again, I'd have a workable suppressant. I just... I think it makes sense, and... I don't know... I know I want a baby with you someday, so why are we waiting when now is the right time?"

I let out a disbelieving laugh. "Spirits, Eventh."

She came over to sit down next to me. "You're not saying anything."

"Uh... no, I'm on board. I want to get you pregnant. I want you to have my baby. I... if you're sure..." I reached over to touch her.

She grinned. "I thought you did." She climbed into my lap and straddled me and we kissed hungrily. She pulled away and rubbed her nose against mine. "You're going to be the best dad in the history of the entire galaxy, and I am going to figure all this out. I'm going to make a life for us where I get to discover things and solve problems and have you and be a mom and... and... it's going to be everything."

I didn't know if I'd ever been quite this happy in my life. "It is. Everything."

We kissed again.

I pulled away, groaning. "When I get you pregnant, I think your father is going to want to *kill* me."

She smirked. "No way. He's going to come around. I think you guys will end up, you know, friends."

I arched an eyebrow.

"Okay, well... you'll tolerate each other anyway."

"I don't know about that," I muttered.

"For me, you will tolerate him." She put her finger in my face.

I grinned at her. "Anything for you, baby girl."

www.ingramcontent.com/pod-product-compliance
Lightning Source LLC
Chambersburg PA
CBHW020910160726
47993CB00005B/1908